Governing Sustainability in the EU

Governing Sustainability in the EU examines the recent novelties in the EU agenda for sustainable development, illustrating how the process of policy change has occurred at different levels, comprising general priorities, specific objectives and policy instruments.

The book focuses on the evolution of the principle of policy integration and analyses its implementation by specific policy instruments across three policy areas: energy efficiency (the Covenant of Mayors), innovation (the Eco-Innovation Programme) and regional development (ERDF regional programmes regarding sustainable urban development). It specifically examines two domestic contexts (Italy and the UK) with the aim of understanding how the goals and means envisaged by the EU have been translated into concrete policy practices on the ground, and which factors have influenced the creation of new policy and governance practices necessary for the achievement of sustainable development objectives.

This text will be of key interest to scholars, students and practitioners of sustainable development, European Union Politics, and Environmental Politics.

Ekaterina Domorenok is Associate Professor of Political Science at the University of Padua, Italy.

Routledge Studies on Government and the European Union

Edited by Andy Smith, University of Bordeaux, France

Policy Change in the Area of Freedom, Security and Justice
How EU Institutions Matter
Edited by Florian Trauner and Ariadna Ripoll Servent

The Mechanisms of Institutional Conflict in the European Union
Ludvig Norman

Public Ethics at the European Commission
Politics, Reform and Individual Views
Andreea Năstase

Parliaments and the Economic Governance of the European Union
Talking Shops or Deliberative Bodies?
Aleksandra Maatsch

EU Presidencies between Politics and Administration
The Governmentality of the Polish, Danish and Cypriot Trio Presidency in 2011–2012
Mads Dagnis Jensen and Peter Nedergaard

Governing Europe in a Globalizing World
Neoliberalism and its Alternatives following the 1973 Oil Crisis
Laurent Warlouzet

European Values
Challenges and Opportunities for EU Governance
Edited by François Foret and Oriane Calligaro

Governing Sustainability in the EU
From Political Discourse to Policy Practices
Ekaterina Domorenok

For more information about this series, please visit: www.routledge.com/Routledge-Studies-on-Government-and-the-European-Union/book-series/RSGEU

Governing Sustainability in the EU

From Political Discourse to Policy Practices

Ekaterina Domorenok

Routledge
Taylor & Francis Group
LONDON AND NEW YORK

First published 2019
byRoutledge
2 Park Square, Milton Park, Abingdon, Oxon OX14 4RN

and by Routledge
52 Vanderbilt Avenue, New York, NY 10017

First issued in paperback 2020

Routledge is an imprint of the Taylor & Francis Group, an informa business

British Library Cataloguing-in-Publication Data
A catalogue record for this book is available from the British Library

Library of Congress Cataloging-in-Publication Data
Names: Domorenok, Ekaterina, author.
Title: Governing sustainability in the EU : from political discourse to policy practices / Ekaterina Domorenok.
Other titles: Governing sustainability in the European Union
Description: Abingdon, Oxon ; New York, NY : Routledge, 2019. | Series: Routledge studies on government and the European Union | Includes bibliographical references and index.
Identifiers: LCCN 2018036985 | ISBN 9781138231559 (hardback) | ISBN 9781315314990 (web pdf) | ISBN 9781315314983 (epub) | ISBN 9781315314976 (mobipocket/kindle)
Subjects: LCSH: Sustainable development—Government policy—European Union countries. | Energy consumption—Government policy—European Union countries. | Regional planning—European Union countries. | City planning—European Union countries.
Classification: LCC HC240.9.E5 D65 2019 | DDC 338.94/07—dc23
LC record available at https://lccn.loc.gov/2018036985

ISBN 13: 978-0-367-66469-5 (pbk)
ISBN 13: 978-1-138-23155-9 (hbk)

Typeset in Times New Roman
by Apex CoVantage, LLC

To my parents for their enduring support, drive and encouragement

Contents

Figures

Tables

Interviews

Interview 1	Emilia-Romagna, ERDF Managing Authority, June 2017
Interview 2	Veneto, ERDF Managing Authority, June 2017
Interview 3	Scotland, ERDF Managing Authority, November 2017
Interview 4	Bologna, City officer (senior), May 2017
Interview 5	Bologna, City officer, October 2016
Interview 6	Padova, City officer (senior), October 2016
Interview 7	Padova, City officer (junior), October 2016
Interview 8	Glasgow, City energy officer (senior), June 2017
Interview 9	Glasgow, City economic development officer (senior), November 2017
Interview 10	Glasgow, City officer (junior), November 2017
Interview 11	Poole, City officer (senior), June 2017
Interview 12	Durham, City officer, June 2017
Interview 13	Leeds, City officer, June
Interview 14	Palermo, City officer, July 2017
Interview 15	Pesaro, City Officer, September 2017
Interview 16	Venice, City officer, June 2017
Interview 17	Benetton Group srl, October 2016
Interview 18	Olimpias Group srl, October 2016
Interview 19	Europrogetti srl, October 2016
Interview 20	Nuova Ompi srl, October 2016
Interview 21	SOGESCA, Energy manager, October 2016, 2017

Acknowledgements

I would like to express my very great appreciation to Elena Ceretta, Duilio Magri and Simona Carmen Garofalo. Their support has been crucial for collecting empirical data for different parts of research presented in this volume. I wish also to acknowledge the help provided by Giuseppe Acconcia in conducting interviews referred to in Chapter 5, and thank all interviewees for their time and precious insights. Finally, my grateful thanks are also extended to Sophie Iddamalgoda and Chris Mathews from the Routledge editing team for their patience and helpful assistance in editing the volume, and to Andy Smith for his valuable guidance in improving the original draft.

The research upon which this volume is based was funded by the Department of Political Science, Law and International Studies, University of Padua, and formed part of a wider research project on climate change policies and governance in the EU.

Introduction

Over the last decade, the issue of sustainable development has acquired increasing prominence in political agendas across the globe, as dramatic environmental, social and economic consequences of climate change have been hitting worldwide. At the same time, the awareness about the complexity and multidimensionality of policy measures required to meet the challenge of sustainability have unavoidably triggered questions about the capacity of national and supranational institutions to govern the transition to a more sustainable regime (Jordan *et al.*, 2015) by fostering profound social and economic transformations. The recently approved Agenda 2030 has established a list of 17 ambitious objectives that can be attained only if all the parties concerned really commit to this joint action.

As is known, the European Union (EU) has been one of the most relevant actors supporting the sustainability agenda at the international level while simultaneously promoting its own policies aimed at decreasing pollution and depletion of natural resources, and improving the level of well-being and quality of life of its citizens. However, a lot of concerns and criticism have been expressed with regard to both the EU ambition for leadership in the United Nations sustainable development agenda and the coherence of its internally and externally oriented policies for achieving the sustainability objectives (Lightfoot and Burchell, 2005).

Far from the lofty ambition of providing a comprehensive assessment of the EU strategy for sustainable development, this book focuses on addressing a number of issues related to the design and implementation of its internal policies with the objective of appraising the EU capacity to guide policy changes towards sustainability, through the perspective of the following four dimensions.

First, several studies have highlighted how the EU-wide political discourse on sustainability has consolidated over time by progressively becoming a context in which decisions are made about how to resolve the tension existing between economic growth, environmental protection and social justice (Barnes and Hoerber, 2013). However, although the need to prioritise the objective of sustainable development has been widely shared at the level of European institutions and across member states' governments, a number of contradictions have been observed over time, in particular with regard to the prioritisation of policy goals and the consistency of objectives. Some scholars have pointed out that as a consequence of the recent economic crisis, a further shift from the original idea of sustainable development embodied by the Brundland report to a model based on ecological modernisation as the dominant ideology (Eadson, 2013) has occurred. The Europe 2020 Strategy for smart, sustainable and inclusive growth (European Commission, 2010a) appears to have further strengthened the economic rationale of reforms, increasingly overriding the principle of Environmental Policy Integration (EPI), which has been considered for decades the "first-order operational principle to implement and institutionalise the idea of sustainable development" (Lenschow, 2002). Furthermore, with the consolidation of the climate change narrative, the attention seems to have definitely moved from a more general concern about sustainability to transitioning towards the low-carbon economy (Oberthür and Dupont, 2015). Unsurprisingly, the aforementioned trends trigger questions about the existence of preconditions for a meta-governance (Jessop, 2016) of sustainable development in the EU, as well as about the overall consistency of its policy agenda in this field (Baker, 2007). Despite the overall growing salience of sustainability in policy discourse and principles, the problematic relationship between economic growth, environmental sustainability and social inclusion has arguably been solved in the EU policy agenda (Bulkeley *et al.*, 2013), and its underlying principles seem to be yet unsettled.

A second relevant issue is the way in which the EU political discourse on sustainable development has shaped concrete policy measures, practices and outcomes. The EU has progressively developed a complex mix of policy instruments with the purpose of meeting the challenge of sustainability, but our knowledge about how successfully EU objectives have been implemented is still limited and the research agenda on this issue has been fragmented. On the one hand, a compliance-oriented research on Europeanisation has revealed a very different scenario of implementation of EU environmental policies, shedding some light on how the principle of EPI became embedded in a range of EU policies through a variety of policy instruments. The study of the so-called New Environmental Policy Instruments (NEPIs) has provided an important account (Wurzel *et al.*, 2013) of how specific novel forms of policy intervention relying on information, financial incentives and coordination have diffused across EU countries and how they have contributed to reshaping the governance of EU environmental policies. However, the relevance of these instruments in a wider perspective of sustainable development agenda has not been explored, disregarding their impacts on wider social and economic domains.

Third, although it has been claimed that the ideas underpinning the concept of sustainable development have generated high levels of commitment amongst those who implement EU policies, no clear evidence has been provided to demonstrate that these ideas have indeed been successfully internalised by national and sub-state policies to ensure effective implementation of sustainability goals on the ground (Barnes and Hoerber, 2013). Moreover, little attention has been paid so far to the role of EU financial and voluntary schemes that target sub-state or non-state actors, while the impact of the recently adopted sustainable development mainstreaming approach has not been appraised yet.

Last but not least, the EU governance architecture for sustainable development offers several insights for unveiling the puzzling relation between governance and sustainability, with particular regard to flexible forms of coordination and bottom-up partnership underlying the mushrooming networks for sustainable development and more recently climate change worldwide (Bulkeley *et al.*, 2012). While the effectiveness of the Open Method of Coordination (OMC), which has been the main governance tool for the implementation of sustainable development in the EU, has been heavily criticised (Berger and Steurer, 2007), our knowledge about other experimental forms of governance promoted by the EU across a variety of policy areas (Zeitlin, 2016) has been limited. Being underpinned by the principles of flexible coordination and learning, these new modes of governance have been expected to become a valuable tool for improving policy implementation in the EU by increasingly involving local authorities and private actors in different forms of strategic partnership (Bulkeley *et al.*, 2012). However, there is still not enough evidence on whether and how these forms of governance actually improve policy effectiveness and enable the achievement of better policy outcomes.

Against this background and in view of the profound crisis that the EU currently faces in terms of political credibility, a deeper reflection on the impact, relevance and potential of its policies is urgently needed. In this context, understanding the EU governing capacity in the field of sustainable development appears to be compelling considering both the utmost importance of this agenda and the fact that no overwhelming steering mechanism could be reasonably adopted in this field. The question spontaneously arises if the EU is and has been able to shape all relevant actors' behaviour by creating an appropriate regulatory context and promoting a mix of incentives encouraging policy actors to align their strategies towards pro-sustainability patterns.

Therefore, distinct from previous research that has mainly focused either on the success of macro policy coordination within the OMC or on member states' compliance with the EU environmental regulations, this study adopts a policy design perspective in order to unpack the changes of the EU policy agenda for sustainability over time and assesses whether and how its selected policy programmes have enhanced policy and governance transformations on the ground. Hence, drawing on analytical insights provided by the concept of usage (Jacquot and Woll, 2003; Woll and Jacquot, 2010), the EU governing capacity is here conceived in terms of its relevance for enabling (Kern and Bulkeley, 2009) and shaping target actors' strategies, which deploy various EU opportunities and work around constraints. From there the aim has been to understand whether and under which conditions a mix of EU regulatory, financial and coordination measures embedded in policy programmes, underpinned by the so-called sustainable development mainstreaming approach, have contributed to modify actors' strategies and performance by producing better convergence to and ownership of common objectives and principles.

Thus, after having outlined the main characteristics of the EU political agenda on sustainable development, including its normative foundations and governance architecture, the analysis presented in the volume will focus on the design and implementation of selected policy programmes with the objective to spell out the nature of the target policy actors' response to policy inputs and incentives channelled by the EU throughout these programmes.

Based on the assumption that policy actors do not simply respond to the institutional contexts, but "can choose and learn, thus engaging with, interpreting, appropriating or ignoring the dynamics of European integration" (Woll and Jacquot, 2010: 220), particular attention has been paid to the scenarios of usage of EU instruments by their policy addressees. To this end, the relevance of such policy variables as actors' existing strategies, objectives, interests and underlying motivations has been considered, reflecting also on whether and how domestic context conditions may provide additional explanations of actors' behaviour. Remarkably, these aspects have been largely overlooked in the research on EU policies so far, which has put an overarching emphasis on the institutional accounts of policy change (Radaelli *et al.*, 2012).

The following three policy areas, with their respective policy programmes underpinned by the sustainable development mainstreaming approach, have been selected for in-depth analysis: EU cohesion policy and its regional programming for sustainable urban development; the Covenant of Mayors programme for promoting sustainable energy policies at the local level and the Eco-Innovation Programme launched within the framework of innovation in order to promote the development and market uptake of environmental technological innovations. Although their specific objectives differ from each other, the common rationale of their design is to encourage the prioritisation of sustainable development objectives in a cross-sectoral manner and increase coordination between sectors, scales and actors in the long run. Significantly, these programmes do not target central governments, but identify regional and local authorities, and private companies as their main policy addressees. An integrated policy approach and multilevel governance architectures involving public and private actors have been at the core of the operational scheme of these programmes.

More specifically, the objective of sustainable urban development has been mainstreamed into national and regional development programmes supported by EU cohesion policies and co-financed by the European Regional Development Fund (ERDF) since 2007. These interventions aimed, among others, at boosting local economic potential, encouraging physical regeneration and social inclusion, and improving the environmental conditions in urban areas. A highly decentralised pattern of implementation of measures was expected to be established by these programmes, allowing for a major role for local authorities in the definition and implementation of policy interventions.

The Covenant of Mayors (CoM) programme was launched by the EU Commission in 2008 within the EU Climate and Energy package, with the objective of promoting local sustainable energy strategies by mobilising a great number of local authorities to develop their Sustainable Energy Action Plans (SEAPs) and direct investments towards climate change mitigation measures. This programme has been based on the voluntary commitment of signatories, who are coordinated and supported by a dedicated CoM Office at the EU Commission in their effort to meet and exceed the EU 20% CO_2 reduction target by developing cross-sectoral energy efficiency and renewable energy measures at the local level.

The Eco-Innovation Programme was implemented by the EU Commission between 2008 and 2013 as a pilot initiative to support the development and market uptake of technological innovations reducing the environmental impact of production processes and products, especially among small and medium-size enterprises (SMEs). Beyond advanced level of technological innovations, the creation of transnational partnerships involving private companies, research and public bodies has been defined as an important added value for obtaining financial support from this programme.

In sum, the core governing principle underlying these programmes implied that target actors would pro-actively deploy a set of EU policy guidance and incentives in order to align their strategies to common policy goals. The process of policy change and convergence was supposed to be driven by a series of thematic guidelines, methodologies, coordination and socialisation mechanisms instead of relying on steering and compliance mechanisms. As a result, the implementation success of these programmes has been associated with the degree to which policy addressees increased their ownership of EU policy objectives and adopted their strategies to common policy targets and operational principles by deploying all available resources (financial, political, relational, etc.).

Thus, a detailed analysis of implementation of the aforementioned programmes has been carried out in order to understand whether and how the EU has shaped target actors' strategies in the perspective of specific sustainable development goals. Besides an extensive desk-source analysis, including EU legislation and guidance; national, regional and local plans and other relevant documents; statistic data, etc., a survey and a number of interviews with policy addressees have been conducted with the purpose of revealing their perceptions and opinions with regard to the programmes under examination.

Considering that the great variety of contextual conditions across EU member states has been considered one of the crucial difficulties for effective policy-making and implementation, two very different countries – Italy and the UK – were chosen for in-depth analysis in order to spell out the interplay of policy and institutional variables determining the success and failures of the selected programmes.

The analysis presented in the volume confirms the validity of policy variables for explaining the scenario of policy implementation and change in the EU, illustrating how a closer look at policy actors and their response to EU guidance and incentives may be extremely helpful for understanding the potential and limits of given policy solutions. By providing evidence of the divergent scenario of usage of EU resources by policy addressees within and between the two countries, the empirical research brings to light how implementation dynamics have been largely determined by such variables as pre-existing target actors' strategies, motivations, interests, capacities and resources. In addition, this approach has allowed for a more nuanced view on contextual factors that also matter and on the way in which they may shape actors' choices.

Overall, the research presented in this volume enriches our knowledge on policy-making in the EU in two important ways. First, it provides a rich cross-sectoral empirical evidence of how the novel modes of governance (Héritier and Rhodes, 2011) have been evolving in the EU, contributing to further consolidate the trend according to which the border between hard and soft forms of regulation has increasingly blurred (Graziano and Halpern, 2016). In fact, in the EU strategy for sustainable development, the method of "governing by authority" (regulations and directives) (Kern and Bulkeley, 2009) applied for promoting the EPI principles across sectors during the past decades, has progressively been complemented and replaced by the sustainable development mainstreaming approach underpinned by the principle "governing through enabling" (e.g. networking, persuasion, subsidies, etc.). This approach has encouraged the diffusion of integrated policies and inclusive governance architectures across different territorial levels, which complement EU regulatory measures across a variety of policy sectors (e.g. energy, innovation, transport, etc.).

Second, by illustrating that under certain conditions policy actors effectively deploy a mix of regulations, guidelines and incentives to adjust their policy strategies to EU objectives and targets, this research has offered a promising analytical pathway contributing to a better understanding of drivers of policy change in the EU, as the logic of compliance seems to have exhausted its expected impact, and there are also signs of fatigue (Graziano and Halpern, 2016) in analytically grasping the relevance of the ever-changing governance architectures such as OMC or post-Lisbon Strategy (Europe 2020). The presented findings appear to confirm the feasibility of the hypothesis that socialisation and learning may be effective in bringing to the alignment to common goals in the EU (Radaelli, 2008), especially among actors other than national governments. At the same time, evidence is provided that EU policy instruments that intended to lead to bottom-up learning need to be carefully fine-tuned, taking into account the peculiarities of contexts in terms of existing policy needs, resources and capacities.

Having presented here our research perspective in broad-brush terms, the volume proceeds as follows.

Chapter 1 introduces the field of study in full, highlighting matters that remained underexplored by previous research and illustrating the methodological approach adopted by the book. Stemming from the literature on policy design and the research on EU public policies, this research elaborates on the concept of usage, illustrating how it may further improve our understanding of policy-making in the EU if applied to the policy domain. Chapter 2 presents an overview of the EU policies and governance architecture for sustainable development, focusing in particular on its recent development and policy programmes developed within the framework of the so-called sustainable development mainstreaming approach. A comparative analysis of the UK and Italian national strategies for sustainable development is provided in Chapter 3, paying particular attention to the degree of political commitment, ambition of goals and specific policy priorities and instruments identified at the national level. The scenarios of implementation of the selected policy programmes in the two countries are presented in Chapter 4, which focuses on actions for sustainable urban development; Chapter 5, focusing on analysing the implementation of the Covenant of Mayors and Chapter 6, which analyses the Eco-Innovation programme. Conclusions are drawn in Chapter 7.

The findings presented in the book contribute to a better understanding of the current dynamics and change of the EU sustainable development policies and governance by providing answers to the following questions: What has been the scenario of policy change in the EU strategy for sustainable development? To what extent has an alteration of policy objectives affected the design of EU policy programmes? To what extent do policy variables account for the *macro* (policy) and *meso* (programme) level goals to be successfully translated into policy practices on the ground and how do they shape the scenario of policy and governance change in different contexts?

References

Baker, S. (2007). Sustainable development as symbolic commitment: Declaratory politics and the seductive appeal of ecological modernisation in the European Union. *Environmental Politics*, 16 (2), pp. 297–317.

Barnes, P.M. and Hoerber, T.C. (eds.) (2013). *Sustainable Development and Governance in Europe: The Evolution of the Discourse on Sustainability*. London and New York: Routledge.

Berger, G. and Steurer, R. (2007). *The EU SDS process in the member states: SDS coordinators, national progress reports and the open method of coordination*. ESDN quarterly report, March. Available at: www.sd-network.eu/?k=quarterly%20reports&report_id=4 [Accessed 2 March 2011].

Bulkeley, H., Andonova, L., Bäckstrand, K., Betsill, M., Compagnon, D., Duff, R., Kolk, A., Hoffmann, M., Levy, D., Newell, P., Milledge, T., Paterson, M., Pattberg, P. and VanDeveer, S. (2012). Governing climate change transnationally: Assessing the evidence from a database of sixty initiatives. *Environment and Planning C: Politics and Space*, 30, pp. 591–612.

Bulkeley, H., Jordan, A., Perkins, R. and Selin, H. (2013). Governing sustainability: Rio+20 and the road beyond. *Environment and Planning C: Government and Policy*, 31, pp. 958–970.

Eadson, W. (2013). The evolution of carbon capitalism in the English regions: Sustainable mitigation, carbon modernization, and selective carbon economies. In: Barnes, P.M. and Hoerber, T.C. eds., *Sustainable Development and Governance in Europe: The Evolution of the Discourse on Sustainability*. London and New York: Routledge.

Graziano, P. and Halpern, C. (2016). EU governance in times of crisis: Inclusiveness and effectiveness beyond the 'hard' and 'soft' law divide. *Comparative European Politics*, 14 (1), pp. 1–19.

Héritier, A. and Rhodes, M. (eds.) (2011). *New Modes of Governance in Europe Governing in the Shadow of Hierarchy*. Basingstoke: Palgrave Macmillan.

Jacquot, S. and Woll, C. (2003). Usage of European integration – Europeanisation from a sociological perspective. *European Integration Online Papers (EIoP)*, 7, available at: http://eiop.or.at/eiop/texte/2003-012a.htm.

Jessop, B. (2016). Territory, politics, governance and multi-spatial meta-governance. *Territory, Politics, Governance*, 4 (2), pp. 8–32.

Jordan, A., Huitema, D., Hildén, M., van Asselt, H., Rayner T.J., Schoenefeld, J.J., Tosun, J., Forster, J., and Boasson, E.L. (2015). Emergence of polycentric climate governance and its future prospects. *Nature Climate Change*, 5, pp. 977–982.

Kern, C. and Bulkeley, H. (2009). Cities, Europeanization and multi-level governance: Governing climate change through transnational municipal networks. *Journal of Common Market Studies*, 47 (2), pp. 309–332.

Lenschow, A. (2002). *Environmental Policy Integration: Greening Sectoral Policies in Europe*. London: Earthscan.

Lightfoot, S. and Burchell, J. (2005). The European Union and the World Summit on sustainable development: Normative power Europe in action? *Journal of Common Market Studies*, 43 (1), pp. 75–95.

Oberthür, S. and Dupont, C. (eds.) (2015). *Decarbonization in the European Union Internal Policies and External Strategies*. Basingstoke: Palgrave Macmillan.

Radaelli, C. (2008). Europeanization, policy learning, and new modes of governance. *Journal of Comparative Policy Analysis*, 10 (3), pp. 239–254.

Radaelli, C., Dente, B. and Dossi S. (2012). Recasting institutionalism: Institutional analysis and public policy. *European Political Science*, 11 (4), pp. 537–550.

Woll, C. and Jacquot, S. (2010). Using Europe: Strategic action in multi-level politics. *Comparative European Politics*, 8 (1), pp. 110–126.

Wurzel, R.K.W., Zito, A.R. and Jordan, A.J. (2013). *Environmental Governance in Europe: A Comparative Analysis of New Environmental Policy Instruments*. Cheltenham: Edward Elgar.

Zeitlin, J. (2016). EU experimentalist governance in times of crisis. *West European Politics*, 39 (5), pp. 1073–1094.

1 Understanding policy change in the EU

What is missing in our knowledge of policy implementation?

1.1 Perspectives on policy change in the EU: policy discourse and practice

As is commonly known, a policy perspective in the research on the European Union has developed over two main phases. A "first generation studies" on European integration has focused on explaining the process of construction of a European sphere characterised by the debate between intergovernmental and neo-functional perspectives, while a "second generation" of studies has analysed the process of adjustment of national policies and systems of governance through the perspective of the process of Europeanisation (Schmidt and Radaelli, 2004). In the scholarly debate on the latter, different explanations have been provided regarding factors that best explain policy change in the process of adjustment to the EU – whether these are external pressures and problems, the "fit" between EU policies and national policy legacies or actors' preferences and problem-solving capacities in a given political-institutional setting (Héritier, 2001; Cowles *et al.*, 2001; Graziano and Vink, 2008).

An attempt to provide a comprehensive view on the aforementioned factors has been made by discursive institutionalism (Schmidt and Radaelli, 2004), which tried to bring components of interest-based rationality, historical and institutional path-dependence and social construction and identity into a single conceptual framework. This approach has stressed the need to integrate structure and agency for explaining policy change in the EU, emphasising how discourse matters in this sense, in terms of both institutional settings embedded in a vast rage of culturally framed and path-dependent rules, as well as policy ideas guided by interest-based rationality affecting policy-making in any given socio-political setting (Schmidt and Radaelli, 2004: 184). Thus, the discourse has been conceived as one of five main mediating factors of policy change, assuming that ideas represent the necessary conditions for collective action by serving to redefine interests and reconfigure interest-based political coalitions, constituting also the policy narratives and frames of reference that serve to reconstruct actors' understandings of interests and redirect their actions within institutions (Schmidt and Radaelli, 2004: 195).While providing a convincing argument about how the ideational and interactive dimensions of discourse matter at the stage of policy formulation, as well as how they influence the diffusion of EU policy ideas across the national political arenas in terms of narratives, this approach lacks accounts of how and why the acceptance of the EU ideas and the usage of the related policy resources varies not only across but also within the countries, and whether and how the diffusion of EU ideas is related to the nature of instruments the EU adopts to channel its policy priorities into national policies. If it is true that policy ideas speak to soundness and appropriateness of policy programmes (Schmidt, 2000) and there is an intrinsic linkage between policy discourse and policy design, how can we explain a significant variability in implementation scenarios and divergent policy responses to EU inputs across member states? In fact, despite a wide consensus and consolidated policy narratives on a range of issues, including sustainable development, the implementation gap remains among the most puzzling aspects for the research agenda on European integration (Knill and Tosun, 2012; Treib, 2014; Heidbreder, 2017). Thus, the relation between the rhetoric dimension and substantive impact of discourse on policy programmes and policy practices appears to be far from unproblematic, and this gap in our knowledge of EU policy process is still to be filled in.

The research on policy implementation in the EU, which has mainly developed within the framework of Europeanisation studies, has adopted a top-down institutionalist perspective, suggesting that the degree of compatibility between EU demands and domestic institutions and policy traditions (goodness of fit) is one of the central factors determining implementation performance (Duina, 1997, 2007; Knill and Lenschow, 1998, 2000) and the degree of compliance (Börzel *et al.*, 2010) in the EU. In this perspective, policy variables related to agency were most often conceived as "mediating factors" to be considered only if the institutional context was not able to explain the outcomes (Cowles *et al.*, 2001; Featherstone and Radaelli, 2003).

Although a limited explanatory capacity of the aforementioned approach has been recognised (Falkner *et al.*, 2005; Knill and Lenschow, 1998, 2001; Mastenbroek, 2005; Treib, 2014), a relatively low number of studies have attempted to assess the impact of actor-relevant factors on policy implementation, such as political preferences of governments or political parties (Treib, 2003), or more general mobilisation of domestic actors that might pressurise public authorities to implement the "misfitting" policy (Börzel, 2000). These studies have suggested that voluntary and involuntary non-alignment depends on costs and benefits of adaptation and on the costs of defiance (Héritier *et al.*, 2001), as well as on political will or administrative capacity (Treib, 2014).

Over the last decade, the issue of practical implementation of EU legislation has been more closely addressed, opening a more nuanced bottom-up perspective on how EU policies are translated into practice. Some studies have brought to light the fact that member states can not only transpose, but also enforce (Liefferink *et al.*, 2011; Falkner, 2016) and "customise" common policy guidance (Thomann, 2015), going even beyond the minimum requirements prescribed by the EU.

Overall, the EU impact has been mainly analysed in the areas of application of "hard" forms of regulation (i.e. regulations and directives) focusing mainly on the role of national governments, while considerable blank spots still exist in our knowledge base about policy change within those domains in which the EU influence is exercised through voluntary coordination and funding schemes that aim to influence the policy behaviour of a wider range of target actors by providing them with a system of flexible guidance and incentives, and leaving them ample margins of manoeuvre within which they can develop their policy response to EU initiatives.

Therefore, as nowadays the EU capacity to solve problems more effectively than individual member states appears to be at stake as never before (Graziano and Halpern, 2016), a deeper understanding of the policy process in the EU is clearly needed, supported by a wider reflection on its policy outputs and results. With this in mind, assessing how different policy addressees (regional and local governments, enterprises, organised civil society and individual citizens) engage with, interpret, appropriate or ignore the opportunities created by the process of integration appears to be fundamental for spelling out the critical junctions of the EU problem-solving capacity and finding clues on how the EU may increase its fragile legitimacy on the side of output (Scharpf, 2003).

Against such backdrop, this book aims to shed light on the EU governing capacity in the field of sustainable development by examining a number of recent policy programmes that have been promoted by the EU with the objective of channelling the energies of disparate actors towards acting for common sustainability goals through a variety of instruments. Such a vital policy sphere represents indeed an inspiring case for assessing whether and to what extent the EU can claim the existence of *meta-governance* (Jessop, 2016), with it being viewed as a policy space where common guiding objectives and principles are established and implemented relying on diffused ownership, willingness to coordinate and learn by different policy actors. In fact, the EU exceptionally combines the formal transfer of decision-making authority to a supranational centre, which has progressively limited the margins of what national governments can do and the instruments they can employ, with a range of soft guidance policy mechanisms (Kassim and Le Gales, 2010). At the same time, however, some studies on policy implementation in the EU has shown that despite the EU effort to promote common policy goals and convergence, the restrictions on national governments' abilities to employ various policy tools on their own have been less significant than often assumed (Halpern, 2010).

Over the last two decades, aware of the aforementioned weaknesses and the limits of compliance mechanisms (European Commission, 2001), the EU Commission has increasingly promoted EU soft law and the so-called "new policy instruments" in an attempt to increase policy effectiveness and reduce the "democratic deficit" (Smismans, 2006) through decentralised and participatory policy-making. Policy networks have been at the basis of the implementation scheme of these new instruments (Jordan and Schout, 2006), representing a new way to "circumvent the traditional limitations (budgetary, formal competence) that characterise the EU by new methods of rulemaking and norm-shaping, and developing imaginative ways to overcome vetoes" (Heritier, 1999). Although the relevance of new decision-making modes for strengthening the democratic legitimacy of EU policy-making have been extensively discussed by the literature, their impact on policy performance has been underexplored.

A policy design perspective has been primarily adopted in the study of EU policy instruments in the environmental field by addressing the question of whether national governments are influenced by the EU in the selection of policy instruments (Damonte, 2014; Halpern, 2010) or by comparing the degree to which the New Environmental Policy Instruments (NEPIs) have diffused in the EU and individual member states' environmental policies (Wurzel *et al.*, 2013). As a result, the EU capacity to make member states' governments to comply with common rules and objectives established at the EU level has been considered the main indicator of policy effectiveness, though many gaps still exist in our knowledge of how EU policy ideas are translated into policy programmes and how the actions promoted by these programmes are perceived and reacted upon by policy addressees that are different from central governments.

Instead, a wider perspective on policy design embracing all three policy levels (policy agenda, programmes and instruments) may provide additional advantages for understanding EU individual policies and its more complex agendas. While embracing a great wide variety of instrument-centred approaches and methodologies (Wurzel *et al.*, 2013), the literature on policy design (Howlett, 2011) provides an insightful framework for bridging discourses and ideas underlying EU policy programmes and their impacts viewed in the perspective of policy response by target actors that deploy the related policy resources. First of all, this perspective invites a more comprehensive view of how particular policy philosophies translate into goals and outlooks, while at the same time providing for concrete manifestations of policy actions (Hall, 1993). Second, it implies looking at a complex activity conducted by a number of actors with the purpose of improving policy outcomes through the application of policy-relevant and policy-specific knowledge to the policy-making process (Cahill and Overman, 1990), and specifically in the crafting of possible alternative courses of action intended to address social, political, economic and other kinds of policy problems (Bobrow, 2006). Finally, a policy design perspective looks at how resources are mobilised in the use of instruments and assesses the effectiveness of policy implementation in terms of institutional, administrative, territorial, distributive and other consequences that are greatly relevant for improving our understanding of EU policies. Hence, this analytical angle connects policy ideas with the necessary policy actions by drawing attention to linkages existing between different levels of public policy and considering how different governing modes and strategies are reflected in the use of particular policy instruments.

Drawing on this analytical perspective, this study analyses the EU strategy for sustainable development aiming to understand whether and how EU policy programmes underpinned by the principle of sustainable development mainstreaming and composed of a mix of instruments (regulations, guidance, financial incentive, soft coordination, etc.) have been deployed by target actors and what kind of impact they have produced on the ground in terms of the enhancement of target actors' ownership of EU objectives, their commitment to common targets and the propensity to adopt to the related governance principles. Thus, in contrast to previous studies on policy implementation in the EU, which have mainly focused on the *macro* policy level, this study will explore the *meso* and *micro* dimensions of policy change, exploring whether and how a set of policy arrangements established by the EU has enabled a range of policy actors to address the challenge of sustainable development in a coordinated manner.

1.2 EU strategy for sustainable development: shifting policy discourse and evolving governance architectures

As already mentioned, the EU policy agenda for sustainable development offers several important insights for understanding EU governing capacity and policy change. As is known, since its origin it has been characterised by a double-fold nature, being composed of two policy agendas initiated at the very beginning of the 21st century aiming to respond to the challenge of global economic competition on the one hand, and climate change on the other. After the launch of the Lisbon Strategy for growth and jobs (European Council, 2000), which mainly focused on social and economic dimensions, the EU Sustainable Development Strategy (SDS) was adopted at the Gothenburg European Council with the purpose of providing an EU-wide policy framework "to meet the needs of the present without compromising the ability of future generations to meet their own needs" (European Council, 2001). The strategy called for a coordinated approach to policy-making, meaning that the economic, social and environmental consequences of all policies are taken into account when those policies are being drawn up and adopted. To improve synergies and reduce trade-offs, a more integrated approach to policy-making was proposed, based, among others, on better regulation and impact assessments, enhancing in particular the precautionary and the polluter pays principles (European Commission, 2001, 2005), which have been progressively integrated in various sectors.

Initially, the implementation of both strategies mainly relied on an iterative and coordinated process of evaluation and revision of national strategies, while their governance architectures aimed at establishing a strategic framework within which to develop common objectives, identify means for achieving them, monitor the progress and learn from results. The founding principles of this mechanism emphasised a crucial role of networks in procedural and institutional aspects, highlighting the need for horizontal (cross-sectoral) and vertical (territorial) integration, participatory practices and high political commitment of all concerned. Monitoring and reviewing were considered crucial for the process of evidence-based learning about success and failures of the strategy. However, a more structured version of the so-called Open Method of Coordination (OMC) was adopted within the framework of the Lisbon Agenda, envisaging a new governance architecture in the EU (Borrás and Jacobsson, 2004; Radaelli and Borrás, 2011), which was based on the following four founding pillars: (i) fixing guidelines and timetables, (ii) establishing indicators as a means of benchmarking best practice, (iii) translating the European guidelines into national policies, and (iv) periodic monitoring and peer reviewing to support mutual learning (European Council, 2000: However, no definite EU governance scheme was created for the implementation of the Gothenburg objectives until 2006, when a "light form of OMC" was established (Berger and Steurer, 2007; Berger and Zwirner, 2008), within which individual member states relied on sets of loose guidelines formulated by the United Nations (UN) and Organisation for Economic Cooperation and Development (OECD) (UNCED, 1992; IIED, 2002), combining formal planning and incremental learning (Steurer and Martinuzzi, 2005). The actual implementation of the EU guidelines in national contexts was totally left to the discretion of the member states.

Despite the efforts to bring the two strategies into a single framework, the EU capacity to guarantee their true complementarity and coherence (Steurer and Berger, 2011; European Council, 2006) has been consistently doubted. The revised EU SDS (European Council, 2006) has claimed to have complemented the Lisbon Strategy by including in its perspective such components as the quality of life, intra- and intergenerational equity and coherence between all policy areas, including external aspects, and by recognising the role of economic development in facilitating the transition to a more sustainable society. The Lisbon strategy, in its turn, was expected to make an essential contribution to the overarching objective of sustainable development focusing primarily on actions and measures aimed at increasing competitiveness, economic growth and employment (European Council, 2006: 6). However, evidence has been provided that the Council rhetoric regarding the horizontal complementarity of the two strategies did not materialise in everyday governance routines and strong horizontal linkages (Steurer and Berger, 2011). Moreover, although the overall political consensus about its general objectives has been high and widely diffused, the degree of coherence in terms of policy and governance architectures established across EU countries within the framework of implementation of the EU sustainable development agenda has been considered rather low (Jordan and Lenschow, 2008).

The essential divide between these two strategies could hardly be overcome as two distinguished governance architecture have been reproduced over time. Strong coordination and enduring review have characterised the Lisbon process, with the key role of the Secretariat-General, annual assessment of the progress at the March European Council at the EU level and the commitment of high-level politicians (often ministers) or public administrators from economic affairs ministries at the national level. The implementation of the SDS has been definitely less structured and its political salience has been significantly lower. Since 2006, the SDS progress was supposed to be reviewed bi-annually at December European Council, with mid-level public administrators – most often from environment ministries –engaged at the national level. But the "SDS coordinators group" was convened only twice in 2007, and never since. Bi-annual reports on SDS indicators have been published by EUROSTAT, but no comprehensive assessments or benchmarking by the European Commission has been produced, except for a few peer reviews of national SD strategies. A certain number of initiatives for coordination and learning has been carried out within the European Sustainable Development Network (ESDN), which brings together in an informal network public administrators and experts dealing with SDS in Europe, but the low frequency and restricted scope of these activities appear to be insufficient for substantiating the ambition of the EU to act as a wide-scale coordinating and learning platform (Radaelli, 2000).

The loose mechanism of intergovernmental coordination in the field of SDS described above has further declined over the last decade. In parallel, taking into account several limitations and implementation failures of both agendas (European Commission, 2007; European Council, 2006), a range of additional policy instruments has been endorsed by the EU. As far as SDS is concerned, beyond specific regulations and directives aimed at strengthening the legal foundations of environmental protection through specific principles (e.g. precaution, polluter pays, etc.) and procedures (Environmental Impact Assessment, Strategic Impact Assessment) across different sectors, the New Environmental Policy Instruments (NEPIs) have been increasingly promoted, including economic incentives, communication, self-regulation and voluntary schemes (Wurzel *et al.*, 2013), in order to encourage a better environmental sustainability. Subsequently, the so-called sustainable development mainstreaming approach has been endorsed by the Europe 2020 Strategy for smart, sustainable and inclusive growth (European Commission, 2010a) with the purpose of enlarging the scope of cross-sectoral policy action and engaging a wider array of actors, comprising industries, public institutions at different territorial levels, organised civil society as well as citizens, in the implementation of the agenda.

While strengthening the economic pillar of action and introducing some measures for enhancing social inclusion, the renewed strategy has also definitely diluted the environmental dimension across energy, transport and innovation packages. Accordingly, the related policy measures and targets have mainly been developed within the aforementioned thematic areas, being shaped by a series of overlapping policy narratives strongly underpinned by the economic rationale (low-carbon economy, circular economy, bio-economy, sustainable mobility, etc.) (Steurer, 2016). Importantly, a structured political guidance, a well-defined coordination mechanism and a dedicated monitoring scheme has been established only for the economic and employment parts of the agenda, leaving the governance setting of the environmental dimension unspecified and split across a number of specific sectors. Such a trend can be seen as the consolidation of the paradigmatic shift moving the EU further away from the original version of the SD strategy, in which a more ambitious vision of the principle of Environmental Policy Integration (EPI) has been promoted (Lafferty and Knudsen, 2007), to the concept of ecological modernisation (Mol and Sonnenfeld, 2000). Notably, the new strategy has stressed the need to strengthen the coherence and deploy all available policies, legal instruments and financial resources to pursue the EU strategic objectives.

A renewed attention to sustainable development agenda has re-emerged at the highest political level in EU in 2015 on the occasion of the launch of the United Nations Agenda 2030. The EU has clearly delineated its position in support to the global action framework and formulated a list of internal and external priorities to pursue in order to implement the ambitious 17 Sustainable Development Goals (SDG). However, there is still much uncertainty about how the announced priorities are going to be achieved, as neither a list of well-defined actions with a clearly identifiable European added value has been formulated, nor has a clear governance architecture for the implementation of the renewed strategy been designed. The EU Commission has presented an overview of various actions currently performed by the EU to enhance the sustainability objectives across different sectors (European Commission, 2016), but no ambitious and forward-looking action plan has been formulated so far. In the absence of such a plan, there is a high risk that the commitment of the Commission to carry out detailed and regular monitoring of the Sustainable Development Goals in EU will not provide solid knowledge-based grounds for evaluating the progress of the strategy, until a precise framework of concrete lines of intervention is designed and indicators are fine-tuned for measuring specific policy impacts instead of tracing a wide range of trends related to the existing indicators across various policy areas.

In the same way, the contours of the new governance architecture appear to be rather blurred. It has been emphasised that Agencies, European External Action Service, and Member State Cities and local authorities will have a particular role to play in the 2030 Agenda implementation with a specific dedicated goal (SDG 11), as well as the other urban targets. Moreover, the Commission's guidance stresses the importance of a joint effort of citizens, civil society, organisations and businesses in order to fulfil the SDS goals, but the only concrete tool proposed for such a purpose appears to be a multi-stakeholder platform with "a role in the follow-up and exchange of best practices on SDG implementation across sectors in Member States and at EU level, in order to create a dynamic space bringing together different stakeholders of the public and private sphere" (European Commission, 2016). This platform is expected to act as a peer-learning hub where stakeholders can engage in debates about sustainability activities and inform others about ongoing successful initiatives, but it is not clear how far it is going to empower these actors and enhance their ownership of the strategy. In sum, it seems that voluntary commitment and loose coordination have been definitely endorsed by the new strategy as the main pillars for policy and governance transformations across different territorial levels.

Surprisingly, prior to the launch of the new strategy, no comprehensive evaluation of the previous efforts to mainstream sustainable development objectives across various policy sectors has been carried out in order to understand whether and how coordination and learning measures have actually contributed to enhancing ownership and commitment to the strategy objectives among various policy addressees. The aforementioned aspects, along with the linkage between policy discourse and programmes, has been largely overlooked by academic research as well.

Therefore, it seems crucial to address these issues, as previous studies have brought to light that not one but multiple discourses on sustainability exist in Europe and that the lines around which these discourses coalesce are not clearly discernible (Barnes and Hoerber, 2013). The scenario of a Europe of "multiple speeds" based on voluntary commitment of member states certainly threats to jeopardise the idea of political unity on a continental scale.

1.3 Unpacking policy mixes: overcoming institutional determinism and national level bias

Evidently, there are still a number of analytical puzzles to be solved about the effectiveness of policy designs and accordingly, conspicuous amount of research has been carried out over the last decades in the attempt to understand the reasons of policy success and failures (Howlett, 2011). Most of these studies have adopted an instrument perspective, aiming to understand how governments select policy instruments to achieve given policy goals (Wurzel *et al.*, 2013), to what extent the effectiveness of policy implementation depends on the characteristics of the instruments, such as, for example, automaticity, visibility, intrusiveness, cost and precision of targeting (Linder and Peters, 1989) or how policy actors perceive the appropriateness of these instruments for meeting their policy demands (Schneider and Ingram, 1990). The debate on these issues is ongoing, as there are still many gaps in our understanding of factors that determine the effectiveness of policy designs and a more extensive empirical analysis of policy instruments in different sectors, both individually and in combination, appears to be needed (Howlett, 2011).

The EU context shows several blank spots in this perspective, as a policy design perspective has been implicitly but primarily employed by scholars when dealing with the regulatory power of the EU and assessing the appropriateness of policy instruments for better compliance (Knill, 2006; Tömmel and Verdun, 2009) in relation with timely and correct transposition of EU law. Limited knowledge exists on how policy ideas consolidated at the EU level become embedded into specific policy programmes and whether and under which conditions these programmes produce the expected policy impact on target actors' strategies.

In particular, the Europeanisation research has suggested that the implementation performance is not affected by the choice of instruments per se, but by the degree of "misfit" – that is by the degree of incompatibility between EU policies and domestic policy structures (Graziano, 2013; Knill and Lenschow, 1998, 2000; Börzel, 2000). Studies on EU "old" (Knill and Lenschow, 2000) and "new" environmental policy instruments (Wurzel *et al.*, 2013) have suggested that the logic of path-dependence and policy legacies were the main explanatory factors of cross-country variations in implementation performance. However, a number of scholars have brought to light a limited analytical leverage of the "institutional filter", as evidence has been provided to show that the usage of policy instruments varies significantly not only across but also within different political systems (Padgett, 2003; Tews *et al.*, 2003) and that the compatibility of policy instruments with a particular kind of domestic institutional setting may not be the only explanation of implementation effectiveness. Besides, a number of studies have shown how preferences of crucial players (often conceptualised as veto players)

(Treib, 2003) as well as administrative capacities and experiences (Haverland and Romeijn, 2007; Kaeding, 2007) may change the scenario of transposition of EU legislation in the domestic political arenas (Falkner *et al.*, 2005). Therefore, it has been recognised that a lower level of abstraction would be needed, with a more careful analysis of the given interest constellations and the strategic interactions of domestic actors, which have remained seriously under-theorised (Treib, 2014: 9) in the study of policy implementation in the EU.

Obviously, a compliance-oriented approach (Börzel *et al.*, 2012), appears to be of limited help if the objective is to understand the implementation trajectories of the complex and multifaceted nature of the EU agenda for sustainable development, which embodies a mix of regulatory, financial and coordinating tools aiming not only to shape the strategies of central governments but also to directly influence the behaviour of industries, non-governmental organisations, sub-state governments and communities. Oftentimes, EU programmes have applied soft forms of coordination and have not required specific policy implementation provisions at the national level. Instead, they rely on a pro-active action by target actors that are expected to be triggered by voluntary commitment and attracted by a range of opportunities that would help engage them with common principles through coordination and learning. In this bottom-up perspective, Europeanisation has been conceived as a context offering shared solutions to common problems, which leaves sufficient space for tailor-made and context-sensitive solutions (Treib, 2014).

Although an actor-centred perspective (Scharpf, 1997) is not at all new to the study of European integration and the relevance of the micro policy dimension has been recognised as important for explaining cross-country variations in policy performance in the EU (Treib, 2003), only a few studies have elaborated on it (Marks, 1996), as this perspective naturally entails a number of methodological challenges, including the extremely heterogeneous multiplicity of potentially relevant factors to be taken into account, high variability of actors' characteristics, the lack of aggregated quantitative data for a representative sample of EU countries and a problematic qualitative in-depth analysis due to, among other factors, the linguistic diversity in the EU.

Notwithstanding the above limitations and concerns that have been raised with regard to the feasibility of this approach, an actor-centred analytical perspective appears to provide a number of advantages for understanding policy process in the EU, as it offers a much more nuanced view on policy implementation dynamics along with specific insights on how policy addressees respond to EU policy inputs bringing policy failure or success. In fact, some scholars have highlighted the fact that there might be more theoretical leverage in starting from actors' constellations in a given policy domain first, and then adding institutional complexity to account for the variation that policy variables do not explain (Radaelli *et al.*, 2012). The relevance of policy addressees has been particularly emphasised with regard to the processes of policy learning and transfer in the EU (Radaelli, 2000), which mainly develop through voluntary or self-regulatory instruments and for which the importance of institutional accounts appears to have been over-stated too (Bulmer and Padgett, 2005).

The only comprehensive framework that has attempted to develop a bottom-up sociologically inclined perspective to the study of the process of Europeanisation has been offered by the concept of "usage of Europe" (Jacquot and Woll, 2003), which provides a number of valuable insights on how the role of policy actors can be reconsidered in the context of European integration and how we can trace the ways in which governments actually utilise the multiple types of policy arrangements available to them, in particular in the absence of significant institutional pressure from the EU (Jacquot and Woll, 2003, 2010). This perspective has been applied meaningfully to the analysis of whether, where and how EU resources have been mobilised by the main political actors in the course of national welfare reforms (Graziano *et al.*, 2011), though its analytical potential appears to be promising also for understanding the implementation dynamics of wider EU policy agendas in which the question whether and how "Europe matters" (Jacquot and Woll, 2003) seems to be the crucial one. Considering the high political salience of the EU strategy for sustainable development, combined with its complex policy and governance design, elaborating on this approach seems to be indeed suitable for operationalising research efforts aiming to reveal to what extent the EU has been able to encourage a range of target actors to commit to EU governance principles and policy targets.

1.4 The concept of usage and policy implementation in the EU: building missing linkages

The pertinence of the analytical framework that has provided the concept of usage for analysing the relevance of the EU strategy for sustainable development, resides in its double-fold perspective, suggesting that it is not an a priori "degree of coercion" of policy instruments that matters, but the usage that is made of them, their concrete implementation and the meaning that actors attach to them (Jacquot and Woll, 2003). Furthermore, the notion of political usage draws attention to the cognitive and strategic dynamics of European transformations by emphasising the role of agency and suggesting that institutional contexts need to be interpreted and actors do not give automatic responses to political pressure: "they can choose and learn and, thus, develop agency independent of structural conditions" (Jacquot and Woll, 2010: 220). Therefore, actors may choose to engage with, interpret, appropriate or ignore the dynamics of European integration, whereas EU resources and constraints are considered to be important elements that usages are based on, which provide necessary but not sufficient conditions for strategic behaviour (Jacquot and Woll, 2010: 116).

While offering useful insights for understanding general policy-making in the EU, the analytical potential of this approach with regard to policy implementation can be further elaborated on. In particular, this concept helpfully distinguishes between three main types of usage: strategic, cognitive and legitimating, in order to describe how the role of actors materialises and how they appropriate the tools and resources offered by European integration to reach their goals by acting strategically (Jacquot and Woll, 2010). These resources are mainly legal, financial, cognitive, political and institutional (Graziano *et al.*, 2011). Finally, this approach highlights that the explanation of various scenarios of usage lies in actors' motivations and underlying beliefs, while resources and constraints are considered to be necessary but not sufficient condition for strategic behaviour.

Based on such a framework, further reflections on the analytical leverage of the concept of usage for understanding policy implementation can be developed. First of all, there might be situations in which actors' activation within an EU initiative appear to be sporadic and do not bring about any substantial changes, denoting a "symbolic" type of action (Newig, 2007) or usage. Furthermore, the analytical framework according to which different categories of actors are expected to develop specific types of usage appears to be somewhat restricted: for example, it was originally stated that politicians develop the legitimating type of usage, bureaucratic actors the strategic type, while experts the cognitive one, etc. (Jacquot and Woll, 2010: 117). It seems feasible to suggest, however, coherently with the general propositions of the concept, that any of the listed (and other) policy actors (e.g. experts, bureaucracies, politicians) may opt for any type of usage (strategic, cognitive or legitimating) depending on their interests and preferences or context conditions. Besides, many other (nonpolitical) actors, such as private companies, NGOs, etc., are affected by EU policies and are potentially capable of developing a certain type of usage of related policy programmes and, consequently, should be embraced by the framework. Accordingly, the interpretation of the scenarios of usage can be further completed by including additional elements that may take into account characteristics of various actors – not only political but also social and economic ones. Finally, although the original analytical framework of the concept of usage warns against institutionalist analysis that treat individual actors as simple transmission belts (Jacquot and Woll, 2010: 116), this approach has not been clear enough about how to conceive "context conditions" and to what extent they matter in determining the scenario of usage and policy outcomes. It seems, however, that it is implicitly accepted that the underlying beliefs and motivations are somewhat embedded in a system of social norms that actors will generally respect. Consequently, it seems feasible to suggest that along with motivations, such variables as policy actors' orientations and capabilities, as well as actors' constellations and modes of interaction (Scharpf, 1997: 38–39) play a relevant role in shaping actors strategies in the context of European policies.

In this way, when appraising the effectiveness of policy designs in the EU, the analysis will follow a micro policy perspective, observing not only government institutions' capacity "in a plentiful supply of resources, but also a corresponding belief or endowment on the part of target groups which would allow that capacity to be utilized effectively" (Schneider and Ingram, 1990: 92). Accordingly, policy implementation is considered more effective the more policy addressees engage with policy programmes, commit to their targets and adjust their strategies by deploying various EU resources. As a consequence, the EU governing capacity in the field of sustainable development is here conceived in terms of its capacity to resonate with interests, concerns and demands of policy addresses at different territorial levels and in its ability to enhance the required policy transformations through a mix of legal, financial, information and other instruments.

1.5 Research methodology

Building on the theoretical and conceptual insights illustrated above, the main endeavour of this research is to shed light on how "Europe matters" in the field of sustainable development and to what extent policy ideas and principles embedded in EU policies have been internalised by policy addressees as a consequence of participation in specific policy programmes and deployment of policy instruments activated by the EU within the framework of the sustainable development mainstreaming approach.

The analysis will depart from a comprehensive overview of the EU agenda for sustainable development, illustrating the evolution of its normative and legal foundations, and describing the main policy and governance instruments that have been created in order to accomplish sustainability objectives. It will then proceed by unpacking the policy mix embodied by the selected policy programmes that are underpinned by the sustainable development mainstreaming approach, showing how regulatory requirements, financial, learning and coordination tools have been combined in their design. Against this background, the implementation of the three programmes will be analysed in detail, focusing on the target actors' response to the EU system of guidance, opportunities and constraints.

As already mentioned, the three policy programmes (regional programming for sustainable urban development within EU cohesion policy, the Covenant of Mayors Programme for sustainable energy and climate, and the Eco-Innovation Programme within the framework of policies for green and circular economy) aimed at promoting sustainable development objectives into the respective policy sectors, while at the same time encouraging coordination between public authorities at different territorial levels, as well as collaborative networks based on public-private partnership. These programmes targeted respectively regional governments, local authorities and private companies, being underpinned by the idea that target actors have flexibility and autonomy for adjusting EU policies in the light of particular local circumstances, policy needs, and local knowledge. In other words, target actors were expected to adjust their strategies to EU objectives and principles by deploying various resources available through the programmes. Thus, a pro-active approach of target actors has been assumed to be the main driver for successful implementation of these programmes, although once they joined, policy addressees had to comply with a range of rules and well-established procedures, including monitoring and evaluation.

Drawing on the analytical insights discussed in the previous paragraph, the following four scenarios of usage of the three programmes will be considered by this research:

- Symbolic – corresponds to occasional and sporadic activation of policy actors within the EU programmes without any substantive changes in strategic or cognitive terms.

- Strategic – EU resources are actively transformed into practices with the intention of achieving a specific goal. The goal is clearly defined and consciously pursued, be it in order to increase actors' capacity of action or resources.
- Cognitive – refers to policy interpretation and persuasion. It applies to the diffusion of specific ideas and knowledge that provide a framework for developing new strategies or actions.
- Legitimising – includes a mix of cognitive and strategic elements, implying justification of a choice that has already been made by a policy actor. EU policy instruments are employed to strengthen the existing actors' strategies or consolidate positions.

These scenarios indicate different ways in which the participation in EU programmes may bring about transformations in target actors' strategies and behaviour, depending on how and to what extent they are disposed to acquire new policy ideas, adopt innovative operational principles, modify their strategic priorities, etc.

Consequently, the strategic and ideational scenarios of usage are characterised by a more significant degree of policy change, as they entail considerable transformations in target actors' strategies in terms of strategic goals and objectives in the former case, and policy ideas or expertise in the latter. In contrast, the degree of change is limited or null in both symbolic and legitimating types of usage. The scenario of symbolic usage indicates only sporadic and superficial activation of target actors within the framework of programmes, which is not followed either by growing commitment or by transformative learning. In contrast, the legitimating usage can be observed when policy actors possess sufficient policy knowledge in a given field and they have already developed their own strategies showing a high degree of ownership of EU objectives.

In this perspective, the underlying logic of policy change mainly develops along the dimensions of ownership and learning, which at the same time appear to be the ultimate political ambition of the EU policy programmes under examination. While the meaning of ownership is rather straightforward being related to the degree of commitment to common objectives and targets, the process of learning can be effectively captured by the following three typologies: instrumental learning, that is learning about how to redesign instruments for carrying out the policy; social learning – the redefinition of policy problems via new policy discourses; and political learning – that takes place when political actors learn about more sophisticated ways of pushing their favourite solutions (Radaelli, 2008). Literatures also distinguish between thin learning and thick learning (Checkel, 1998), referring in the former case to the situation in which an actor learns how to cope with a problem without changing preferences, whereas thick learning implies a change in preferences. As is known, socialisation, monitoring and benchmarking have been univocally mentioned among the main learning mobilising mechanisms in the EU (Radaelli, 2008). Socialisation makes actors more aware about their interdependence, providing also the preconditions for ideation, while monitoring enables those involved to keep track of progress and to compare what has been achieved by others, individually and as a whole. Benchmarking, in contrast, consists of a process of systemic comparison of results, allowing to compare own performance to that of others, considered to be the best (Vesan, 2008: 249–252) and thus, enhances the shared definitions of success and failure. All three instruments aim to enhance the development of a reflexive policy-making style and encourage policy improvements based on self-evaluation without necessarily conforming to or replicating practices of others.

Thus, the dimensions of ownership and learning appear to be particularly relevant for assessing the success of the selected policy programmes, since their impact is as high as the extent to which they manage to encourage the process of diffusion of common policy ideas, targets and goals, and enhance ownership of EU objectives among policy addressees. Ideally, the process of policy change through these instruments should bring policy convergence, which is different from convergence at the level of discourse – people speak the same language but their preferences do not change as a result of new vocabulary (Radaelli, 2008). Substantive policy change entails variations at the level of ideas, which alter preferences and are translated into decisions and actions following decisions, as well as implementation. Moreover, it has been emphasised that what is learnt is more important than what is actually achieved in terms of other policy results/objectives.

Different scenarios of usage reflect how intensely involved policy actors become in the process of learning and to what extent their sense of ownership of EU policy goals increases as a consequence of participation in specific policy programmes. Figure 1.1 is a graphical representation of this dynamics.

Therefore, when analysing the implementation trajectories of the selected policy programmes, the focus has particularly been on these two dimensions, investigating on how and to what extent target actors have actually aligned their strategies and practices to EU policy priorities and targets, and how much they have learnt through such experience.

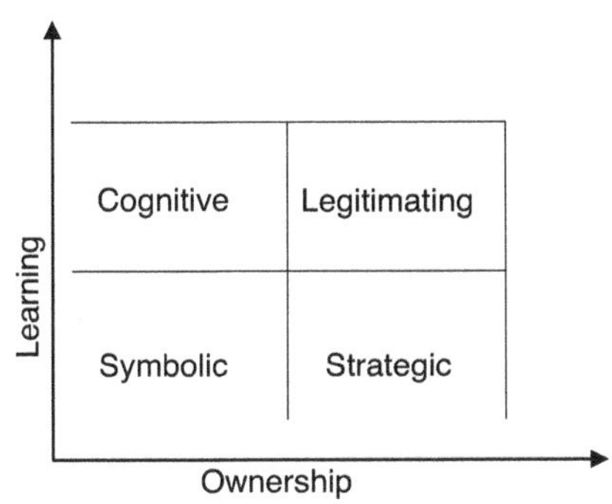

Figure 1.1 Dimensions of policy change and scenario of usage

Accordingly, the empirical enquiry has focused on the following core aspects of target actors' performance:

- The degree of commitment to general and specific objectives promoted by the programmes;
- The extent to which EU policy goals, targets and principles are translated into policy measures and practices through specific operational provisions included into programming and planning documents and projects by deploying a wide range of instruments;
- Policy addressees' perceptions about the importance of EU programmes for acquiring or consolidating specific knowledge and policy ideas in the field of sustainable development.

Beyond describing the implementation trends of the three programmes, the research sheds some light on factors that shape the different scenario of usage by unveiling policy addressees' preferences and their underlying motivations regarding responding to the EU system of incentives and guidance. Consistent with the analytical assumptions of the concept of usage, it has been suggested that the implementation dynamics for all selected programmes would converge along the following characteristics of policy actors, rather than being determined by institutional contextual conditions:

- Motivation (strategic orientation) for action (obtaining new knowledge, financial resources, partnerships, etc.)
- Perceived relevance of the established common objectives
- Existence of previous strategies
- Appropriate capacities (technical expertise, human resources, etc.)

Based on this analytical framework, the analysis will illustrate the degree and direction of policy change, revealing whether, when and how EU policy objectives become embedded in target actors' strategies and practices; how far do they have influenced governance transformations on the ground; to what extent policy actors rely on various EU resources for developing and improving their strategies for sustainable development and whether the uptake of new policy ideas, principles and operational methods promoted by the EU has actually taken place.

Two domestic contexts – Italy and the UK – have been selected for empirical analysis in order to demonstrate the interplay of factors influencing the scenario of policy implementation, as these two countries differ considerably in terms of two core criteria that determine policy and governance preconditions within which target actors develop their policy responses to EU guidance and incentives for sustainable development: the advancement of the national strategy for sustainable development and the pattern of decentralisation. The UK has been among the EU leaders in SD policies and performance, while Italy has showed one of the highest number of infringement procedure in the environmental sector and performed worse than several other EU counterparts, according to EU sustainable development indicators (Eurostat, 2015). As far as the pattern of territorial governance is concerned, over the last decade the UK has gone through significant devolution reforms empowering its four nations (Scotland, Wales, Northern Ireland and England), followed by more recent strengthening of the local level, in particular in the field of economic development policies. Its sub-state system of governance has been characterised by considerable flexibility, with a long tradition of public-private partnerships (PPP) and the presence of numerous non-elected agencies. In contrast, the process of regionalisation in Italy has remained incomplete, although wider legislative competences and powers have been transferred to regions as a consequence of constitutional reforms of 2005. Importantly, the central government still detains the main decision-making power as far as economic development is concerned and establishes the overall legal principles and political guidance in the environmental field. The Italian system of local government is regulated at the national level, and it has been characterised by rather hierarchical and top-down procedures, with very embryonic experience of PPPs.

Against this background, the volume offers a comparative analysis of strategies of the core policy actors targeted by the EU agenda for sustainable development, including national, regional and local governments, as well as enterprises. Therefore, the National Sustainable Development Strategies (NSDS) will be first reviewed in detail, followed by an in-depth analysis of regional operational programmes developed within the framework of cohesion policy, local sustainable energy plans implemented through the CoM and projects realised within the framework of the Eco-Innovation Programme. To this end, two regional and four local cases in each country have been chosen for in-depth analysis, representing similar territorial contexts with regard to such relevant characteristics for the definition of sustainable development strategies as the level of social and economic development and industrialisation, investments in research and development (R&D) and population. An analysis of regional operational programmes, with regard to their actions for sustainable urban development, will consider the Emilia-Romagna and Veneto Regions in Italy, and England and Scotland in the UK. One city in each of these regions: Bologna for Emilia-Romagna, Padua for Veneto, Glasgow for Scotland and Poole for England have been selected based on the population criteria, taking also into consideration their long-term experience of participation in the CoM. The study of the Eco-Innovation Programme has taken into consideration the entire population of enterprises that have taken part in the programme in the two domestic contexts.

The empirical research covers the decade between 2007 and 2017, and relies on a mix of quantitative and qualitative methods. The data and information collected from desk sources, including regional programming documents, local sustainable energy plans, eco-innovation projects, the EU legislation and other official documents, statistics, reports, etc. has been completed by in-depth interviews and a survey. All regional Managing Authorities (MA) except for England have been interviewed for the regional development programmes co-financed by the ERDF. Seven in-depth interviews were conducted in Italy and four in the UK in the cities participating in the Covenant of Mayors. As for the

Eco-Innovation Programme, a survey has been administered to all lead partners of projects implemented in the two countries: 28 completed questionnaires (18 from Italy and 10 from the UK) were collected and analysed by the research against the total number of 45 and 21 project lead partners respectively in Italy and the UK. Four in-depth interviews with Italian enterprises that acted as lead project partners have been carried out.

References

Barnes, P.M. and Hoerber, T.C. (eds.) (2013). *Sustainable Development and Governance in Europe: The Evolution of the Discourse on Sustainability*. London and New York: Routledge.

Berger, G. and Steurer, R. (2007). *The EU SDS process in the member states: SDS coordinators, national progress reports and the open method of coordination*. ESDN quarterly report, March. Available at: www.sd-network.eu/?k=quarterly%20reports&report_id=4 [Accessed 2 March 2016].

Berger, G. and Zwirner, W. (2008). *The interfaces between the EU SDS and the Lisbon strategy: Objectives, governance provisions, coordination and future developments*. ESDN quarterly report, December. Available at: www.sdnetwork.eu/?k=quarterly%20 reports&report_id=11 [Accessed 2 March 2016].

Bobrow, D.B. (2006). Policy design: Ubiquitous, necessary and difficult. In: Peters, G.B., Pierre, J. eds., *Handbook of Public Policy*. London: Sage, pp. 75–95.

Borrás, S. and Jacobsson, K. (2004). The open method of co-ordination and new governance patterns in the EU. *Journal of European Public Policy*, 11 (2), pp. 185–208.

Börzel, T.A. (2000). Why there is no Southern problem: On environmental leaders and laggards in the European Union. *Journal of European Public Policy*, 7 (1), pp. 141–162.

Börzel, T.A., Hofmann, T. and Panke, D. (2012). Caving in or sitting it out? Longitudinal patterns of non-compliance in the European Union. *Journal of European Public Policy*, 19 (4), pp. 454–471.

Börzel, T.A., Hofmann, T., Panke, D. and Sprungk, C. (2010). Obstinate and inefficient: Why member states do not comply with European law. *Comparative Political Studies*, 43 (11), pp. 1363–1390.

Bulmer, S. and Padgett, S. (2005). Policy transfer in the European Union: An institutionalist perspective. *British Journal of Political Science*, 35 (1), pp. 103–126.

Cahill, A.G. and Overman, E.S. (1990). Information policy: A study of values in the policy process. *Review of Policy Research*, 9 (4), pp. 803–818.

Checkel, J. (1998). The constructivist turn in international relations theory. *World Politics*, 50 (2), pp. 324–348.

Cowles, M.G., Caporaso, J. and Risse, T. (eds.) (2001). *Transforming Europe: Europeanization and Domestic Change*. Ithaca and London: Cornell University Press.

Damonte, A. (2014). Policy tools for green growth in the EU15: A qualitative comparative analysis, *Environmental Politics*, 23 (1), pp. 18–40.

Duina, F. (2007). Domestic actors and Europeanization: Why 'fit' still matters. *Comparative European Politics*, 5 (3), pp. 339–341.

Duina, F. (1997). Explaining legal implementation in the European Union. *International Journal of the Sociology of Law*, 25 (2), pp. 155–179.

European Commission (2001). *Communication a sustainable Europe for a better world: A European Union strategy for sustainable development* [COM(2001)264final]. Available at: http://eurlex.europa.eu [Accessed 5 May 2018].

European Commission (2005). *Communication on the review of the sustainable development strategy: A platform for action* [COM(2005)658final]. Available at: http://eurlex.europa.eu [Accessed 5 May 2018].

European Commission (2007). *Progress report on the sustainable development strategy 2007* [COM(2007) 642 final]. Available at: http://eurlex.europa.eu [Accessed 5 May 2018].

European Commission (2010a). *Communication Europe 2020: A strategy for smart, sustainable and inclusive growth* [COM(2010)2020final]. Available at: https://eur-lex.europa.eu [Accessed 5 May 2018].

European Commission (2010b). *Communication next steps for a sustainable European future European action for sustainability* [COM(2016)739 final]. Available at: http://eurlex.europa.eu [Accessed 5 May 2018].

European Commission (2016). *Communication next steps for a sustainable European future European action for sustainability* [COM(2016)739 final].

European Council (2000). *The presidency conclusions: Lisbon European Council*, 23–24 March [100/1/00].

European Council (2001). *The presidency conclusions of the Göteborg*, 15–16 June. Available at: www.consilium.europa.eu/media/20983/00200-r1en1.pdf.

European Council (2006). *Review of the EU Sustainable Development Strategy (EU SDS): Renewed strategy*. Available at: http://register.consilium.europa.eu [Accessed 5 May 2018].

Eurostat (2015). Sustainable development in the European Union. 2015 monitoring report of the EU Sustainable Development Strategy. Available at: https://ec.europa.eu/eurostat/documents/3217494/6975281/KS-GT-15-001-EN-N.pdf

Falkner, G. (2016). The EU's current crisis and its policy effects: Research design and comparative findings. *Journal of European Integration*, 38 (3), pp. 219–235.

Falkner, G., Treib, O., Hartlapp, M. and Leiber, S. (2005). *Complying with Europe? The Impact of EU Minimum Harmonisation and Soft Law in the Member States*. Cambridge: Cambridge University Press.

Featherstone, K. and Radaelli, C.M. (2003). *The Politics of Europeanization*. Oxford: Oxford University Press.

Graziano, P. (2013). *Europeanization and Domestic Policy Change: The Case of Italy*. London and New York: Routledge.

Graziano, P., Jacqout S. and Pallier, B. (2011). *The EU and the Domestic Politics of Welfare Reforms*. Basingstoke: Palgrave MacMillan.

Graziano, P. and Halpern, C. (2016). EU governance in times of crisis: Inclusiveness and effectiveness beyond the 'hard' and 'soft' law divide. *Comparative European Politics*, 14 (1), pp. 1–19.

Graziano, P. and Vink, M. (eds.) (2008). *Europeanization New Research Agendas*. Basingstoke: Palgrave MacMillan.

Hall, R. (1993). Policy paradigms, social learning, and the state. *Comparative Politics*, 25 (3), pp. 975–296.

Halpern, C. (2010). Governing despite its instruments? Instrumentation in EU environmental policy. *West European Politics*, 33 (1), pp. 39–57.

Haverland, M and Romeijn, M. (2007). Do member states make European politics work? Analysing the EU transposition deficit. *Public Administration*, 85 (3), pp. 757–778.

Heidbreder, E.G. (2017). Strategies in multilevel policy implementation: Moving beyond the limited focus on compliance. *Journal of European Public Policy*, 24 (8), pp. 1367–1384.

Héritier, A. (2001). *New modes of governance in Europe: Policy-making without legislating?* Research Paper. Rennen Institut. Available at: www.renner-institut.at/fileadmin/user_upload/downloads/eEuropa_buch/heritier.pdf.

Héritier, A., Kerwer, D., Knill, C., Lehmkuhl, D., Teutsch, M. and Douillet, A. (2001). *Differential Europe: New Opportunities and Restrictions for Policymaking in the Member States*. Lanham, MD: Rowman & Littlefield.

Howlett, M. (2011). *Designing Public Policies: Principles and Instruments*. London and New York: Routledge.

IIED (2002). *Sustainable development strategies: A resource book*. Compiled by Barry Dalal-Clayton and Stephen Bass for OECD and UNDP. Available at: www.poptel.org.uk/nssd/pdf/resource_book/SDStrat-Prel.pdf [Accessed 10 March 2015].

Jacquot, S. and Woll, C. (2003). Usage of European integration: Europeanisation from a sociological perspective. *European Integration Online Papers*, 7, 12.

Jacquot, S. and Woll, C. (2010). Using Europe: Strategic action in multi-level politics. *Comparative European Politics*, 8 (1), pp. 110–126.

Jessop, B. (2016). Territory, politics, governance and multispatial meta-governance. *Territory, Politics, Governance*, 4 (2), pp. 8–32.

Jordan, A. and Lenschow, A. (2008). *Innovation in Environmental Policy? Integrating the Environment for Sustainability*. Cheltenham: Edward Elgar Publishing.

Jordan, A. and Schout, A., (2006). *The Coordination of the European Union. Exploring the Capacities of Networked Governance*. Oxford: Oxford University Press.Kassim, H. and Le Gales, P. (2010). Exploring governance in a multi-level polity: A policy instruments approach. *West European Politics*, 33 (1), pp. 1–21.

Kaeding, M. (2008). Lost in translation or full steam ahead? The transposition of EU transport directives across member states. *European Union Politics*, 9 (1), pp.115–143.

Knill, C. (2006). Implementation. In Richardson, J. ed., *European Union: Power and Policy-Making*. London and New York: Routledge.

Knill, C. and Lenschow, A. (1998). Coping with Europe: The impact of British and German administrations on the implementation of EU environmental policy. *Journal of European Public Policy*, 5 (4), pp. 595–614.

Knill, C. and Lenschow, A. (2000). *Implementing EU Environmental Policy: New Directions Old Problems*. Manchester: Manchester University Press.

Knill, C. and Lenschow, A. (2001). Adjusting to EU environmental policy: Change and persistence of domestic administrations. In: Cowles, M.G., Caporaso, J. and Risse, T. eds., *Transforming Europe: Europeanization and Domestic Change*. Ithaca and London: Cornell University Press.

Knill, C. and Tosun, J. (2012). Governance institutions and policy implementation in the European Union. In: Richardson, J. ed., *Constructing a Policy-Making State? Policy Dynamics in the EU*. Oxford: Oxford University Press, pp. 308–333.

Lafferty, W. and Knudsen, J. (2007). The issue of 'Balance' and Trade-offs in Environmental Policy Integration. EPIGOV Working Paper. Berlin: Ecologic.

Liefferink, D., Wiering, M. and Uitenboogaart, Y. (2011). The EU water framework directive: A multidimensional analysis of implementation and domestic impact. *Land Use Policy*, 28 (4), pp. 712–722.

Linder, S.H. and Peters, G.B. (1989). Instruments of government: Perceptions and contexts. *Journal of Public Policy*, 9, pp. 35–58.

Marks, G. (1996). An actor-centred approach to multi-level governance. *Regional & Federal Studies*, 6 (2), pp. 20–38.

Mastenbroek, E. (2005). EU compliance: Still a 'black hole'? *Journal of European Public Policy*, 12 (6), pp. 1103–1120.

Mol, P.J. and Sonnenfeld, D.A. (2000). Ecological modernisation around the world: An introduction. *Environmental Politics*, 9 (1), pp. 1–14.

Newig, J. (2007). Symbolic environmental legislation and societal self-deception. *Environmental Politics*, 16 (2), pp. 276–296.

Padgett, S. (2003). Between synthesis and emulation: EU policy transfer in the power sector. *Journal of European Public Policy*, 10 (2), pp. 227–245.

Radaelli, C.M. (2000). Policy transfer in the European Union: Institutional isomorphism as a source of legitimacy. *Governance*, 13 (1), pp. 25–43.

Radaelli, C.M. (2008). Europeanization, policy learning, and new modes of governance. *Journal of Comparative Policy Analysis*, 10 (3), pp. 239–254.

Radaelli, C.M. and Borrás, S. (2011). The politics of governance architectures: Creation, change and effects of the EU Lisbon Strategy. *Journal of European Public Policy*, 18 (4), pp. 463–484.

Radaelli, C.M., Dente, B. and Dossi, S. (2012). Recasting institutionalism: Institutional analysis and public policy. *European Political Science*, 11 (4), pp. 537–550.

Scharpf, F.W. (1997). *Games Real Actors Play: Actor-Centered Institutionalism in Policy Research*. New York: Avalon Publishing.

Scharpf, F.W. (2003). Problem-Solving Effectiveness and Democratic Accountability in the EU, MPIfG Working Paper 03/1, Max Planck Institute for the Study of Societies February 2003. Available at: www.mpifg.de/pu/workpap/wp03-1/wp03-1.html.

Schmidt, V. (2000). Democracy and discourse in an integrated Europe and a globalizing world. *European Law Journal*, 6 (3), pp. 277–300.

Schmidt, V. and Radaelli, C. (2004). Policy change and discourse in Europe: Conceptual and methodological issues. *West European Politics*, 27 (2), pp. 183–210.

Schneider, A.L. and Ingram, H. (1990). The behavioral assumptions of policy tools. *The Journal of Politics*, 52 (2), pp. 510–529.

Smismans, S. (ed.) (2006). *European Governance and Civil Society*. Cheltenham: Edward Elgar.

Steurer, R. (2016). The Proliferation of Environmental Concepts in EU Policymaking: Serious Omnipresence, Diluted Focus, or Excessive Rhetoric? Paper presented at the ECPR Joint Research Sessions. Pisa, April 24–28.

Steurer, R. and Berger, G. (2011). The EU's double-track pursuit of sustainable development in the 2000s: How Lisbon and sustainable development strategies ran past each other. *International Journal of Sustainable Development & World Ecology*, 18 (2), pp. 99–108.

Steurer, R. and Martinuzzi, A. (2005). Towards new patterns of strategy formation in the public sector: First experiences with national strategies for sustainable development in Europe. *Environment and Planning C: Government and Policy*, 23, pp. 455–472.

Thomann, E. (2015). Customizing Europe: Transposition as bottom-up implementation. *Journal of European Public Policy*, 22 (10), pp. 1368–1387.

Tews, K., Busch, P. and Jörgens, H. (2003). The diffusion of new environmental policy instruments. *European Journal of Political Research*, 42 (4), pp. 569–600.

Tömmel, I. and Verdun, A. (2009). *Innovative Governance in the European Union: The Politics of Multilevel Policymaking*. Boulder: Lynne Rienner Publishers.

Treib, O. (2003). *EU governance, misfit, and the partisan logic of domestic adaptation: An actor-centred perspective on the transposition of EU Directives*, EUSA 8th Biennial International Conference, Nashville, Tennessee, conference paper online version available at: http://aei.pitt.edu/6566/.

Treib, O. (2014). Implementing and complying with EU governance outputs. *Living Reviews in European Governance*, 9 (1), pp. 1–47.

UNCED (1992). Agenda 21. Available at: https://sustainabledevelopment.un.org/content/documents/Agenda21.pdf.

Vesan P. (2008). Conoscenza e apprendimento nella governance europea. In Ferrera, M. and Giuliani, M. eds., *Governance e politiche nell'Unione europea*. Bologna: Il Mulino, pp. 241–269.

Wurzel, R.K.W., Zito, A.R. and Jordan, A.J. (2013). *Environmental Governance in Europe: A Comparative Analysis of New Environmental Policy Instruments*. Cheltenham: Edward Elgar.

2 EU agenda for sustainable development

Evolving policy instruments and governance architectures

2.1 Political discourse on sustainable development in the EU: legal and normative foundations

As both past and current scholarly and political debates clearly show, the conceptualisation of sustainable development in the EU has been far from unproblematic. According to some studies, an EU-wide political discourse on sustainability has consolidated over the recent decades, progressively becoming a context in which decisions are made about how to resolve the tension existing between economic growth, environmental protection and social justice (Barnes and Hoerber, 2013). Other scholars have emphasised that the development and implementation of the EU's policies for sustainable development has so far been disappointing (Pallemaerts, 2013), despite a legally formalised commitment to this principle included in the treaties. Moreover, there is no consensus even on the interpretation of the principle of environmental policy integration (EPI), which has been conceived as an essential pillar of sustainable development allowing for channelling sustainable development goals across sectoral policies (Lafferty, 2004). A contrasting view on this aspect exists, according to which these two related concepts have developed in parallel rather than together, with EPI being mainly concerned with ensuring that environmental protection is factored into all governmental decision-making, whereas sustainable development is concerned with balancing economic, social and environmental issues (Steurer, 2008). In fact, several tensions and ambiguities can be observed in the evolving EU agenda for sustainable development in terms of both prioritisation of goals in the context of a problematic balance between environmental, economic and social pillars, and policy and governance tools for achieving them.

Hence, the normative concept of sustainable development has started to make headway since the early 1990s, being increasingly embedded in EU treaties and secondary legislation. Following the growing political acknowledgement of the need to promote sustainable development announced in the fifth Environmental Action Programme (EAP) in 1992, the EU first established the legal basis for this commitment through the Treaty of Amsterdam (1997), stating that the "Union shall set itself [. . .] to promote a harmonious, balanced and sustainable development" (Art. 2, Treaty on European Union (TEU)). Therefore, the obligation to integrate environmental protection requirements into the definition and implementation of other Community policies and activities has been included in Article 6 of the Treaty (now Art. 11, Treaty on the Functioning of the European Union (TFEU)).

Since then, the EU legal commitments to sustainable development have significantly amplified, primarily through the codification of the principle of environmental policy integration, as well as through provisions aiming at the prevention and remedying of the environmental damage, ensured by the polluter pays, precautionary and prevention principles.

Beyond EU secondary legislation that has widely incorporated the aforementioned principles since the end of the 1990s, a renewed legal commitment to these principles, has been enshrined in the Lisbon Treaty. A general commitment to sustainability was announced in Article 3(3) TEU, stating that "the Union . . . shall work for the sustainable development in Europe based on balanced economic growth . . . and a high level of protection and improvement of the quality of the environment", while Article 5 enlarged the scope of action stating that "the Union . . . shall contribute to the sustainable development of the Earth". The Treaty has also emphasised that with regard to the external policy dimension, "EU policies commit to foster sustainable economic, social and environmental development of developing countries . . . help develop international measures preserve quality environment and sustainable management global natural resources, in order to ensure sustainable development" (Art. 21(2) TEU). It was further specified that the Union shall respect the principles and pursue the objectives set out in paragraphs 1 and 2 (check) in the development and implementation of the different areas of the Union's external action . . . and of the external aspects of its other policies (Art. 21(3) TEU).

The principle of EPI has been further strengthened by the new Article 11 and Article 191 (TFEU). Accordingly, EU policies commit to contribute to preserving, protecting and improving the quality of the environment, protecting human health, prudent and rational utilisation of natural resources, promoting measures at international level to deal with regional or worldwide environmental problems, and in particular combating climate change. Furthermore, the *prevention principle* has been confirmed (Art. 191(2)TFEU) as already defined by the Single European Act, establishing that preventive action should be taken, that environmental damage should as a priority be rectified at source and that the polluter should pay. The *precautionary principle* states that scientific uncertainty must not be used as excuse to postpone measures against potential environmental damage. Lastly, the Treaty has recognised the need to extend the use of scientific and technical data in the evaluation of the potential benefits and costs of action or lack of action, and define environmental policies in close junction with the economic and social development of the Union as a whole and the balanced development of its regions (Art. 191 (3) TFEU).

Regardless of the increased recognition of the normative value of sustainable development in EU policy-making, along with the consolidation of its legal foundations concerning environmental protection, the political ambition of this strategy appears to have gradually declined over the last decade, while its operational scope still remains to be defined. Thus, after a decade of growing political attention to sustainability agenda, which followed the Rio Earth Summit in 1992 and culminated with the approval of the EU Strategy for sustainable development in 2001, the EU's political priorities have definitely turned to economic concerns, guided by the concept of "sustainable growth respecting the environment" first announced by the Treaty of Maastricht. As will be illustrated in greater detail, this process has progressively evolved from the original idea of a stronger version of environmental sustainability built on the EPI principle towards the concept of ecological modernisation (Steurer and Meadowcroft, 2013), which considers economic growth and environmental protection not as antagonistic, but rather as mutually reinforcing.

Such trend has definitely consolidated with the "Europe 2020" Strategy that explicitly promotes the "win win" approach, highlighting synergies between economic, social and environmental objectives. Putting its primary emphasis on economic growth, this new strategy has restricted the environmental component to energy and resource efficiency targets, while very modestly addressing the social dimension in terms of employment, education and inclusion measures. Besides, the increasing prioritisation of climate policy objectives, which have not been clearly framed in the perspective of a wider policy agenda for sustainability, seems to have further undermined the consistency of the latter.

Remarkably, the very words "sustainable development" have not been mentioned in the main Europe 2020 policy document, and it was considered ironic that at the very moment of its elevation to an overriding objective of the EU in the Lisbon Treaty, sustainable development was fading from high-level political discourse to be replaced by the reductionist notions of "sustainable growth" or "green economy" (Pallemaerts, 2013).

The United Nations Organisation's Agenda 2030 with its 17 ambitious development goals has put forward a number of new challenges for the EU, offering also the opportunity to carry out a comprehensive review of the EU strategy for sustainable development, which has been missing since 2006. Surprisingly, neither a systematic political assessment of implemented actions has been carried out – except for the Commission's overview of how the existing policies have been contributing to the achievement of a number of these objectives (European Commission, 2016), nor a detailed policy guidance has been formulated in order to identify a clear European added value of the EU commitments to Agenda 2030. Although for the first time the EU Commission has endeavoured to bring the internal and external dimensions of the EU action for sustainable development within a unique framework (European Commission, 2016), it still appears to lack a clear vision of how the coherence and complementarity of these two components will be guaranteed and in what way their progress and impact will be evaluated in the medium and long term.

To proceed in this direction, it appears to be crucial to reconsider the relevance of the substantive normative and legal foundations of the concept of sustainability developed by EU legislation, along with the impacts produced by the implementation of the so-called "sustainable development mainstreaming" approach that has aimed to promote sustainable development objectives across various sectors since 2008. In sum, a number of challenges are still to be addressed for the principle of sustainable development to be conceptualised as a *meta-principle* (Cordonier Segger and Khalfan, 2004) of EU policy-making, which is an overarching cross-sectoral policy paradigm covering both the internal policy drivers, as well as the external relations and cooperation.

First, some scholars emphasise the uncertain legal consequences and limitations of EU treaty provisions for sustainable development (Nowag, 2016), highlighting that they lack the coherence and clarity needed in a legal context, rather embodying a political compromise with which everyone can agree and which can be given its political content according to the political actors who use it (Kingston, 2013). Moreover, it seems that the legal basis for the EU sustainable development agenda shows a number of features of "symbolic" legislation (Newig, 2007), as it is characterised by a low prospective issue-related effectiveness and a high prospective political-strategic effectiveness. In fact, they have been positioned at the top of the EU legal rule and its main provisions were primarily passed at a tactically "right" point in time, coinciding with major international agreements on sustainable development and climate change in order to ensure more public attention and political support to action. No doubt that these provisions were highly suited to enhance political acceptance but the legal consequences in the case of non-compliance appear to be not sufficiently clear. In fact, the appropriateness of these provisions for attaining the objectives of the Treaty and their enforceability has been considered limited, as is the availability of resources required by the implementing administration or the structural ability and disposition of the addressees to comply with the law (Van Hees, 2014).

The attempt to guarantee the respect for this principle ex ante through the Better Regulation agenda has been assessed as rather modest too. Since 2009, the EU Commission has been promoting horizontal policy coordination as the central means of placing sustainable development at the core of EU policy-making, including impact assessment covering both new internal and external Commission policy initiatives, stakeholder consultation and regulatory simplification. The quality of this process was expected to be guaranteed, primarily through the Better Regulation Guidance and Reports of the European Commission, but a number of outstanding challenges have been identified for the Better Regulation agenda to really embrace the sustainable development goals (Renda, 2017), particularly in the way in which the indicators associated with each of the SDGs refer to similar values and benchmarks. For example, the following elements appear to be unsettled in the current better regulation framework: (i) a methodological framework that considers sustainable development as the framework within which to locate policy impacts, rather than one of several policy impacts; (ii) a way to measure distance from SDG targets; and (iii) criteria to prioritise certain impacts over others in the case of trade-offs (Renda, 2017: 9).

Overall, although ideas and principles related to environmental sustainability have progressively diffused in the political discourse at the EU level, no substantial empirical evidence exists to show how and to what extent these transformations have entailed changes at the *meso* level of policy instruments and at the *micro* level encompassing policy styles, perceptions and behaviour of policy actors.

Bearing in mind these weaknesses in the political narrative and legal framework for sustainability, the next few paragraphs will illustrate policy and governance framework as well as the main instruments that have been designed by the EU to translate the sustainable development mainstreaming approach into concrete policy practices on the ground.

2.2 Policy and governance architectures for sustainable development

As numerous studies of international and European contexts have brought to light (Berger and Steurer, 2007; Bulkeley *et al.*, 2013; Jordan and Lenschow, 2008; Jordan and Lenschow, 2010), the overall relevance of the concept of sustainable development in policy and governance terms can be summarised (Table 2.1) through the three governing principles: cross-sectoral integration, cross-jurisdictional coordination and inclusive patterns of decision-making.

Accordingly, integrated policy approach requires combining different sectoral policy measures in a unique operational design and establish appropriate governance settings enabling both the coordination of different organisational units and participatory modes of decision-making involving all actors concerned, across different territorial and functional jurisdictions.

As the overview given above has illustrated, the normative and legal foundations of the EU strategy for sustainable development has mainly contributed to the implementation of the EPI principle, which implies taking into particular consideration environmental concerns when making decisions in any policy sector. The EU has committed to this principle since the end of the 1980s, applying it as a driver for policy change across a number of sectors. Originally, the EU approach was totally in line with the spirit of the seminal report "Our Common Future" (1987), that paved the way to the international agenda for sustainable development, conceiving EPI as an essential tool for achieving sustainability goals and attributing foremost priority to environmental objectives in the process of "balancing" economic, social and environmental concerns (Lafferty and Hovden, 2003).

Table 2.1 Governing principles of sustainable development

Governing principle	*Components to integrate*
Cross-sectoral integration	Sectors: economic, social, environmental, transport, energy, etc.
Cross-jurisdictional coordination	Sectors and scales: EU, national, regional, local
Inclusiveness/partnership	Actors: public authorities, civil society, economic and social interests, enterprises, etc.

Source: Author's elaboration on Steurer (2008)

In fact, the pattern of policy integration developed between 1980s and 1990s has promoted a rather "strong" idea of EPI (Lafferty, 2004), by promoting specifically two core policy directions established by Environmental Actions Programmes (EAPs). On the one hand, the need to incorporate environmental objectives into all stages of policy-making in non-environmental policy sectors was emphasised, with a specific recognition of this goal as a guiding principle for the planning and execution of policy. On the other, a commitment was taken to aggregate presumed environmental consequences into an overall evaluation of policy and minimise contradictions between environmental and sectoral policies by giving principled priority to the former over the latter. In sum, the primacy of environmental dimension over any other sectoral interest has been stressed, aiming to ensure that environmental objectives become principle or overarching societal objectives, referring to both a state of affairs, which is the aim of policy-making, as well as to the process necessary for achieving change (Lafferty, 2002).

In this perspective, the Cardiff process that took its name after the meeting of the European Council in Cardiff, was launched in June 1998. It required different Council formations to integrate environmental considerations into their respective activities, putting article 6 of the EC Treaty into practice. This process has been considered one of the most ambitious projects ever launched for EPI, as numerous legislative and policy provisions were formulated to guide the EU effort of "greening" the various sectors through specific regulatory and organisational instruments, such as, for example, Environmental Impact Assessment (EIA) introduced by Directive 85/337/EEC (amended and codified by Directive 2011/92/EU) and Strategic Environmental Assessment (SEA) established by Directive 2001/42/EC. Moreover, a significant number of regulations and directives were adopted across different sectors, encouraging higher environmental standards, including water, agriculture, etc. (Jordan and Lenschow, 2008).

However, the effectiveness of this process still remains to be assessed and sceptical views have been expressed with regard to its success, emphasising that the various instruments that were supposed to deliver more integration have themselves been poorly coordinated with one another (Jordan *et al.*, 2005) and the normative principle of EPI has failed to permeate all the stages of the policy-making process, especially the earliest ones (Jordan and Lenschow, 2010).

Against this background, some observers have further highlighted that the launch of the EU agenda for sustainable development in 2001 and the subsequent shift from EPI to an equilibrium between the economic, social and environmental dimensions of sustainability was not a semantic matter. In fact, such a shift in the political discourse has entailed the move from the "principle priority" of environmental factors in decision-making to a process of balancing of the three factors, which would conceivably involve weakening the last (Jordan and Lenschow, 2008).

More specifically, the Gothenburg declaration included in the Presidency Conclusions Document of June 2001 welcomed the EU Commission's communication on sustainable development (European Council, 2001) and announced the decision to launch a strategy for sustainable development, aiming to complete the Union's political commitment to economic and social renewal by adding a third, environmental dimension to the Lisbon process initiated in 2000 (European Council, 2000).

Besides affirming EU commitment to promote sustainable development at a global level, which was further explicated in the declaration of the European Council in Barcelona held in view of the World Summit on Sustainable Development in Johannesburg (2002), the EU strategy targeted the following four areas for pursuing environmental priorities in internal policies: climate change, transport, public health and natural resources. A list of actions to be promoted in these areas was drawn, building on the Commission's communication on sustainable development (European Commission, 2001), the 6th EAP and the sector strategies for environmental integration. The principle of EPI was referred to at §32 of the Strategy, which invited the European Council to complete and further develop sectoral strategies for integrating environment into all relevant community policy areas.

However, no concrete proposals in this sense have followed. Instead, according to some observers, the adding of an environmental dimension to the Lisbon priorities on growth and jobs appeared to be imbalanced and ineffective from the outset (Steurer and Berger, 2011). In fact, evidence has been provided that the political commitment to EPI – which was more sharply and forcefully expressed in the 1990s – tangibly weakened, as jurisdiction has pledged itself to implement the somewhat broader and less explicitly environmentally focused goal of sustainable development (Jordan and Lenschow, 2008). In the course of re-conceptualisation of the EPI foundations aimed at integration of this principle in the newly formulated sustainable development strategy, concerns about the economic competitiveness and employment became more pronounced than environmental objectives. This trend has further consolidated as a consequence of subsequent revisions of the SDS.

In 2006, at the explicit request of the Council (European Council 2005) and following the commitment of the EU Commission to review the strategy at the start of each new mandate, the strategy was revised by the new office guided by José Manuel Barroso. Based on the assessment of progress since 2001 and acknowledging a number of drawbacks in the implementation of the strategy, the initial proposal of the Commission highlighted the challenge of reconciling economic development, social cohesion, north/south equity and protection of the environment (European Commission, 2005a), reiterating the need to strengthen the linkage and complementarity between the Lisbon process for growth and jobs and sustainable development. When defining its strategic objectives for the next five years, the Commission suggested that policy coherence and coordination should be improved within the framework of the Cardiff process by increasing the use of market and coordination mechanisms, encouraging investments in science and technology, and involving social and economic stakeholders and civil society.

Hence, the revised strategy emphasised the need to further integrate sustainable development objectives into the Lisbon process and increase the role of economic factors in facilitating the transition to a more sustainable society. In continuity with the previous strategic guidance adapted in 2001, such areas as climate change, sustainable energy, public health, social inclusion, sustainable management of natural resources and transport, sustainable production and consumption, global poverty and development were included among the strategic fields of action (European Commission, 2005a). At the same time, the attention to EPI has further declined: neither specific indicators related to this principle were included in the final text, nor dedicated policy instruments were designed in order to maintain the importance of environmental objectives that were placed high in the new integrated strategy (European Council, 2006a), establishing four principal objectives: environmental protection, social equality and cohesion, economic prosperity and international responsibilities. The revised strategy has committed to a wider version of the principle of policy integration, suggesting to bring economic, social and environmental considerations together. It called for coherent and mutually reinforcing action across the three dimensions, also by making full use of instruments for better regulation, such as balanced impact assessment and stakeholder consultations, best use of available knowledge, precautionary principle and polluter pays principle. Importantly, a number of relevant governance principles have been formulated in the strategy, including the promotion and protection of fundamental rights, inter and intra-generational equity, open and democratic society, involvement of citizens, business and social partners, policy integration, coherence and governance (European Council, 2006a).

In the review carried out in 2009, the Commission traced the main achievements and unsustainable trends across a number of EU policies, anticipating the data presented by Eurostat in its extensive report on sustainable development (Eurostat, 2009). This new document has endorsed a three-dimensional nature of sustainable development as the cornerstone of the strategy: "a development that can only be achieved if economic growth, social inclusion and environmental protection go hand in hand, both in Europe and in other parts of the world" (European Commission, 2009: 19). A number of policy achievements have been registered across several sectors, in particular the "greening" of energy and transport, sustainable production and consumption, including eco-labelling and other types of environmental certification, eco-innovation, green public procurement and resource efficiency.

The Commission's document (European Commission, 2009) has once again highlighted a number of weaknesses of the strategy, stressing the need for improvement, especially with regard to the definition of its specific objectives compared to other EU strategies (Lisbon strategy, Climate and Energy package, etc.). The necessity of establishing more effective monitoring and evaluation instruments has been emphasised, but no specific proposals were advanced in this sense. Instead, the linkage between Lisbon and SD strategies has been further strengthened, mainstreaming eco-innovation, resource efficiency and green growth as leading themes for developing measures with visible positive results on growth, jobs and environment. Importantly, although the EU Commission urged the EU Council to decide on a revised strategy by 2011, when a comprehensive review of the strategy was supposed to be launched, the Council has shown a rather weak sense of ownership and commitment to the strategy, and no comprehensive political revision of the SDS followed. The Council's Presidency Report of 2009 recognised that the results of EU actions for SDS were limited and generally reiterated that the EU SDS should contribute to a further change in order to avoid irreparable damage and to create a future of prosperity, equity and well-being. The Report emphasised the need to ensure that the SDS had a real influence on EU policies, including other cross-cutting EU strategies, and called for a better coherence between short and long-term objectives and between different sectors. Accordingly, the Commission was invited to propose appropriate measures to enhance the links and synergies between the SDS and the upcoming EU 2020 strategy, as well as to integrate sustainability objectives in its 5-year work programmes and in the future EU budgetary proposals. However, no comprehensive review of the strategy's progress since 2006 has been conducted (European Council, 2009a).

In 2015 the EU confirmed its commitment to sustainable development goals announced by the UN Agenda 2030. Following the EU Commission's Communications (2013, 2014), the Council of the EU (European Council 2015) invited the European Commission to elaborate, by mid-2018, an implementation strategy outlining timelines, objectives and concrete measures to reflect the 2030 Agenda in all relevant EU internal and external policies, taking into account the global impacts of the EU's domestic actions. This strategy should be based on a clear vision of how all relevant EU policies will contribute to the realisation of the 2030 Agenda, by considering existing gaps in all relevant policy areas in order to assess what more needs to be done until 2030 in terms of EU policy, legislation, governance structure for horizontal coherence and means of implementation. The EU's better regulation agenda has been suggested to be one of the key instruments for enhancing policy coordination in the implementation of the strategy, although it was recognised that the current tools and methods used in both ex ante impact assessment and ex post policy evaluation need to be improved in order to link better regulation with SDGs more effectively (European Commission, 2016).

The developments reported above bring to light a number of critical aspects in the EU policy framework for sustainable development. Not only has it lacked consistency over time, but it often failed to provide a clear concept of how to integrate and balance environmental, social and economic objectives. Moreover, the challenge of identifying a specific added value of EU actions within the framework of the global agenda for sustainable development has so far not been met. Lastly, no systematic monitoring and evaluation mechanisms have been established to measure the impact and results of specific policies and programmes in the medium-long term, although an extensive set of social, environmental and economic indicators has been built by Eurostat in order to collect data on the EU member states' performance in relation to SDGs.

2.3 Governance architecture for sustainable development: loose patterns of intergovernmental coordination

Since its early years, the EU SDS has aimed to establish an appropriate governance architecture in order to enable the achievement of shared objectives, but it still remains largely dependent on member states' action. The fundamental weakness of the EU in this sense consists in the fact that the EU has mainly relied on the Open Method of Coordination (OMC) for implementing this agenda, within which the EU mainly supports, coordinates and complements member states' policies. A similar pattern of intergovernmental coordination has been adopted for its "sister" Lisbon Strategy that, however, has gradually strengthened the system of mutual monitoring and the political leadership of the Council ensuring a better accountability of national governments for specific commitments.

Thus, member states were invited to develop their own SDS as well as a set of indicators that would be in line with those designed by Eurostat in order to enable a periodic informal exchange of information between governments. However, although bi-annual reporting obligations at the EU level were recommended by the Commission, neither a regular assessment mechanism was designed, nor was systematic monitoring of progress launched. In the same way, the benchmarking exercise that was supposed to enhance the process of learning and policy innovation among states was limited too due to a very low number of peer reviews of national strategies drawn by the EU Commission. Additionally, while the annual review of the Lisbon process was scheduled for the March meeting of the European Council, the evaluation of results and recommendations for SDS was planned to take place in autumn.

As a consequence of the revision in 2006, the intergovernmental coordination mechanism of the strategy was expected to be strengthened by a new enhanced policy coordination approach, according to which "the economic, social and environmental effects of all policies should be examined in a coordinated way and taken into account in decision-making" (European Council, 2006a). The EU institutions were invited to improve policy coordination between different sectors, whereas the Commission was asked to include this new principle in its action plan for better regulation mechanism to ensure that all major policy proposals "include a sustainability impact assessment covering their potential economic, social and environmental consequences". Moreover, the EU Council called on member states to make use of the existing European Sustainable Development Network (ESDN) in order to facilitate the exchange of good practices and experiences, enhance the mainstreaming of sustainable development issues across sectoral policies, and promote vertical integration and coherence between the EU, national and sub-national levels of policy-making. National governments were invited to set up or strengthen national advisory bodies for involving stakeholders and were suggested to improve horizontal coordination at the level of EU institutions to verify the coherence of strategy implementation in their respective areas.

Unlike previous times, a range of measures and targets to be promoted directly by the EU through its regulatory and financial instruments was clearly listed (European Council, 2006a) and the EU Commission's commitment to mainstream sustainable development across policies and communication campaigns was announced (European Commission, 2005a). As in the case of the NEPIs (Wurzel *et al.*, 2013), the EU Commission aimed to empower social and market actors in implementing environmental policies, in those policy fields where the impact of public authorities was limited or insignificant (e.g. green technologies, consumption, buildings and constructions, etc.). Although characterised by uneven diffusion and scope of action, these instruments have widely relied on self-regulation, as well as on market-based and information devices for achieving their objectives, and contributed in increasing the involvement of non-state actors in sustainable development governance.

However, no substantial measures have been designed for monitoring the strategy, and bi-annual reviews by the EU Council and Parliament based on EU Commission's reports remained the only tool for assessing its progress. It is also worth mentioning that by that time, many of the EU member states had already developed their SDS, following in particular the international guidance provide by the United Nations framework and best practices (Steurer and Martinuzzi, 2005).

In sum, although the existence of National Sustainable Development Strategies (NSDS) can be considered in itself an important indicator of political commitment to the role that the EU plays in the achievement of sustainable development goals, the overview of the national documents shows that the implementation of SDS has been quite poor (European Commission, 2004). By 2009, only a few countries had collected and shared the data required by the system of indicators on social, economic and environmental dimensions of sustainable development strategy, showing a deep gap between the general commitment to the strategy in terms of political discourse and the respective political action on the ground (Steurer, 2008). Significantly, no mechanisms were established to guarantee that coordination and complementarity between the NSDS and EU regulatory and other policy instruments underpinned by EPI are ensured at both EU and domestic levels.

Finally, the citizens' mobilisation and individual action have been considered crucial for the implementation success of the EU SDS. In fact, EU institutions (European Commission, 2001; European Council, 2001) have stressed that in order to channel SD objectives crosswise policies and levels, a widespread popular "ownership" of the goal of sustainable development is needed, depending not only on more openness in policy-making but also on the perception that individuals can, through their own actions, make a real difference. While emphasising that public authorities have a key role in providing a clear long-term framework, the EU Commission has highlighted that clear, stable, long-term objectives should be established in order to deliver the changes in consumption and investment patterns by creating the conditions in which businesses have the confidence to invest in innovative solutions, and to create new, high-quality jobs. It also stressed the fact that public policy has a key role to play in encouraging a greater sense of corporate social responsibility and in establishing a framework to ensure that businesses integrate environmental and social considerations in their activities. In this context, sustainable development was seen as an opportunity for business that should be encouraged to take a pro-active approach and adopt investments strategy accordingly.

The Europe 2020 Strategy has highlighted the importance of establishing an appropriate governance framework as a powerful tool for promoting sustainable development through cross-jurisdictional integration. More specifically, it suggested a stronger role for the European Parliament not only in its responsibility as co-legislator on key initiatives, but also as a driving force for mobilising citizens and their national parliaments. It also emphasised that the partnership approach should extend to EU committees, to national parliaments and national, local and regional authorities, to social partners and to stakeholders and civil society – so that everyone is involved in delivering on the vision. The role of public authorities at different levels has been considered to be crucial, as they should explain clearly why reforms are necessary and what contribution they are looking for from citizens, businesses and their representative organisations. Against this background, it is striking that the role and contribution of sub-state governments has not been duly taken into account in the definition of various actions and no specific governance settings have been created for enhancing the multilevel perspective of the strategy already developed in many EU member states (Committee of the Regions, 2009).

In continuity with this framework, the EU Commission guidance for the implementation of the 2030 Agenda has stated the objective to create a dynamic space bringing together the different stakeholders of the public and private sphere. Thus, the Commission has committed to launch a multi-stakeholder platform with a role in the follow-up and exchange of best practices on SDG implementation across sectors, at member state and EU level. This platform is expected to act as a peer-learning hub where stakeholders can engage in debates about sustainability activities and inform others about ongoing successful initiatives. Moreover, a European Sustainability Prize has been established to award initiatives that bring relevant contribution to the achievement of the global 2030 Agenda. The Commission has highlighted that in line with the principle of subsidiarity, the EU will only act in areas outside its exclusive competences when the objectives can be better achieved at Union level rather than by action of member states. Therefore, close cooperation with member states would be required on many issues affecting sustainable development as national governments are currently in the process of establishing their own national frameworks for the achievement of the SDGs and for reporting to their own citizens and to the UN. In sum, a very loose pattern of intergovernmental coordination has been confirmed as the main governance tool for the strategy's implementation, whilst also highlighting the relevance of local authorities and especially cities for its success. In this context, the Commission intends to play a central role by implementing the Urban Agenda for the EU, keeping in mind the diversity of cities and their responsibilities and interactions with the wider territory, providing expertise, implementing actions and facilitating the multilevel governance process (European Commission, 2016: 16).

2.4 Sustainable development mainstreaming: towards a new generation of policy instruments?

As already mentioned, the efforts for increasing horizontal policy coordination within the sustainable development mainstreaming approach has developed after the last review of the SDS in 2006. In the premise to its first progress report published in 2007, the EU Commission has highlighted the need to increase convergence between the overarching long-term objectives of sustainable development, namely, focusing on quality of life, equity between generations, the long-term viability of European society; and the medium-term goal of growth and jobs under the Lisbon Strategy. Therefore, it has committed to build a long-term vision and an overarching policy framework providing guidance for all EU policies and strategies and including a global dimension, with a timeframe of up to 2050 (European Commission, 2007). This commitment came in response to the European Council (2007) invitation to provide a second progress report on SDS and to propose appropriate measures to enhance the links and synergies between sustainable development goals, as well as to integrate sustainability objectives in its 5-year work programmes and in future EU budgetary proposals.

However, in its communication "Mainstreaming sustainable development into EU policies: 2009 review of the European Union Strategy for Sustainable Development", the EU Commission has presented an overview of policy measures implemented across various sectors to promote sustainable development goals and provided a few suggestions on the future strategy, without delivering an in-depth analysis on achievements and implementation gaps. While generally recognising that "there may still be room for further clarification of the specific role of the EU SDS in relation to other EU strategies and for it to be streamlined accordingly" (European Commission, 2009: 14), the Commission identified a set of cross-cutting issues considered crucial for the strategy's success, including education, training, research and development, financial and economic instruments. Energy security, adaptation to climate change, food security, and land use were mentioned among the new challenges on which the EU SDS should focus.

Particular emphasis has been put on the need to strengthen the monitoring mechanism of the strategy and improve its coordination with domestic systems of monitoring, as individual States and regions have developed their own strategies in line with international recommendations of best practice (European Commission, 2009: 13). For this purpose, the Commission has committed to developing a sustainable development scoreboard, based on the SDIs suggested by Eurostat, while the intergovernmental coordination was suggested to be the main tool for facilitating exchange of best practices or innovative approaches across member states.

The Europe 2020 Strategy for "smart, sustainable and inclusive growth" (European Commission, 2010), which is considered to be the next step in the development of the EU SDS, has brought a number of novelties. While keeping the main focus on economic growth, it has attempted to mainstream environmental objectives into a range of sectors and tackled the problems of social inclusion and poverty reduction under the social dimension.

Within this framework, the environmental component has been mainstreamed into energy and climate policy measures, being translated more specifically into measures for "promoting a more resource efficient, greener and more competitive economy", targeting the "20/20/20 energy package". Furthermore, the environmental dimension has been spotlighted in one out of seven "flagship initiatives" of the strategy "Resource efficient Europe", calling for decoupling of economic growth from the use of resources and for the shift towards a low-carbon economy based on an increased use of renewable energy sources, modernisation of transport sector and higher energy efficiency. Member states were expected to translate the aforementioned priorities into national targets and trajectories, while the EU Commission committed to undertake actions for mainstreaming the strategy objectives in the following non-energy development sectors: disaster prevention and response, harnessing the contribution of cohesion, agricultural and rural development, maritime policies to address climate change, in particular through adaptation measures based on more efficient use of resources, which will also contribute to improving global food security (European Commission, 2010). Remarkably, reference to the term sustainable development has been used only once in the documents when referring to the international context of the EU strategy (European Commission, 2010: 16), while the concept of sustainable growth has become the red thread running through the document. Moreover, the environmental dimension has not been included in the monitoring grid proposed by the Commission for evaluating the implementation progress to be carried out in conjunction with the Stability and Growth Pact annual evaluation, which focused on macro-economic and investment policies and fiscal and social issues of reform (European Commission, 2010).

Instead, a separate scoreboard has been created by Eurostat in relation to the Roadmap to a Resource Efficient Europe (European Commission, 2011b), which outlined how Europe's economy can be transformed into a sustainable one by 2050. The EU Commission has proposed a number of measures to increase resource productivity and decouple economic growth from resource use and its environmental impact, focusing in particular on the evaluation of whether the EU as a whole is using resources more efficiently, decreasing pressures on "natural capital" like biodiversity and ecosystems, addressing key sectors and shifting towards a circular economy. Key resources (land, water and carbon) were analysed from a life cycle and value-chain perspective. Nutrition, housing and mobility were suggested to be the sectors primarily responsible for environmental impacts and actions in these areas are being proposed to complement existing measures. Scoreboard was updated for three years from 2013 through 2014–2016. While providing an extensive overview of the trends in resource efficiency, these reports do not provide insights on whether and how EU measures have affected these trends in different states.

Overall, a significant shift in the EU political discourse on sustainability can be observed (European Commission, 2010), as it has become strongly underpinned by the focus on the dimension of economic growth that embraced the environmental component within its priority for "building a resource efficient, sustainable and competitive economy, exploiting Europe's leadership in the race to develop new processes and technologies, including green technologies, accelerating the roll out of smart grids using ICTs, exploiting EU-scale networks, etc.". Such approach was expected to help in moving out from the devastating economic crisis 2008–2009 and prosper by investing in cleaner, low-carbon technologies, fighting climate change and creating new business and employment opportunities.

Thus, while enhancing the sustainable development mainstreaming approach, the EU has shifted further from the original idea of sustainable development based on a "stronger" EPI to a policy framework underpinned by the concept of ecological modernisation as the dominant ideology (Eadson, 2013), in which strong environmental commitments have been "watered down" being overridden by the economic rationale for reforms (Kernevez, 2013).

The analysis above has shown how the EU has gradually moved in this direction, elaborating on how the environment might benefit through the innovation encouraged by market mechanisms and vice versa. This trend is in line with the so-called ecological modernisation theory, assuming that "policies to protect the environment can enhance efficiency and accelerate innovation, thereby providing an engine for further economic development" (Baker, 2007: 299). Although a significant variety of approaches exists in the conceptual development of ecological modernisation, the Europe 2020 Strategy appears to have adopted all five fundamental clusters (Mol and Sonnenfeld, 2000: 7) constituting the core of this approach:

- *Changing role of science and technology* – actual and potential impact in curing and preventing environmental problems;
- *Increasing importance of markets and economic agents* – producers, customers, consumers, etc. as carriers of economic restructuring and reform;
- *Transformations in the role of nation states* – more decentralised, flexible and consensual styles of governance emerge, with less top-down, national command-and-control environmental regulation and emergent supranational institutions playing important roles in environmental reforms;
- *Modifications in the position, role and ideology of social movements* – those that are increasingly involved in public and private decision-making institutions regarding environmental reforms;
- *Changing discursive practices and emerging new ideologies* – overcoming counterpositioning of economic and environmental interests (Hajer, 1995), increasing support to the principle of intergenerational solidarity in dealing with the sustenance base.

The first explicit reference of this shift can be traced back to the fourth edition of the EAP and it was definitely consolidated in the EAP7. The former document laid down the basis for this approach by stating that "the protection of the environment can help to improve economic growth and facilitate job creation" and that environmental protection has become "an essential element in the future economic success of the Community" (Council of European Communities, 1987). In its turn, the 7th EAP has promoted a wider vision of the Union's commitment to transforming itself into an inclusive green economy that "secures growth and development, safeguards human health and well-being, provides decent jobs, reduces inequalities and invests in, and preserves biodiversity, including the ecosystem services it provides (natural capital), for its intrinsic value and for its essential contribution to human well-being and economic prosperity" (European Council, 2013a).

These developments seem to confirm that the Cardiff process that has pushed for implementation of the EPI principle since the end of the 1990s has been definitely overshadowed by the Lisbon Process. Remarkably, no overwhelming appraisal of the EU SDS progress has been carried out since 2006, and its political leadership appeared definitely weak compared to the Lisbon agenda for growth and jobs.

Against this background, a comprehensive assessment would have been indeed essential for developing EU actions for fulfilling the Agenda 2030 goals. However, while declaring full commitment to be a frontrunner in implementing this agenda (European Commission, 2016), the EU has so far failed to articulate sustainable development goals into a system of specific objectives and targets for its context. While stressing that economic, social and environmental dimensions of sustainable development should be addressed together, the EU Commission has announced a two-step process for implementing the strategy by fully integrating the SDGs in the current European policy framework and identifying the most relevant sustainability concerns in the long-term perspective after 2020. In his way, the ten political priorities covering the internal EU policies have been defined in continuity of the strategy Europe 2020 and refer to actions to be implemented in order to enhance synergies between SDGs and the EU current policy agenda, including such aspects as a new boost for growth, jobs and investments, circular economy, climate change and resilience, sustainable finance and capital market, a deeper economic union and social pillar, corporate social responsibility, area of justice and fundamental rights, gender equality and a new migration policy. In this context, most environmental priorities, especially those related to waste and pollution, have been interpreted in the perspective of circular economy agenda, while the implementation of the EU's environmental acquis has been considered vital for long-term sustainability and is inseparable from the broader economic and societal challenges (European Commission, 2016). The main directions of the international role of the EU have been set out in two dedicated communications of the EU Commission, "A new European consensus on development" and "A renewed partnership with African, Caribbean and Pacific (ACP) countries, tracing the path for the foreign and security policy, and cooperation for development".

In the run-up to the adoption of the 2030 Agenda, the Commission issued the first communication, "A decent life for all: ending poverty and giving the world a sustainable future" in February 2013. It was followed by Council Conclusions on "An overarching post-2015 framework" in June 2013. A second communication titled "A decent life for all: from vision to collective action" was issued in June 2014 and was followed by Council Conclusions on "A transformative post-2015 agenda" in December 2014. On 5 February 2015 the Commission published its third communication, "A global partnership for poverty eradication and sustainable development after 2015", which puts forward ideas on the appropriate enabling policy environment; on financing – public and private, national and international; and on monitoring and accountability. This was followed by Council Conclusions on "A global partnership for Poverty Eradication and Sustainable Development after 2015" on 26 May 2015.

An overview of key existing European initiatives related to the achievement of the 2030 Agenda for Sustainable Development has been presented in the EU Commission Staff Working Document "Key European action supporting the 2030 Agenda and the Sustainable Development Goals" (European Commission, 2016). It has summarised EU actions and policy tools for each of the 17 Sustainable Development Goals (SDGs), including both domestically oriented and external actions.

Notably, the EU system of SD indicators managed by Eurostat has been rapidly updated by reorganising them in line with the 17 SDGs announced by Agenda 2030. However, the aforementioned weakness in the system of monitoring appears to persist, as the indicators are not attributable to precise EU policy measures and therefore does not allow us to assess impacts and outcomes of policy programmes implemented across various sectors over time.

Hence, the overall scenario of policy change in this field seems to have followed the logic of incremental layering rather than the one of a comprehensive and strategic development and reconsideration. The recent attempts to balance economic, social and environmental objectives across different sectors have contributed to strengthen the social dimension, while at the same time bringing replacement of EPI as a guiding political principle of the strategy. Indeed, a progressive decline of the EU environmental regulation has brought about the hypothesis of dismantling of EU environmental policy (Gravey and Jordan, 2016).

In this way, the principle of policy integration has remained at the core of the EU strategy for sustainable development. But it currently embodies rather complex patterns of policy coordination across various sectors. At the same time, the political discourse on sustainability has acquired a much wider perspective compared to the past, developing beyond the EPI normative and legal foundations that have consolidated in the treaties and secondary legislation over the last two decades (i.e. Water Framework Directive CE/60/2000; Air Framework Directive 2008/50/EC).

The proliferation of integrative environmental concepts in the field of sustainable development has taken place since 2009 onwards, referring to sustainable growth in a low-carbon, bio-based, climate resilient economy and bringing above all the integration of climate change mitigation in all carbon-emitting sectors. At the same time, a strong project-based logic has underpinned thematic programmes promoted by the EU, including those co-financed by the EU budget (Life+; Horizon; Territorial Cooperation, etc.).

Such a high complexity and the absence of a detailed evaluation scheme of results risk undermining the credibility of the strategy. The question whether ex ante tools for sustainable development mainstreaming could suffice for ensuring its overall effectiveness spontaneously arises, as the continued effort to mainstream SD into new policy initiatives has recently been reiterated by the EU Commission, as well as the necessity to enable policies and funds into practice and showcase concrete results on the ground (European Commission, 2016: 2).

In this perspective, an in-depth understanding is needed of whether and to what extent the EU insights have been collected by the target actors and to what extent they have shaped their action within the perspective of SD. To this end, more knowledge would be required on the impact of complex policy programmes that have been promoted by the EU Commission since 2008 with the purpose of encouraging the implementation of the policy integration principle across various sectors. These programmes have targeted in particular regional and local authorities, business and civil society, aiming to engage them with the EU sustainable development agenda through a system of opportunities and guidance.

The analysis presented in the next paragraphs will unpack the complex policy mix boxes developed on the initiative of the EU Commission in the field of regional development, energy efficiency and innovation policy, focusing respectively on sustainable urban development programmes, the Covenant of Mayors programme and the Eco-Innovation Programme.

These policy programmes were launched shortly before the adoption of the Strategy Europe 2020. Distinct from the past generation of environmental policy instruments, these programmes were underpinned by the sustainable development mainstreaming approach aiming at integrating environmental concerns into policies having broader socio-economic impacts. While important progress had been made in dealing with traditional environmental policies by that time, we know little about the effectiveness and impact of the aforementioned programmes.

Moreover, the design and operational logic of the three programmes under examination differ significantly from the so-called New Environmental Policy Instruments that have contributed to the transformation of environmental governance by integrating the environmental dimension increasingly into sectoral policies and involving non-state actors, private companies and communities into decision-making over the previous decades (Wurzel *et al.*, 2013)

Being reinforced by the sustainable development mainstreaming approach, the new generation of programmes oftentimes do not target national governments and administrations, but aims at promoting a more strategic bottom-up approach encouraging sub-state authorities, private companies or citizens to develop their own strategies in order to achieve the EU sustainable development goals. Second, even if no steering mechanisms are established to implement these programmes, specific commitments and requirements should be met by those who are willing to join. Third, these programmes rely on networked or polycentric patterns of governance and promote a strategic approach, leaving ample margins of manoeuvre to policy addressees. Fourth, they highlight the role of awareness, commitment and learning as the main factors of policy change and innovation. Lastly, these programmes rely on a combination of various policy tools, combining regulations, financial incentives, knowledge and capacity building activities in their operational designs.

The characteristics of these programmes will be described in greater details in the next paragraphs, describing the pattern of policy integration and governance settings adopted to promote sustainable development goals in specific sectors.

2.4.1 Regional policies for sustainable urban development

Regional policy was among the first EU policy areas to have embraced the principles of policy integration and sustainable development. In fact, the need to adopt an integrated approach to regional development policies can be traced back to the first programming period of structural funds (1989–1993), when early embryonic forms of substantive and procedural elements aiming to enhance cross-sectoral policy integration and inclusive modes of governance were introduced. In the 2000–2006 programming period environmental sustainability was included in the SF regulations as a horizontal theme, while Article17 of the SF general regulation for the 2007–2013 programming has made the framework of sustainable development a binding principle for all funding objectives, establishing that "The objectives of the funds shall be pursued in the framework of sustainable development and the Community promotion of the goal of protecting and improving the environment as set out in art.6 of the Treaty" (Ferry *et al.*, 2008).

The consolidation of these elements has been particularly dynamic in the field of urban development policies, which called for similar policy process in which a multisectoral and multilevel coordination challenge could be met. It was highlighted already in the first programming period in 1989 that the various dimensions of urban life, including its environmental, economic, social and cultural components, were interwoven and thus, the success in urban development could only be achieved through an integrated and participatory approach (European Commission, 1998). Therefore, policy measures for physical urban renewal were to be combined with actions promoting education, economic development, social inclusion and environmental protection and required the development of strong partnerships between local communities, business and the various levels of government as a pre-requisite (European Commission, 1998, 2000).

During the subsequent decades, the design of EU policies for sustainable urban development (SUD) has progressively acquired the ambition to replace, to say it with Rayner and Howlett (2009), "patchworks of public policies in specific issue areas with a more coordinated of integrated policy strategies". Hence, the earliest attempts to promote an integrated approach with specific regard to urban areas have been undertaken with the launch of the Urban Pilot Projects (UPP), which were promoted within the framework of innovative actions foreseen by art.10 of the European Regional Development Fund (ERDF) (Council of European Communities, 1988). In 1994, the URBAN Community Initiative Programme (CIP) was launched declaring the objective of promoting an integrated approach to urban regeneration by taking account of all dimensions of urban life. In this way, a package of actions was proposed at EU level in order to combine the rehabilitation of obsolete infrastructures with economic and labour market actions, as well as measures to combat the social exclusion inherent in run-down neighbourhoods, and measures to upgrade the quality of the environment. A participatory bottom-up approach to the design and implementation of interventions was encouraged, being underpinned by the principle of partnership intended to bring together public authorities, social and economic stakeholders and civil society. Hence, the Managing Authorities of Urban CIPs, which were responsible for running the programmes and normally coincided with municipal administrations, were required to work in partnership with social and economic actors and civil society. In this way, a number of operational bodies were established, such as *steering committees* composed of public authorities at different territorial levels concerned (national, regional and local) and *local forums* encompassing wider local networks made of social and economic stakeholders and local community representatives (non-governmental organisations, district committees, spontaneous groups of individuals, etc.). Such networked form of governance was expected to enable cooperation and coordination between different parties across all phases of CIPs: from the definition of actions to implement to the selection of projects to finance. The commitment of the URBAN CIPs to including local citizens in the development and implementation of the programmes was stressed by the Commission, highlighting the belief that the problems of urban deprivation should be solved at grass root level (European Commission, 2014b).

After being implemented throughout two successive periods, 1994–1999 and 2000–2006, the CIP URBAN was not renewed for the 2007–2013 programming, though the objective of sustainable urban development and the related operational method (entitled URBAN) were to be mainstreamed as a horizontal priority into three main cohesion policy objectives (Convergence, Regional Competiveness and Territorial Cooperation). Therefore, wider potential possibilities to implement actions for integrated urban development were enshrined in the Regulations for the 2007–2013, allowing for an increase of both the geographical scope of their application and the amount of investments. The Community Strategic Guidelines (European Commission, 2005b) and the Commission's communication on "Cohesion policy and cities" (European Commission, 2006) have provided a more specific outline of how actions for integrated urban development could be included in the National Strategic Reference Frameworks (main national programming documents) and Operational Programmes co-financed by the ERDF at national and regional levels. Hence, either a specific operational programme could be designed or a priority axis could be included within an operational programme, absorbing up to 10% of resources or up to 15% under the regional competitiveness and employment objective falling within the scope of regulation (EC) No 1081/2006 (European Council, 2006b).

By adopting a wider perspective on sustainable development, the regulation has highlighted that specific problems of the urban areas such as social exclusion, high and rising crime rates, and the general worsening of the quality of life in deprived areas should be accounted for. The ERDF Regulation further specified (Art.4, European Council, 2006b) that as far as the convergence areas were concerned, the assistance had to focus on supporting sustainable integrated regional and local economic development and employment by mobilising and strengthening endogenous capacity through operational programmes aimed at the modernisation and diversification of economic structures and at the creation and safeguarding of sustainable jobs.

In its turn, the objective "Territorial Cooperation" (Art.6, European Council, 2006b) suggested that the development of transnational networks should be conducive to integrated territorial development, concentrating primarily on the following priority areas: innovation, environment, accessibility and sustainable urban development. In regard to urban areas, the regulation (Art.8, European Council, 2006b) has further specified that the ERDF may, where appropriate, support the development of participative, integrated and sustainable strategies to tackle the high concentration of economic, environmental and social problems. These strategies aimed to promote sustainable urban development through such activities as strengthening economic growth, rehabilitating physical environment, brownfield redevelopment, the preservation and development of natural and cultural heritage, the promotion of entrepreneurship, local employment and community development, and the provision of services to the population, taking account of changing demographic structures.

The regulation stressed, however, that the precise policy mix to implement depended on the specificities of each member state, which could combine the following priorities: research and technological development, innovation and entrepreneurship, information society, environment, prevention of risks, tourism, investments in culture, transport, energy.

Finally, the relevance of participatory and integrated strategies capable of tackling the high concentration of economic, environmental and social problems affecting urban agglomerations was highlighted, with particular attention to the role of cities and local authorities in achieving regional policy objectives. Therefore, the preparation of a medium-to-long-term development plan for urban regeneration has been suggested to be a precondition for success of integrated strategies, as it would ensure the coherence of investments and of their environmental quality, also helping to secure the commitment and participation of the private sector in urban renewal. Under the new legislative framework, member states were given the possibility to delegate the management of funds addressing urban issues to cities, with the responsibility of designing and implementing the sub-delegated portion of the programme (European Commission, 2005b).

As far as urban governance more in general is concerned, the Commission has proposed a range of actions aimed at establishing good cooperation between the different territorial levels (e.g. by developing partnerships between cities, regions and the state or improving coordination between urban, rural and regional authorities), raising the participation and involvement of citizens and establishing networks for the exchange of experience (European Commission, 2006).

In sum, the diffusion of integrated approach in EU policies for sustainable urban development has evolved in parallel with the consolidation of the territorial dimension of cohesion policy, which was also associated with a holistic approach to development, combining different sectoral measures so as to enable their complementarity and coherence in a given territorial context.

In the same period, 2007–2013, a new initiative for SUD – Joint European Support for Sustainable Investment in City Areas (JESSICA) – was launched with the purpose of increasing resources, strengthening public-private cooperation and attracting private investments for integrated sustainable urban development. The implementation mechanism of this initiative required the establishment of Urban Development Funds (Urban Authority) that would be based on well-established public-private partnerships and to which regional or national MA could delegate the management of the part of funding for sustainable urban development. The JESSICA mechanism offered the possibility of financing expenditures to support financial engineering instruments for enterprises, primarily small and medium-sized, such as venture capital funds; guarantee funds and loan funds, as well as guarantee for urban development funds, that is, funds investing in public-private partnerships and other projects included in the respective local integrated plan for sustainable urban development (Art. 44, 78, European Council, 2006b). Thus, a strong inter-sectoral nature and an evident objective intending to involve private companies and investments has characterised this initiative.

As the analysis of 316 ERDF Operational Programmes covering all three EU Cohesion Policy Objectives showed (Van der Zwet *et al.*, 2014), the availability of funding to cities has progressively increased as a consequence of the introduction of specific actions for SUD in the period 2007–2013. Around 3% of the ERDF budget (approx. €10 billion) was specifically programmed for urban development at Priority Axis level. At the same time, it has been recognised that the mainstreaming of the URBAN approach into operational programmes has led to a stronger sectoral focus (especially in "convergence regions") and that community involvement seems weaker than it was in the context of the URBAN Community Initiative Programme (European Commission, 2010). In fact, though the objective of integrated urban development has been highlighted throughout the EU policy guidelines, no specific guidance has been provided on how the integrated approach should be operationalised, which sectors should be integrated, how they should be balanced and most importantly, how the results should be monitored and measured.

Remarkably, since its very origins, the principle of policy integration principle in the field of regional policy has been conceptualised in a wider perspective, aiming to bring together economic growth, infrastructural restructuring, environmental protection, employment and social inclusion, combined with participatory governance.

It is also worth mentioning that in parallel to this top-down trend, a bottom-up coordination process has developed around the issue of sustainable urban development in Europe, being supported by a series of declarations and agreements – the so-called "Urban Acquis" – approved in Lille (2000), Rotterdam (2004), Bristol (2005), Leipzig (2007), Marseille (2008), Toledo (2010), Riga (2015), Amsterdam (2016). These documents have established a set of shared common principles and strategies for sustainable urban development policy agreed by ministers responsible for Urban Development of EU member states, who committed themselves to initiate a political debate in their states on how to integrate the common principles and strategies into national, regional and local development policies, and how to use the tool of integrated urban development and the related governance for its implementation by establishing any necessary framework at national level. In line with the EU guidelines described above, these declarations highlight that all dimensions of sustainable development should be taken into account at the same time and with the same weight, including economic prosperity, social balance and a healthy environment. They have also highlighted the relevance of holistic, participatory and coordinated action at local level in order to develop a new sense of responsibility for integrated urban development policy. To this end, an integrated approach has been considered crucial, as it has offered a set of instruments that proved their effectiveness in numerous European cities in developing modern, cooperative and effective governance structures, which are indispensable for facilitating early beneficial coordination of housing, economic, infrastructure and services development by taking into account, inter alia, of the impact of existing ageing, migration trends and energy policy conditions (Leipzig Charter, 2007).

The regulatory framework for the programming period 2014–2020 aimed to embrace the above propositions, recognising that an integrated approach is especially important at this time, given the seriousness of the challenges European cities currently face, which range from specific demographic changes to the consequences of economic stagnation in terms of job creation and service providing, to the impact of climate change. The ability to meet these challenges has been considered to be critical for achieving the smart, sustainable, inclusive society envisaged in the Europe 2020 Strategy, and a number of provisions have been introduced aiming to foster integrated urban policies and enhance sustainable urban development.

The policy frame for sustainable development of the programming period 2014–2020 has been characterised by increased attention to coordination between the European Structural and Investment Funds (ESIF), cross-sectoral policy integration and integrated strategies to develop at national, regional and local levels. In fact, not only does the new ESI policy guidance based on the Strategy Europe 2020 require tackling of environmental, social and economic challenges simultaneously, but it also calls for expanding the number of sub-systems involved in the policy-making processes, which are expected to enhance the implementation of integrated strategies offering more effective solutions for cross-cutting development problems in EU countries and regions.

Overall, the principle of policy integration has been reinforced, as the General Regulation highlighted the need to strengthen the arrangements to promote an integrated use of the ESIF, the arrangements for coordination between the ESIF and other relevant Union policies and instruments, horizontal principles and cross-cutting policy objectives for the implementation of the ESIF, the arrangements to address key territorial challenges and priority areas for cooperation activities under the ESIF (European Council, 2013a). Due to the complex and interrelated nature of these challenges, the regulation suggested that the solutions supported by the ESI funds should be of an integrated nature, multisectoral and multidimensional. Moreover, in order to increase the effectiveness and efficiency of the policies, it should be possible for the ESI funds to be combined into integrated packages which are tailor-made to fit the specific territorial needs (§18).

An integrated approach designed by the Common Strategic Framework shall establish arrangements to promote an integrated use of the ESIF at EU level. Accordingly, Partnership Agreements (PA) (Art.15, European Council, 2013a) had to indicate an integrated approach to territorial development supported by the ESIF, based on the content of the OP, setting out, among others, the arrangements to ensure an integrated approach to the use of the ESIF for the territorial development of specific sub-regional areas, in particular the implementation arrangements for Articles 32, 33 and 36 (European Council, 2013a) accompanied by the principles for identifying the urban areas where integrated actions for sustainable urban development are to be implemented.

More specifically, member states were asked to ensure that the selection of thematic objectives, investments and Union priorities addresses development needs and territorial challenges in an integrated manner and seek to make maximum use of the possibilities for ensuring coordinated and integrated delivery of the ESI funds. Moreover, member states and where appropriate, regions, were invited to ensure that the interventions supported through the ESIF are complementary and are implemented in a coordinated manner with a view to creating synergies. They were required to ensure the existence of arrangements for the effective coordination of the ESIF in order to increase the impact and effectiveness of the funds, including, where appropriate, through the use of multi-fund programmes encouraging cooperation between managing authorities of different ESIF in the areas of monitoring, evaluation, management and control, and audit (Annex 1, European Council, 2013a). The operational programmes should set out the contribution to the integrated approach for territorial development, including – where appropriate – a planned integrated approach to the development of urban areas (Art. 11, 14, 87, European Council, 2013a).

Thus, the sustainable urban development approach has been shaped by the principle of policy integration, requiring to addressing the specific needs of geographical areas most affected by poverty, or of target groups at highest risk of discrimination or exclusion – as set out in the Partnership Agreement and the operational programmes.

A number of specific governance instruments were established in order to enhance the development of integrated strategies across member states. The regulations stressed that member states should, where appropriate, combine the ESI funds into integrated packages at local, regional or national level, which are tailor-made to address specific territorial challenges in order to support the achievement of the objectives set out in the PA and OP. This could be done using different policy instruments foreseen by the regulations, namely, Integrated Operations, Joint Action Plans, Integrated Territorial Investments (ITIs) and Community-Led Local Development (CLLD).

The adoption of the aforementioned instruments has been suggested to be particularly suitable for sustainable urban development, as they allow to combine resources from different funds in order to support integrated investment strategies with a more strategic and holistic approach. As a basic principle, the ERDF committed to support sustainable urban development through integrated strategies that tackle the economic, environmental, climate and social challenges of the urban areas (Art. 7, 8, European Council, 2013c). The meaning of this principle is twofold: it signifies that resources should be concentrated in an integrated manner to target areas with specific urban challenges; and at the same time, that ERDF-funded projects in urban areas should be integrated into the wider objectives of the programmes. EU member states were encouraged to use the European Social Fund (ESF) in synergy with the ERDF, to support measures related to employment, education, social inclusion and institutional capacity, designed and implemented under the integrated strategies. Moreover, at least 5 % of the ERDF resources at national level were to be invested into integrated actions for sustainable urban development where cities, sub-regional or local bodies responsible for implementing sustainable urban strategies ("Urban Authorities") shall be responsible for tasks relating, at least, to the selection of operations (Art.7(2), European Council, 2013c).

According to the regulations, the implementation of integrated urban development strategies could be enhanced by the possibility of combining actions financed by ERDF, ESF and CF either at programme or operation level, and the instrument of ITI would be ideal to support integrated actions in urban areas, as it offers the possibility to combine funding linked to different thematic objectives, including the combination of funding from those priority axes and operational programmes supported by the ERDF, ESF and Cohesion Fund (Art. 88, European Council, 2013b). The indicative amount to be dedicated for ITIs had to be set out in the operational programme or programmes concerned, while cross-financing between ERDF and ESF of a part of an operation (up to 5 % of each priority axis of an Operational Programme) will remain to complement the multi-fund approach (Art.55, 88, European Council, 2013b).

The actions were to be concentrated on four thematic priorities listed under art.5 of the ERDF regulation (European Council, 2013c), aiming at promoting low-carbon strategies for urban areas, an improved urban environment, sustainable urban mobility, and social inclusion through supporting the physical and economic regeneration of deprived urban areas, embedding them in the integrated urban development strategy of the city to implement the principle of integrated urban development.

Finally, the creation of urban development platform and networking mechanism was proposed for making the contribution of cities under cohesion policy to the Europe 2020 Strategy more visible, facilitating integrated and innovative actions for sustainable urban development and capitalising on the results (Art. 9, European Council, 2013b).

Overall, since 2007 all EU regions have been encouraged to develop policies for sustainable urban development, based on an integrated policy approach combining complementary measures from different sectors and enhancing local ownership of interventions through the creation of participatory governance arrangements.

2.4.2 Local sustainable energy strategies: the EU Covenant of Mayors

While the EU urban agenda has aimed at enhancing the potential of cities within the framework of social and economic development policies, in particular at regional level, the Covenant of Mayors has targeted local authorities with the purpose of addressing some specific climate and energy policy challenges.

There were two main reasons behind the creation of the programme. On the one hand, local authorities in most countries have direct jurisdiction over a number of sectors relevant for greenhouse gas emission and energy efficiency. Besides, they are also in charge of managing energy relevant local public services, including public lighting, waste and water management, municipal fleet and public transportation. Thus, they are directly concerned with energy saving and renewable energy production in the aforementioned sectors. Last but not least, local authorities are central in influencing the behaviour of local productive sector and local communities. It has been estimated that behavioural change and raising awareness of the public contribute with 26 % to the total estimated GHG emission reduction by 2020, being one of the major policy instrument deployed by local authorities to mobilise public interest in sustainable energy policies and climate change. Establishing monitoring and management standards, green public procurement and financial incentives available at local level represent important policy instruments that can be used by local authorities to promote energy efficiency and deployment of renewables.

Therefore, the programme was launched by the European Commission's Climate and Energy Package in 2008 to endorse and support the efforts deployed by local authorities in the implementation of sustainable energy policies, in collaboration with a number of influential networks of local authorities such as Energy Cities, Climate Alliance, CEMR, EUROCITIES and FEDARENE, working in close cooperation with ECOFYS, Fresh Thoughts and IFOK. The main top pillars of the CoM's governance architecture have been composed of the Covenant of Mayors Office (COMO) established at the EU Commission and the EU Commission's Joint Research Centre (JRC). Besides being in charge of the overall coordination of the initiative, the COMO had the task of administering the Covenant web-page and coordinating all the related activities of the network, providing also local authorities with the necessary technical guidance at all stages of development and implementation of Sustainable Energy Action Plans (SEAPs). The JRC was expected to contribute to the implementation of the programme by providing specific methodological expertise required for the development of local Baseline Emissions Inventories (BEIs), SEAPs, the system of monitoring and benchmarking. Hence, the initiative has been underpinned by a number of instruments aiming at enhancing learning, innovation, coordination and mutual trust among its participants.

The main objective of the CoM has been to bringing together local authorities voluntarily committing to reduce CO_2 emissions through a range of cross-sectoral local interventions. Such commitment should be formalised by a SEAP to be prepared and implemented by each municipality participating in the Covenant. The SEAP has been conceived as the main tool of policy innovation at local level, contributing to identify the appropriate mixture of actions for the reduction of emissions, improving energy efficiency and increasing the use of local renewable source, while at the same time encouraging the integration of energy systems across several policy sectors (transport, buildings, industry, etc.) covered by the so-called Effort Sharing Decision (European Council, 2009). Templates have been prepared by the COMO in collaboration with JRC for all types of activities (BEIs, SEAPs and monitoring) in order to ensure a common framework of reference for developing and implementing local sustainable energy strategies. Moreover, local authorities were invited to develop or reinforce public-private partnerships, and increase public and private investments in energy efficiency. These actions were considered crucial to local economic growth, employment, innovation and a reduction in fuel poverty in households, positively contributing to economic, social and territorial cohesion.

The CoM activities were significantly strengthened as a consequence of the approval of the Energy Efficiency Directive (European Council, 2012) that acknowledged the importance of local governments in achieving significant energy savings. It called for member states to encourage municipalities and other public bodies to adopt integrated and sustainable energy efficiency plans by "developing innovative practices in the transition towards a more competitive, secure and sustainable energy system with an internal energy market at its core".

The ambition and the scope of the programme have amplified over time. The minimum commitment for local authorities to reduce the emissions was originally established by the initiative at 20%, compared to the BEIs reference year. In 2015, with the launch of the "Mayors Adapt" initiative, which full title was "The Covenant of Mayors Initiative on Climate Change Adaptation", the programme's target increased. When joining the programme, new signatories pledged to reduce CO_2 emissions by at least 40% by 2030 and to adopt an integrated approach tackling mitigation and adaptation to climate change together. Accordingly, starting from 2016, SEAPs were substituted by Sustainable Energy and Climate Action Plans (SECAPs), amplifying the scope of local actions for sustainable energy in a wider climate policies perspective. During the same year, the CoM signatories endorsed a shared vision until 2050: accelerating the decarbonisation of their territories, strengthening their capacity to adapt to unavoidable climate change impact, and allowing their citizens to access secure, sustainable and affordable energy (CoM, 2015).

In sum, the CoM's design has combined a flexible pattern of coordination with a number of learning tools encouraging policy and governance transformations on the ground. More specifically, several specific tasks had to be performed by local administration in order to comply with the CoM activities, including the construction BEIs, filling in the templates for SEAP and monitoring, identifying best practices, etc. After having been approved first by the respective municipal council and then by the COMO, SEAPs had to be published on the CoM website. The monitoring activity has been considered crucial for the effectiveness of the programme and signatories were required to design and implement monitoring within two years after approval of SEAPs, thereby enabling greater transparency, accountability and mutual trust among participating municipalities. Although the accomplishment of the aforementioned steps is based on voluntary commitment, once joined, local authorities had to comply with the CoM rules, procedures and targets.

Furthermore, a number of capacity building activities, such as joint training, thematic webinars and guidance, benchmarking, conferences and workshops have been organised in order to help local authorities to develop, implement and improve their sustainable energy strategies. Besides, the CoM has established a complex system of territorial coordinators and supports in order to enhance wider cooperation and partnerships between local authorities, intermediate territorial bodies (i.e. regions and provinces) and other entities having specific expertise or technical capacity in the field of sustainable energy. These networks were expected to help in mobilising local authorities' efforts to reach the CoM objectives and develop synergies with other existing national and EU initiatives.

Finally, a number of financial opportunities have been envisaged in the EU budgetary framework in order to support the various activities related to the preparation and implementation of SEAPs. Although there was no an ad-hoc financial heading for this objective, a number of EU direct thematic programmes, including ELENA initiative, Life, Horizon 2020, as well as EU structural funds introduced specific actions for funding local actions related to the implementation of the CoM.

In ten years of activity, the membership of the CoM has reached 7.204 signatories and 5.679 SEAPs were approved by the JRC (as of January 2017), with the highest number of participants coming from Italy and Spain. Recently, the geographical scope of the CoM has further expanded, involving the Eastern Partnership, Central Asia and ten southern Mediterranean countries. Regional offices in North and Latin America will soon follow, while at the beginning of 2017 a new partnership with the Compact of Mayors and the global Covenant of Mayors for Climate Change and Energy was launched thereby strengthening the cross-cutting links between the CoM and other transnational city networks, such as ICLEI, C40 or Climate Alliance, in which it has been strongly embedded since its very origins (Busch, 2015).

2.4.3 Technological innovation for environment: the Eco-Innovation Programme

The Eco-Innovation Programme, or as it is officially entitled "The Competiveness and Innovation Programme. Eco-Innovation Application and Market Replication Projects" (European Commission, 2005c), was implemented between 2008 and 2013 with the objective to support innovation among SMEs and to improve their competitiveness while at the same time developing products, techniques, services and processes that reduce CO_2emissions and increase resources efficiently. This pioneer grant scheme, with the total budget of nearly 200 million euros has offered support to the first application and further market uptake of a range of advanced eco-innovative products and services in Europe, showing how this kind of support may contribute to overcome the existing critical barriers to the diffusion of eco-innovation in the productive sector and its commercial success.

Initially, the Eco-Innovation Programme was part of the Competitiveness and Innovation Framework Programme (CIP) – in particular under the Entrepreneurship and Innovation Programme (EIP), aimed at encouraging the competitiveness of European companies, in particular SMEs. In the EU Commission terminology, eco-innovation refered to any form of innovation aiming at significant and demonstrable progress towards the goal of sustainable development. This can be achieved either by reducing the environmental impact or achieving a more efficient and responsible use of resources. Therefore, eco-innovation projects aim to produce quality products with less environmental impact, whilst innovation may include moving towards more environmentally friendly production processes and services.

Starting from 2011, the EIP has been included as one of the measures to implement the EU Eco-innovation Plan (EcoAP), which aims at accelerating market uptake of eco-innovation by addressing its barriers and drivers. Currently, the EcoAP pursues a wider objective of promoting eco-innovation policies across Europe though enhanced policy coordination, indicators and common certification schemes, including the Eco-Management and Audit Scheme (EMAS), the EU Ecolabel, the Environmental Technology Verification (ETV) scheme as well as the Product Environmental Footprint pilot. The Eco-Innovation Scoreboard (Eco-IS) has been established in order to provide a comparative assessment of how EU member states perform in this field.

During the period 2008–2013, the Eco-Innovation Programme awarded grants in the following five sectors:

- Recycling and recycling processes;
- Sustainable building products;
- Food and drink sector;
- Water efficiency;
- Treatment and distribution and greening business.

Besides the criteria related to the ability of companies in terms of technological innovation, environmental benefits, replication potential, marketability and economic impact, the programme highlighted the value of building transnational networks and public-private partnerships. According to it, anyone from an individual legal entity to a large consortium could apply for financing, but the needed to demonstrate "European added value" was highlighted, implying that the benefits of the project on a European scale must be clearly shown, as required by award criterion 5 of the Call for Proposals. The EAV indicates the benefits of addressing the proposal at European level as opposed to purely national/regional/local projects, and the level of European cooperation in the project (EASME, 2008).

The projects submitted to the Eco-Innovation Programme had to share the same strategic approach, that is consider the entire life cycle of the proposed solution, from production to disposal, covering the whole supply chain and not focusing on a single domain i.e. energy consumption. Although it was not a legal requirement or a precondition for an applicant to conduct a Life Cycle Assessment (LCA), but they had to demonstrate that their proposals take a life cycle oriented approach.

Each project could receive a maximum EU contribution of 50% of its total eligible costs (the "grant"). This means that the funding rate per participant could be higher or lower, as long as the total requested funding from the EU would not exceed half of the total eligible costs of the project. The remaining 50% had to be co-funded from applicant's own resources, from other private or public sources or from income generated through the project. If it came from income, the proposed project should not be profitable during the project lifetime. There was no formal minimum or maximum amount for the grant. On average, an eco-innovation project had an approximate budget of €1.6 million – of which €800.000 is EU funding (EASME, 2016).

The Programme was managed by the Executive Agency for Small and Medium-sized Enterprises (EASME), set up by the European Commission to manage on its behalf several EU programmes, including, more recently, SME instrument, COSME, Enterprise Europe Network, in close cooperation with the European Commission's Environment Directorate General.

The description of project activities has been shared through the web-page, providing detailed information on objectives, financing, partnerships and results. Moreover, the Programme has established stringent reporting obligations. Projects had to submit financial and technical progress reports at different stages of the project in order to help keeping track of progress, and enable the EASME to ensure the funds are properly used. The frequency and number of reports, usually five, was defined in the grant agreement for each project. The payments – set out in the Model Grant Agreement – were generally divided into three installments (EASME, 2008). First pre-financing amounting to 30% of the EU grant within 45 calendar days from the date when the signed grant agreement and all the mandates are officially received by the EASME. Second pre-financing could be requested by project coordinators if the first 30% of the total budget was spent. All requests had to be accompanied by a report including technical and financial descriptions, proving the transfer of the funds made available under the first pre-financing agreement. The final payment could be carried out only when all project activities were completed.

All eco-innovation funded projects had to undertake a variety of communication/dissemination activities, including the creation of project website, project information sheets, additional information materials (e.g. videos and pictures), contribution to events and conferences, production of a layman's report, evaluation of project's economic and environmental impacts for contractual obligation (European Commission, 2013). In these activities beneficiaries were required to use the European emblem to acknowledge the support received, mentioning "Co-funded by the Eco-innovation Initiative of the European Union".

In sum, the programmes were underpinned by the idea that technological innovation for environment can be achieved is more effectively and efficiently if private companies and public bodies operating in this sphere collaborate, exchange knowledge and invest their own and the available EU resources into joint projects developed at the transnational level.

In fact, the majority of projects financed by the Programme (more than 70%) based on international partnerships. The highest share of EU funding was obtained by organisations from Italy, Spain, Germany, Netherlands, the UK, and France. Although most consortia were led by private companies (mostly SMEs), academic and research institutes as well as industry associations and chambers of commerce also played a significant role. The evaluation reports highlight that even if the eco-innovation initiative is now closed, the lessons learnt from the initiative inform EU action under the LIFE and Horizon programmes in the current period 2014–2020, and around 60% of all respondents reported that the knowledge content of their innovation can easily be copied or further developed by other market operators in the EU (EASME, 2016).

Against this backdrop, the questions that arise are whether and how the EU sustainable development agenda and discourse has generated commitment among those policy actors who were supposed to implement them; whether and how they used various resources offered by the EU; to what extent they have changed their priorities and habitual practices and whether they have ultimately become socialised to new knowledge and policy ideas.

While evidence has been provided to prove that multiple discourses on sustainability exist in Europe and the lines around which these discourses coalesce are not clearly discernable (Barnes and Hoerber, 2013), the effectiveness of policy programmes that have been implemented across EU countries in order to enable tangible improvements in the achievement of a variety of ambitious policy goals will be further explored in the following chapters.

References

Baker, S. (2007). Sustainable development as symbolic commitment: Declaratory politics and the seductive appeal of ecological modernisation in the European Union. *Environmental Politics*, 16 (2), pp. 297–317.

Barnes, P.M. and Hoerber, T.C. (eds.) (2013). *Sustainable Development and Governance in Europe: The Evolution of the Discourse on Sustainability*. London and New York: Routledge.

Berger, G. and Steurer, R. (2007). *The EU SDS process in the member states: SDS coordinators, national progress reports and the open method of coordination*. ESDN quarterly report, March. Available at: www.sd-network.eu/?k=quarterly%20reports&report_id=4 [Accessed 2 March 2011].

Bulkeley, H. and Jordan, A. (2012). Transnational environmental governance: New findings and emerging research agendas. *Environment and Planning C: Government and Policy*, 30, 4, pp. 556–570.

Bulkeley, H., Jordan, A., Perkins, R. and Selin, H. (2013). Governing sustainability: Rio+20 and the road beyond. *Environment and Planning C: Government and Policy*, 31, pp. 958–970.

Busch, H. (2015). Linked for action? An analysis of transnational municipal networks in Germany. *International Journal of Urban Sustainable Development*. Available at: http://dx.doi.org/10.1080/19463138.2015.1057144.

Cordonier Segger, M.C. and Khalfan, A. (eds.) (2004). *Sustainable Development Law: Principles, Practices, and Prospects*. Oxford: Oxford Scholarship Online.

Covenant of Mayors (2015). Press Release. Available at: www.covenantofmayors.eu/about/covenant-of-mayors_en.html.

Committee of the Regions (2009). Contributions of the Regional and Local Authorities to Sustainable Development Strategies. The study written by the Research Institute for Managing Sustainability (RIMAS), Vienna University of Economics and Business Administration. Available at: https://cor.europa.eu/en/engage/studies/Documents/Contributions-LRA-Sustanable-Developement.pdf [Accessed 6 June 2018].

Council of European Communities (1987). Resolution on the continuation and implementation of a European Community policy and action programme on the environment (1987–1992). OJ C 328, 7.12.87.

Council of European Communities (1988). Council Regulation (EEC) No 2052/88 of 24 June 1988 on the tasks of the structural funds and their effectiveness and on coordination of their activities between themselves and with the operations of the European Investment Bank and the other existing financial instruments. OJ L 185/9.

Eadson, W. (2013). The evolution of carbon capitalism in the English regions: Sustainable mitigation, carbon modernization, and selective carbon economies. In: Barnes, P.M. and Hoerber, T.C. eds., *Sustainable Development and Governance in Europe: The Evolution of the Discourse on Sustainability*. London and New York: Routledge.

Executive Agency for Small and Medium-sized Enterprises (EASME). (2008). Financial guidelines for co-ordinators and co-beneficiaries. Available at: http://ec.europa.eu/environment/eco-innovation/files/docs/contract/financial_guidelines_en.pdf.

EASME (2016). Report Analysis of the results achieved by CIP Eco-innovation market replication project. Available at: http://ec.europa.eu/environment/eco-innovation/discover/publications/index_en.htm.

European Commission (1998). Communication sustainable urban development in the European Union: A framework for action (COM(1998)605).

European Commission (2000). Communication from the Commission to the member states of 28.4.00 laying down guidelines for a community initiative URBAN II 2000–2006 C(2000)1100.

European Commission (2001). A sustainable Europe for a better world: A European Union strategy for sustainable development, Brussels: Commission of the European Communities. Available at: http://eurlex.europa.eu/LexUriServ/LexUriServ.do?uri=CELEX:52001DC0264:EN:HTML.

European Commission (2004). National sustainable development strategies in the European Union: A first analysis by the European Commission. Available at: http://europe.eu.int/comm/sustainable/docs/sustainable_development_strategies.pdf.

European Commission (2005a). Communication draft declaration on guiding principles for sustainable development (COM(2005) 218 final).

European Commission (2005b). Communication Cohesion Policy in Support of Growth and Jobs: Community Strategic Guidelines, 2007–2013, (COM(2005) 299 final).

European Commission (2005c). Proposal for a Decision of the European Parliament and of the Council establishing a Competitiveness and Innovation Framework Programme (2007–2013), (COM(2005) 121 final).

European Commission (2006). A year of delivery. Communication from the commission to the Spring European Council. Implementing the renewed Lisbon strategy for growth and jobs (COM(2006) 816 final).

European Commission (2007). Progress report on the Sustainable Development Strategy 2007 (COM(2007) 642 final).

European Commission (2008a). Fostering the urban dimension. Analysis of the operational programmes co-financed by the European regional development fund (2007–2013). Working document of the DG regional policy. Belgium: Brussels.

European Commission (2008b). *EIP WORK PROGRAMME 2008*. Available at: http://ec.europa.eu/cip/files/docs/eip_wp2008_consolidatedversion_dec2008_en.pdf.

European Commission (2009). Communication Mainstreaming sustainable development into EU policies: 2009 Review of the European Union strategy for sustainable development (COM(2009) 400 final).

European Commission (2010). Communication Europe 2020: A strategy for smart, sustainable and inclusive growth (COM(2010)2020).

European Commission (2011a). Communication a budget for Europe 2020 of 29 June 2011 (COM(2011)500) final. Brussels: Commission of the European Communities.

European Commission (2011b). Roadmap to a resource efficient Europe (COM(2011) 571 final). The scoreboard is available at: http://ec.europa.eu/environment/resource_efficiency/targets_indicators/scoreboard/.

European Commission (2013). Communication a decent life for all: Ending poverty and giving the world a sustainable future (COM(2013) 92 final).

European Commission (2014a). Communication a global partnership for poverty eradication and sustainable development after 2015 (COM(2015) 44 final).

European Commission (2014b). Integrated sustainable urban development, factsheet. Available at: http://ec.europa.eu/regional_policy/sources/docgener/informat/2014/urban_en.pdf.

European Commission (2015). Guidance for member states on integrated sustainable urban development. Available at: http://ec.europa.eu/regional_policy/en/information/publications/guidelines/2015/.

European Commission (2016). Communication next steps for a sustainable European future European action for sustainability (COM(2016) 739 final).

European Council (2000). Presidency conclusions – Lisbon European Council, 23–24 March.

European Council (2001). Presidency conclusions – Gothenburg European Council, 15–16 June.

European Council (2005). Presidency conclusions – Brussels European Council, 22–23 March.

European Council (2006a). Review of the EU Sustainable Development Strategy (EU SDS) – Renewed Strategy.

European Council (2006b). Regulation (EC) No 1080/2006 of the European Parliament and of the Council of 5 July 2006 on the European Regional Development Fund and repealing Regulation (EC) No 1783/1999. OJ L 210, 31.7.2006.

European Council (2007). Presidency conclusions – Brussels European Council, 8–9 March.

European Council (2009a). Presidency conclusions – Brussels European Council, 10–11 December.

European Council (2009b). Council Decision 406/2009/EC of the European Parliament and of the Council of 23 April 2009 on the effort of Member States to reduce their greenhouse gas emissions to meet the Community's greenhouse gas emission reduction commitments up to 2020. *Official Journal of the European Communities* OJ L 140, 5.6.2009, pp. 136–148.

European Council (2012). Council Directive 2012/27/EU of the European Parliament and of the Council of 25 October 2012 on energy efficiency, amending Directives 2009/125/EC and 2010/30/EU and repealing Directives 2004/8/EC and 2006/32/EC. *Official Journal of the European Communities* OJ L 315, 14.11.2012, pp. 1–56.

European Council (2013a). Decision No 1386/2013/EU of the European Parliament and of the Council of 20 November 2013 on a General Union Environment Action Programme to 2020 'Living well, within the limits of our planet' Text with EEA relevance.

European Council (2013b). Regulation (EU) No 1303/2013 of the European Parliament and of the Council of 17 December 2013 laying down common provisions on the European Regional Development Fund, the European Social Fund, the Cohesion Fund, the European Agricultural Fund for Rural Development and the European Maritime and Fisheries Fund and laying down general provisions on the European Regional Development Fund, the European Social Fund, the Cohesion Fund and the European Maritime and Fisheries Fund and repealing Council Regulation (EC) No 1083/2006. OJ L 347, 20.12.2013.

European Council (2013c). Regulation (EU) No 1301/2013 of the European Parliament and of the Council of 17 December 2013 on the European Regional Development Fund and on specific provisions concerning the Investment for growth and jobs goal and repealing Regulation (EC) No 1080/2006. *OJ L 347, 20.12.2013.*

European Council (2015). Council conclusions a new global partnership for poverty eradication and sustainable development after 2015, 26 May.

Eurostat (2009). *Sustainable development in the European Union – 2009 monitoring report on the EU sustainable development strategy*. Available at: https://ec.europa.eu/eurostat/web/products-statistical-books/-/KS-78-09-865.

Ferry, M., Mendez, C. and Batchler, J. (2008). From environmental sustainability to sustainable development? Making concepts tangible in structural funds programmes. *IQ-Net Thematic Paper*, 22 (2). Available at: www.eprc-strath.eu/public/.

Gravey, V. and Jordan, A. (2016). Does the European Union have a reverse gear? Policy dismantling in a hyperconsensual polity. *Journal of European Public Policy*, 23 (8), pp. 1180–1198.

Hajer, M. (1995). *The Politics of Environmental Discourse: Ecological Modernization and the Regulation of Acid Rain*. Oxford: Oxford University Press.

Jordan, A. and Lenschow, A. (2008). *Innovation in Environmental Policy? Integrating the Environment for Sustainability*. Cheltenham: Edward Elgar Publishing.

Jordan, A. and Lenschow, A. (2010). Policy paper environmental policy integration: A state of the art review. *Environmental Policy and Governance*, 20, pp. 147–158.

Jordan, A., Schout, A. and Zito, A. (2005). *Coordinating European Union environmental policy: Shifting from passive to active coordination*. CSERGE Working Paper EDM, No. 04–05.

Kernevez, L. (2013). The EU emissions trading scheme: A post political tool for strengthening integration and wide-reaching sustainability? In: Barnes, P.M. and Hoerber, T.C. eds., *Sustainable Development and Governance in Europe: The Evolution of the Discourse on Sustainability*. London and New York: Routledge.

Kingston, S.E.J. (2013). *European Perspectives on Environmental Law and Governance*. London and New York: Routledge.

Lafferty, W.M. (2002). *Adapting government practice to the goals of sustainable development*. Available at: www.oecd.org/pdf/M0032000/M00032075.pdf.

Lafferty, W.M. (ed.) (2004). *Governance for Sustainable Development: The Challenge of Adapting Form to Function*. Cheltenham: Edward Elgar Publishing.

Lafferty, W.M. and Hovden, E. (2003). Environmental policy integration: Towards an analytical framework. *Environmental Politics*, 12 (3), pp. 1–22.

Leipzig Chapter (2007). Available at: http://ec.europa.eu/regional_policy/archive/themes/urban/leipzig_charter.pdf

Mol, A.P.J. and Sonnenfeld, D.A. (2000). Ecological modernisation around the world: An introduction. *Environmental Politics*, 9 (1), pp. 1–14.

Newig, J. (2007). Symbolic environmental legislation and societal self-deception. *Environmental Politics*, 16 (2), pp. 276–296.

Nowag, J. (2016). *Environmental Integration in Competition and Free Movement Laws.* Oxford: Oxford University Press.

Pallemaerts, M. (2013). Developing more sustainably? In: Jordan, A. and Adelle C. eds., *Environmental Policy in the EU: Actors, Institutions and Processes.* London: Routledge, pp. 347–367.

Rayner T., Howlett, M. (2009). Conclusion: Governance arrangements and policy capacity for policy integration. *Policy and Society*, 28, pp.165–172.

Renda, A. (2017). *How can sustainable development goals be 'mainstreamed' in the EU's better regulation agenda?* CEPS, Policy Insights. Available at: www.ceps.eu/publications/.

Steurer, R. (2008). Sustainable development strategies. In: Jordan, A. and Lenschow, A. eds., *Innovation in Environmental Policy? Integrating the Environment for Sustainability.* London: Edward Elgar, pp. 93–113.

Steurer, R. and Berger, G. (2011). The EU's double-track pursuit of sustainable development in the 2000s: How Lisbon and sustainable development strategies ran past each other. *International Journal of Sustainable Development & World Ecology*, 18 (2), pp. 99–108.

Steurer, R. and Martinuzzi, A. (2005). Towards new patterns of strategy formation in the public sector: First experiences with national strategies for sustainable development in Europe. *Environment and Planning C: Government and Policy*, 23, pp. 455–472.

Steurer, R. and Meadowcroft, J. (2013). Assessment practices in the policy and politics cycles: A contribution to reflexive governance for sustainable development? *Journal of Environmental Policy & Planning*, 1–23.

Van der Zwet, A., Miller, S. and Gross, F. (2014). A first stock take: Integrated territorial approaches in cohesion policy 2014–2020. *IQ-Net Thematic Paper*, 35 (2), November.

Van Hees, S.R.W. (2014). Sustainable development in the EU: Redefining and operationalizing the concept. *Utrecht Law Review*, 10 (2). Available at: www.utrechtlawreview.org/articles/.

Wurzel, R.K.W., Zito, A.R. and Jordan, A.J. (2013). *Environmental Governance in Europe: A Comparative Analysis of New Environmental Policy Instruments.* Cheltenham: Edward Elgar.

3 National sustainable development strategies

A comparative overview

3.1 Italy: from laggard to follower

3.1.1 Stepping forward and turning back

The Italian strategy for sustainable development has been described as rather ceremonial with a clear trend for stop and go dynamic (Pizzimenti, 2008). Not only has the implementation of concrete policy instruments related to the sustainability agenda been sporadic and incomplete, but a more general acceptance of the new policy paradigm in the domestic political discourse and policy structures was slow and problematic as well.

In fact, after the initial interest in the new political agenda on the occasion of the Rio Summit in 1992, no substantial steps followed between 1993 and 1996. Although the first National Plan for Sustainable Development was drawn in 1993, it was purely a symbolic document that brought no substantial changes either at the systemic level of political institutions or in terms of policy instruments (Capozza and Garrone, 2007; ISSI, 2004). During that period, the Italian environmental legislation remained strongly framed by the command and control style, with scarce implementation performance and no attempt for cross-sectoral or territorial coordination (Lewanski, 1997; Giuliani, 1998). Between 1997 and 2001, as a consequence of alternation of political majority in the national government that then included the communist party and greens, the sustainable development discourse acquired higher salience. In fact, in 1997 the Agenda for Sustainable Development was approved by the Parliament and a Commission for Sustainable Development was established under the Interministerial Committee for Economic Programming (ICEP – CIPE), which was the main body in charge of economic development. Although the Commission had a very limited role in coordinating decisions with potentially high environmental impacts, its creation has been a very important step, as it was the only body allowing for horizontal coordination and the integration of environmental concerns into national economic policies.

Importantly, as a consequence of administrative decentralisation reform in 1996 (the Bassanini Law) and the constitutional reform of 2001, greater powers in the environmental and development policies were delegated to Regions and their environmental protection agencies. According to the renewed Title V of the

Constitution, Regions were assigned the responsibility of defining environmental priorities, coordinating environmental action and allocating the related financial resources (Capozza and Garrone, 2007).

Moreover, a Sustainable Development Office was established at the Ministry of Environment in 2000, which co-financed the first call for proposals for Agenda 21 local and promoted the creation of a fund for Sustainable Development (Law 388/2000). During subsequent years, a number of institutional innovations aiming to strengthen the institutional framework of reference for sustainable development policies have been introduced, including the establishment of a sustainable development department and a dedicated Directorate General at the Ministry for Environment. In the same period, a new Environmental Action Strategy for Sustainable Development was elaborated and a technical committee for sustainable development was supposed to be established at the ICEP with executive and monitoring functions. The committee was supposed to include a representative forum having the task of encouraging public participation and consultation during the implementation of the strategy.

However, none of the aforementioned reforms have been fulfilled due to the alternation in government from the center-left to the center-right coalition guided by Silvio Berlusconi at the end of 2001. Indeed, the political guidance that aimed to institutionalise the environmental sustainability dimension was disrupted and a step back taken to the sectoral approach focused on economic growth above all else, regardless of the fact that the Environmental Action Strategy for Sustainable Development in Italy (EASSD) drafted by the previous government was formally approved by the ICEP in August 2002. The strategy aimed at mainstreaming the environmental dimension into sectoral policies and achieving a decoupling between economic growth and pressure on the use of natural resources and on the environment, especially in agriculture, energy and transport sectors. Specific indicators for the use of material, soil, energy, water, resources and waste production per unit of economic wealth were defined in order to measure the strategy's outcomes. In line with the EU 6th Environmental Action Plan, the strategy contained four broad priority themes: climate change and protection of ozone layer; protection and valorisation of natural resources and biodiversity; environmental quality and the quality of life in urban areas; resource and waste management (MATT, 2002). This document was considered the most advanced, albeit poorly implemented, document ever drafted in Italy on sustainable development at that time (Diamantini, 2004; ISSI, 2004).

Following the priorities outlined by the strategy, the Institute for Environmental Protection and Research (ISPRA) built a set of 150 indicators covering the key issues. Additionally, the main environmental indicators identified by Barcelona's European Council in 2002 were included in the document. Besides, the "Environmental Data Yearbook" was issued on annual basis, providing a comprehensive overview on the environment and sustainable development performance of the country. This dataset offered a detailed picture of environmental conditions and responses across various productive sectors, with a specific focus on the matter of prevention and recovery interventions. The number and precision of indicators has progressively increased, reaching 311 in the edition of 2017, 167 of which covered the regional level.

Moreover, in 2011, the National Institute for Statistics (Istituto Nazionale di Statistica – ISTAT) and the National Council for Economics and Labour (Consiglio Nazionale Economia e Lavoro – CNEL) established a Steering Committee and a Scientific Commission in charge of identifying a common set of indicators for broader measure of progress within the framework of the international activities on development indicators complementing GDP. The Steering Committee – composed of representatives of civil society – identified 12 dimensions of well-being relevant to the country, while the Scientific Commission then selected 134 high-quality statistical indicators appropriate for measuring the dynamics in the domains identified by the Committee. Extended consultations with public opinion (through online surveys) have also been carried out to fine-tune the dataset. The first comprehensive report of these activities aimed at defining the indicators of the equitable and sustainable well-being ("*benessere equo e sostenibile*" – BES) was published in March 2013. In 2017, the four BES indicators were for the first time introduced in the Economy and Financial Document, coherently with the commitment to integrate these indicators into the national economic programming established by Law 163/2016.

Beyond the aforementioned actions, the implementation of the Strategy's environmental measures has been extremely fragmented and mostly channeled through sector activities that have mainly concentrated in the following areas:

i. Local Agenda 21 (300 projects);
ii. Sustainable development in the depressed areas of Southern Italy;
iii. Promotion of environmental certification for small and medium enterprises;
iv. Promotion of programme agreements with industries for the creation of low emission systems and technologies with high environmental and energetic efficiency;
v. Research and development aimed at experimenting with innovative systems for the production and exploitation of energy by means of renewable sources and hydrogen and of highly efficient technologies for distributed generation of electricity, heat and cold;
vi. Participation of scientific institutions and universities in research programmes, both European and international, for the protection and understanding of global environment.

Starting merely since 2008, Italy has increasingly assigned priority to some specific aspects of sustainable development, such as, for example, the Green Public Procurement (GPP) and the Sustainable Consumption and Production patterns (SCP). A National Action Plan for the environmental sustainability of consumption in the public administration sector was approved (MATT, 2008), setting out the general framework of action and encouraging national and local authorities to adopt a GPP approach. It established the national target of at least 30% of goods to be purchased by the PAs in compliance with ecological criteria, and at least a 30–40% reduction of electricity consumption. Public authorities have been required to include "minimum environmental criteria" in the calls for tenders for goods and services listed in the Plan (e.g. paper for printers, furniture for offices, electrical devices, food services, vehicles, etc.). In subsequent years, a series of criteria have been defined, providing public authorities with further operational instructions and guidelines on how to employ social criteria in the definition of tenders for goods and services, as well as in the execution of interventions. These criteria mainly referred to a range of standards that guarantee fundamental human rights and appropriate working conditions, such as social protection, minimum income, equality, non-discrimination, etc.

Thus, the lack of political leadership for the strategy has been somehow compensated by scientific efforts and administrative provisions contributing to implement selected objectives and principles related mainly to the environmental dimension of sustainability. The issue of sustainable development definitely downscaled in the domestic political agenda as a consequence of the economic crisis of 2008–2009, resurfacing only in 2015, on the occasion of the adoption of the UN Agenda 2030.

A working group was established at the Ministry of the Environment, Land and Sea with the objective of laying the foundations for a renewed strategy and adjusting the path of national reforms in a long-term perspective. The newly formulated strategy aims to integrate the 17 Sustainable Development Goals (SDG) of the 2030 Agenda into the National Sustainable Development Strategy (NSDS) 2017–2030. It is organised in five core areas: People, Planet, Prosperity, Peace and Partnership. The first four areas mainly cover the domestic dimension, while the last one covers the principles and purposes of international cooperation as integrating and qualifying part of Italian foreign policy, drafted by Law 125/2014. The strategic topics identified by the document cover a wide range of issues, including decreasing poverty, inequality, discrimination, unemployment (particularly among youth and women), ensuring an environmentally sustainable economic development, increasing the opportunities for training, education and social progress, restoring the competitiveness of Italian companies through a "fourth industrial revolution" based on innovative and sustainable technologies.

The monitoring activities for the strategy have been naturally incorporated in the system of indicators previously elaborated by the National Statistical System, which has progressively released a new set of indicators covering the 17 SDGs. Many of them are based on the already mentioned BES measures, highlighting the fact that economic parameters alone are inadequate to evaluate the progress of societies and should be complemented by social and environmental information and by measures of inequality and sustainability.

The effort to connect more closely the implementation of this renewed NSDS with the economic programming documents, namely, the National Reform Programme and the Document on Economy and Finance, has been announced. Moreover, in keeping with the binding objectives set by the European Semester (i.e. EU2020 targets), the government has declared its intention to largely deploy the resources of EU structural funds included in the Partnership Agreement

2014–2020 for its strategy for smart, sustainable and inclusive growth. Furthermore, a number of existing national plans and initiatives have been listed under each priority without, however, illustrating how each of them will contribute to the achievement of specific sustainable development goals.

In 2015, the intention to formulate a National Green Act was announced with the purpose of designing a set of integrated measures for environmental protection, energy and climate, which would help bring Italy to an advanced position at the EU level. At the same time, the so-called Environmental Attachment (*collegato ambientale*) was envisaged by Article 31 of Legislative Decree on Economy and Finance (Documento di programmazione economica finanziaria – DEF, 2013), introducing environmental provisions for promoting green economy measures and limiting the excessive use of natural resources. It established a ministerial Committee for Natural Capital with the task to integrate environmental concerns and costs in the main financial law and other governmental legislative acts concerning economic programming and budgetary issues. The Committee is chaired by the Minister for Environment and includes nine other sectoral ministers: Minister of Economy and Finance, Minister of Economic Development, Minister of Jobs and Social Policies, Minister of Infrastructure and Transport, Minister of Agriculture, Minister of Regional Affairs and Territorial Autonomies, Minister of Territorial Cohesion, Minister of Public Administration and Minister of Culture. The Committee also included representatives of the National Association of Italian Municipalities (*Associazione Nazionale dei Comuni Italiani* – ANCI) and of the Conference of Regions, as well as representatives of five public entities for research (ISPRA, CNR, ENEA, *Banca d'Italia*) and nine independent experts nominated by the Ministry of Environment. Soon after, Law 221/2015 was passed, establishing a wide range of measures on environmental protection, sustainable development, energy, green public procurement, waste and water management. This was the first attempt to introduce the concepts of green economy and circular economy in the country's formal institutional political agenda, providing also insights on the integration of environmental dimension into a range of public policies, concerning water and resource management, soil protection, sustainable energy production and consumption, etc.

More specifically, the Committee's task has been to provide the government with appropriate policy instruments for assessing how the state of environment and natural resources affects the economic performance of the country and the level of citizens' well-being, identifying in particular economic and social consequences deriving from the lack of prevention of environmental damage in productive activities. Until now, the Committee has produced two assessment reports (in 2017 and in 2018), contributing to integrate the environmental dimension into sectoral decision-makings by providing specific recommendations on future actions, based on the evidence of major environmental risks and pressures, as well as related economic costs to be taken into account.

Therefore, although the new strategy undoubtedly represents a significant progress in terms of the overall upgrading of the Italian policies for sustainable development and might eventually bring the country from being a group of laggards to one of followers, it has clearly been characterised by the incremental approach that brings together ex post a number policy instruments under a common umbrella rather than developing a new comprehensive strategic framework.

3.1.2 Governance of the Italian strategy for sustainable development

Until recently, the Italian governance architecture for their strategy's implementation has been rather blurred and strongly centralised, although regional and local authorities were assigned increased responsibilities who filed and developed their own strategies that e to varying degree coordinated with the central government agenda. Therefore, the Prime Minister and his office held the overall coordination and management of the strategy, being supported by the Ministry of Environment, Land and Sea and the Ministry of Foreign Affairs, respectively for the internal and external dimensions. The Ministry of Finance had been tasked to identify appropriate models for creating strong synergies between the NSDS implementation and the ordinary economic policies.

While recognising the importance of implementing the SDGs at the local level and considering the fact that several competences and responsibilities in this field lie not only with the central administrations, but also on regional and local authorities, the government has committed to enhance the participation of sub-state authorities in the implementation process, as established by Article34, of Legislative Decree 152/2006, following the constitutional reform of 2005, which transferred some competences in the environmental field from national to regional and local levels. In this framework, the national level has maintained its competence in the definition of general objectives and guiding principles of environmental protection policies. Regions instead were responsible for strategic planning and the definition of specific measure of environmental protection. Within this framework, many Regions have adopted innovative policies and strategies for environmental field and in a wider sustainable development and climate policies perspective, extensively referring to the European and international guidance. More specifically, Regional governments have developed their respective environmental protection plans, along with a number of economic and planning documents, covering such policy areas as public investments, urban planning, social and health services and territorial development. In addition, a network of Regional Environmental Protection Agencies (Agenzie Regionali per la Protezione e Prevenzione Ambientale – ARPAs) has been established in order to enable policy coordination in the field of environmental policies, particularly for monitoring and environmental statistics. The National Institute for Environmental Protection and Research (ISPRA) has worked in close collaboration with all ARPAs, for promoting the implementation of national objectives at the regional level and developing a harmonised methodological and operational guidance.

Local authorities (provinces and municipalities), in their turn, were in charge of implementation of regional plans and programs as well as of control measures on waste, air and noise pollution, and the management of a wide array of environmentally relevant public services. Many Italian cities have developed their

Agenda 21, catching up with multiple European and international networks. A nation-wide network of Agenda 21 municipalities has been established with the purpose of coordinating the local efforts for sustainable development by collecting and sharing data, knowledge and practices delivered by municipalities in this field.

Lastly, the system of "permanent conferences" composed of the State-Regions Conference bringing together regional representatives, and the State-Local Authorities Conference, made of representatives of municipalities, inter-municipal aggregations and metropolitan areas, was expected to enable interactions and coordination between the centre and sub-state authorities in the implementation of the strategy.

Despite the existence of these numerous instruments potentially supporting the overall cooperation between the national and regional levels, the results of this activity appear to have been rather poor so far and indeed, the environmental protection has been a field of frequent clashes of interests between the centre and the periphery.

Importantly, the initiative to create a nation-wide network bringing together Regional Environmental Authorities and the Managing Authorities for the EU Structural Funds was taken in order to facilitate the integration of environmental issues into socio-economic development policies co-financed by EU funding, in particular in the south of the country. Furthermore, the National Observatory for Organisation and Management of regional agencies (Osservatorio Nazionale sull'Organizzazione e sulla Gestione delle ARPA – ONOG – ARPA) was established to prepare technical studies and guidelines on funding and management. These cooperation mechanisms were quite effective at the start, but after an intensive period of work in the early 2000s, their activities slowed down and the ONOG's work was discontinued.

Overall, the Ministry of the Environment, Land and Sea has been the main governmental body in charge of regulations, coordination and control related to environmental management. Its activities are supported by a range of specialised agencies, including the Italian Institute for Environmental Protection and Research (ISPRA – IEPR), the Department of the Marine Environment of the Italian Coast Guard, the Carabinieri Corps for Environmental Protection, an environmental unit of the national military police (*carabinieri*) at the disposal of the Ministry, and the State Forestry Corps, and an autonomous unit of the Ministry of Agriculture, Food and Forestry.

In a broader perspective, the search for horizontal integration and coherence through integrated environmental policies has been one of the most explicit objectives of the NSDS. Therefore, attempts have been made to create a unique forum for dealing with environmental sustainability in development policies, involving Interministerial Committee for European Community Affairs, the National Council for Economy and Labour (an advisory body to the government), the Parliament and the regional governments. Interdepartmental coordination at the central level has been carried out through task forces and steering committees, such as the Steering Committee for preparing the National Action Plan for Green

Public Procurement and the interministerial Technical Committee for Emissions of GHGs.

A number of initiatives have been launched to encourage the private sector to contribute to the strategy by conducting responsible business. In particular, the National Action Plan for Corporate Social Responsibility has been developed by the Ministry of Economic development and Ministry of Labour in compliance with the European Commission Communication 681 (2001) "A renewed EU strategy 2011–14 for corporate social responsibility".

Remarkably, the gap in the national political leadership for sustainable development, which became especially evident between 2009 and 2015, has to a certain extent been filled in by a number of voluntary initiatives undertaken by non-governmental organisations, private foundations or research institutions. There have been two outstanding actors in this field: the Foundation for Sustainable Development (FSD) and the Italian Alliance for Sustainable Development (ASviS). The former was established in 2008 with the objective of promoting policy initiatives for sustainable development with particular regard to climate and economic policies. It was directed by the then-minister for environment (1996–2000) Edo Ronchi and sponsored numerous policy and governance activities for integrating environmental concerns into different sectors, including energy and climate, circular economy, eco-innovation and waste. In fact, besides conducting studies, organising events and drawing policy reports on a wide range of issues, the FSD has consolidated an extensive collaborative network involving private companies, agencies and individual experts working on sustainability issues, also through thematic observatories and working groups. The most important initiative of this organisation has been the "General States of the Green Economy", which aims at developing proposals and recommendations for policy makers in order to enhance the greening of Italian economy by involving companies and business organisations directly. The National Council of the Green Economy has been established within the framework of this activity, in collaboration with the Ministry of Environment and the Ministry of Economic Development, which brings together 64 business organisations. Its activities are conducted through a multi-stakeholder participatory process based on a bottom-up consultation process involving the core green economy actors. The whole process annually concludes with a wide-scale, two-day public event included in the "Ecomondo" initiative held at Rimini Fiera, which gathers over 2000 participants.

The other important actor – the Italian Alliance for Sustainable Development (ASviS) was established in 2016, at the initiative of the Unipolis Foundation and the University of Rome "Tor Vergata". Its mission is to raise awareness among the Italian society, economic stakeholders and institutions about the importance of the Global Agenda 2030 for sustainable development, bringing together actors who already deal with specific aspects related to the Sustainable Development Goals (SDGs). More specifically, the activities of ASviS include the following: making the environment favourable for the development of a culture of sustainability at all levels; reorienting production and consumption models to that end; analysing the implications and opportunities of the sustainable development Agenda for Italy;

contributing to the definition of an Italian strategy for the implementation of the SDGs (also employing analytical and forecasting tools to help define policies for sustainable development) and to the establishment of a monitoring system to track the progress of Italy in attaining the SDGs.

Regardless of its relatively recent history, the Alliance has already built a wide network of supporters, including associations representing social partners (businesses, trade unions and third sector associations); networks of civil society associations operating in specific areas (health, education, employment, environment quality, gender equality, etc.); associations of local public administrations; public and private universities and research centres; associations working in the field of communication and information; organisations that are members of international networks dealing with the SDGs. Among other activities, the Alliance conducts an extensive communication and information campaign through its website and newsletters, providing thousands of readers and users with a continuous flow of information on the implementation of the 2030 Agenda in Italy and worldwide, as well as on the results of ongoing research on issues related to the SDGs.

Lastly, two national research institutes, ENEA (Italian National Agency for New Technologies, Energy and Sustainable Economic Development) and ISPRA, have contributed to build an extensive and solid knowledge base in the fields of environmental policy integration and sustainable development.

In sum, the consolidation of the discourse on and policy agenda for sustainable development has been slow and cumbersome. The low political priority regarding the issue is also reflected in its being one the highest in the EU in number of infringement procedures (Börzel *et al.*, 2012), which has only recently been reduced. After the approval of the early version of the strategy in 2002, no coordinated cross-sectoral action has been performed and only fragmented legislative initiatives have been undertaken, being mainly guided by EU mandatory requirements. In spite of increased awareness about the relevance of environmental and sustainability issues among Italian businesses and society, which is reflected by high scores of the eco-innovation index concerning the propensity to invest into eco-innovation and green jobs, or the participation in environmental certification schemes (European Commission, 2016), as well as by growing community movements for sustainable consumption (Forno and Graziano, 2011), there has been an obvious reluctance of the government to establish a comprehensive policy agenda for sustainability (Ronchi and Colucci, 2011).

A qualitatively new phase has recently opened during the new left-wing government led by Matteo Renzi, which has tried to catch up with the new challenges of the evolving international and EU agenda for sustainability and climate change mitigation and adaptation. However, the country needs to overcome a number of bottlenecks in order to move forward to achieve the 17 ambitious SDGs, which go beyond the concept of environmental sustainability.

Despite some recent efforts to enhance policy coordination "from the top", most domestic policies are still developed within distinct sectoral domains. Thus, the improvement of policy coherence and integration for the pursuit of the goal of sustainable development is on the agenda, requiring institutional efforts for changing policy and governance practices.

In addition, the balance between the economic and environmental dimensions represents a challenge, as the development of policy measures aimed at sustainable growth cannot avoid taking into account the need of cutting public expenditure and inverting the growing public debt, which the country has had to address over the last few decades. Some recent measures, such as the National Action Plan for the reduction of greenhouse gas emissions approved by the Department for Economic Programming and Coordination (CIPE) has undertaken some efforts in this direction, but it is still far from being systematic. Consistent with the goals of the new National Energy Strategy, the plan encourages the process of decarbonisation of the economy through actions supporting the green economy, including the extension of tax reduction for energy efficiency in buildings, the extension 0 of white certificates for energy savings until 2020, the promotion of renewable energy sources, the green technologies database – just to mention a few.

Finally, there has been limited recognition and involvement of regional and local governments as well as of other non-governmental actors in the past NSDS. Instead, as the overview above shows, there has been a considerable amount of initiative aimed at increasing sustainable modes of production and consumption, and at enhancing more general awareness about the opportunities of sustainable development.

In this perspective, the preparatory process that preceded the approval of the new strategy seems to have paved the way for a wider, more inclusive and hopefully, more straightforward strategy. A forum on the strategy for sustainable development was established by the Ministry for the Environment, Land and Sea in order to conduct a multilevel consultation process by ensuring the participation of civil society and relevant stakeholders in the definition of the new strategy.

Fully in line with the spirit of the 2030 Agenda, civil society engagement and consultations with public and private institutions have been organised in order to ensure a reliable context analysis and effective identification of main strengths and weaknesses to be addressed, leading to the definition of widely shared national objectives. More than 200 NGOs have been involved in the consultation procedure, together with a range of public research agencies (for instance, CNR, ISPRA, ENEA, ISTAT) and universities. Public national administrations cooperated throughout an ad hoc process in order to set shared National Strategic Choices and Objectives, as well as to identify viable and existing means of implementation. Regional authorities have been involved too in order to bring together territorial issues and priorities. The final steps in the elaboration of a National Strategy has been conducted in strong coordination with the National Reform Programme (PNR), dealing with social and economic programming in the context of EU policies and processes and containing the bulk of present and future government actions (MATT, 2017).

The new SDS was endorsed by the Italian Council of Ministers in 2017 and a Plan of Action will be developed by the end of 2018, which will include numerical and quantitative targets in 2030, as well as monitoring and review mechanisms and analytical models capable of measuring the impacts of policies on the NSDS objectives. It has been established that the NSDS will undergo an annual review and monitoring process. Moreover, a three-year Strategic and Planning Document for Development Cooperation has been approved for the 2016–2018 period, designing the scope and the structure of actions in this domain. Its macro-areas have been arranged so as to take into account the integrated nature and the structure of the 17 SDGs and include new sectors for action – such as data for development and domestic resources mobilisation – together with those of more traditional engagement. The three-year document served as a basis also for the active commitment of Italy in the elaboration of the new EU Consensus on Development.

3.2 The UK: from leaders to pioneers

3.2.1 The origins and progress of the UK strategy for sustainable development

The current UK policies and governance for sustainable development was built on a long-term experience of environmental institutions and policy integration instruments dating back to the 1970s, when the Department of Environment – the world's first such department (Russel and Jordan, 2010) was created embracing many of the most important central government-level environmental structures. At the same time, a Central Unit on Environmental Pollution in the Cabinet Office and an independent scientific advisory board known as the Royal Commission on Environmental Pollution were established to enhance the environmental dimension of policy-making. In the following years, the UK dissolved its integrated environmental department (Jordan and Lenschow, 2008) by merging the environmental portfolio first with transport (until 2001) and later with agriculture in a newly established Department for Environment, Food and Rural Affairs – DEFRA (Wurzel *et al.*, 2013).

As far as policy instruments are concerned, in particular in view of EU regulatory impact, the development of environmental policy in the UK between the late 1970s and early 1980s has been described as a story of "reluctant Europeanisation" (Bulmer and Burch, 2005), with the central government adopting a minimalist approach to compliance with EU standards and requirements.

Voluntarism, discretion and practicability characterised UK environmental policy throughout the 1970s and 1980s (Weale, 1997), the dominant philosophy of which was that the central government should only ever set the broad legislative or policy framework, leaving the detailed aspects of policy fine-tuning and implementation either to specialist agencies or to local/regional government bureaucracies (Wurzel *et al.*, 2013).

Its overall policy style that developed over subsequent years has been described as embodying "a strong commitment to co-operation, administrative discretion and technical specialisation" (Weale *et al.*, 2000: 180–181), emphasising consultation and negotiation, rather than imposition and confrontation. Contrary to the continental European states that have widely been applying fixed legislative standards and deadlines, the UK more frequently opted for unwritten agreements, general legal guidelines and flexible implementation systems (Wurzel *et al.*, 2013). However, a paradox has been observed in this regard: while the UK can be said to have pioneered the use of voluntary approaches, it has been very selective in promoting the main EU voluntary schemes or market based instruments. In fact, the UK was among the laggards in adopting the EU eco-label scheme, while strongly supporting the use of EMAS and a much broader, integrated product policy approach to greening production referring to international certification schemes (Zito and Egan, 1998).

At the same time, many large businesses in Britain have been opposed to government and EU supported eco-labels and have instead preferred self-declaratory schemes such as "fair trade" and "red tractor" labels (Jordan *et al.*, 2003: 172). Although industry has been broadly committed to the adoption of more voluntary approaches, some economic sectors have warmly embraced voluntary schemes, others have been ambivalent, and some flatly opposed them (Wurzel *et al.*, 2013). At the same time, there is little evidence that UK voluntary schemes were inspired by development abroad. Much more significant were domestic developments between UK regulatory bodies and producer groups, evolving according to a path-dependent pattern based on a sort of gentleman's agreements.

The UK NSDS was launched in 1994, two years after the Rio Summit and largely anticipating the formulation of EU strategy for sustainable development. The UK strategy has predated the EU effort to pursue the EPI principle and strongly advocated EPI at the EU level since the beginning of the 1990s (Jordan, 2002: 41), as a new approach was announced by the White Paper on environment, outlining a comprehensive cross-governmental approach to sustainable development (Russel and Jordan, 2010: 159). Thus, by the end of the 1990s, the UK policy priorities shifted from the EPI approach to a wider perspective of "sustainable development integration", with the Green Ministers renamed Sustainable Development Ministers and environmental policy appraisal supplanted by Regulatory Impact Assessment – RIA (Jordan and Lenschow, 2008).

In 1999, the UK government refined its approach to SD in its new White Paper "A better quality of life: a strategy for sustainable development for the United Kingdom", suggesting a series of headline indicators for measuring how economic, social and environmental outcomes can be simultaneously delivered (HMG, 1999). The following priorities have been defined by the document:

- More investment in people and equipment for a competitive economy;
- Achieving higher growth whilst reducing pollution and use of resources;
- Sharing the benefits of growth more widely and more fairly;
- Improving towns and cities and protecting the quality of the countryside;
- Contributing to sustainable development internationally.

Hence, while clearly prioritising the dimension of economic growth, this strategy included the environmental and – to a less extent – social components while also introducing an explicit territorial focus. Furthermore, the strategy emphasised the role of individuals for achieving sustainability goals and as a consequence, a number of actions were launched with the objective of promoting behaviour change, including the most prolific and high profile campaign "Are you doing your bit (AYDB)?". AYDB was a national awareness initiative that aimed to encourage environmental action and sustainability oriented patterns of behaviour. It distinguished from previous campaigning by a broader definition of sustainable development, supported by the Labour administration, calling for the first time for sustainable consumption. The second important novelty was regarding the method: the strategy used the multimedia channels widely, using short, snappy and clear messages focused on a different type of targetted behavior/lifestyle change each month, such as energy, water, waste. The assumption was that citizens' awareness and information were central to changing behaviour, and that environmental consciousness would enable them to transfer environmental messages into everyday lifestyle with ease (Barr, 2008).

In 1999 the UK was ranked 16th in the World Economic Forum (WEF) Environmental Sustainability Index (ESI) that measured the overall progress towards and the capacity to achieve environmental sustainability for 122 countries, considering a broad spectrum of indicators contributing to long-term sustainability, such as baseline environmental conditions and natural resource endowments, pollution flows and resource stresses, human welfare, social and institutional capacity to respond to environmental challenges and national contributions to global stewardship.

Since 2003, the concept of low-carbon economy has started to make its way, being considered one of the main pillars of sustainable development strategy. The White Paper on Energy has introduced the related policy goal, setting out a long-term target of reducing carbon dioxide emissions by some 60 percent by 2050, with real progress to be shown by 2020 (DTI, 2003).

The NSDS was reviewed again in 2005, taking account of policies and developments since the 1999 Strategy, both domestically and internationally, and covering the period up to 2020 (HMG, 2005). The reviewed Strategy entitled "Securing the future delivering UK sustainable development strategy" called for enhanced action in a number of policy sectors, including in particular energy, transport and waste, and paid particular attention to the territorial and societal dimension of action.

More specifically, it put greater emphasis on the new relationship between the central government and local authorities, also taking into consideration the devolution reforms that empowered Scotland, Wales and Northern Ireland. Thus, the revised strategy established a new set of principles of sustainable development and identified new political priorities that were agreed to by the central and the devolved administrations within the framework of the Community Action 2020 document (HMG, 2005). Building on the 1999 Strategy, the document has promoted a new integrated vision of SD strategy, focusing on a range of environmental and societal challenges and identifying four distinct priorities: sustainable consumption and production, climate change, natural resource protection and sustainable communities.

Therefore, a set of measures for encouraging transformations of models of production and consumption towards green economy has been identified, including the delivery of new products and services with lower environmental impacts across their life cycle. The development of new business models that would meet this challenge while also boosting competitiveness has been welcomed, along with an increased emphasis on reducing waste and on resource efficiency. In regard to these measures, the strategy recognised the crucial importance of people's growing awareness about social and environmental concerns, and the relevance of their roles as citizens and consumers.

A package of interventions was defined with the purpose of promoting the vision of sustainable communities across the country, enhancing the delivery of sustainable development at the local level. Key commitments in this sense can be summarised under the following four main strands:

- Collaborating effectively at the local level around the vision of sustainable communities with the local planning and development strategies, concluding the Local Development Framework (LDF), the Sustainable Community Strategies, the Local Area Agreements, etc.;
- Providing better information and participation of communities in decision-making at the local level;
- Empowering local authorities under the Clean Neighborhoods and Environment Bill;
- Helping to improve international environmental governance.

Moreover, a strong emphasis was put on measures that would enable and encourage behavioural change, enhance the engagement of communities, also looking for ways to catalyse changes helping people to get involved by providing skills training, improved access to funding and mentoring. For example, as far as local communities are concerned, a number of actions have been envisaged aimed at promoting the creation of deliberative forums helping in understanding how to develop more sustainable lifestyles; piloting open and innovative ways to allow stakeholders to influence decisions about the kind of projects that would deliver the goals of the strategy; enhancing new commitments to support education and training in sustainable development.

Besides, within the framework of the Community Action 2020 document, the UK Government and the Devolved Administrations in Scotland, Wales and Northern Ireland agreed to provide a consistent approach to the implementation of the strategy across the UK by producing a strategic framework for sustainable development until 2020. The following five guiding priorities have been set out in order to enable an overarching approach that would be followed by the four separate national strategies (HMG, 2005):

- Living within environmental limits
- Ensuring a strong, healthy and just society
- Achieving a sustainable economy
- Promoting good governance
- Using sound science responsibly

Accordingly, a shared priority for action has been agreed upon in the field of sustainable consumption and production, climate change and energy, natural resource protection and environmental enhancement and sustainable communities. Overall, the strategy has been strongly embedded in the UK international commitments framed by the Millennium Development Goals (MDGs).

The aforementioned changes were a result of a new thinking, supported by DEFRA, concerning the creation of capacity for behaviour change based on the lessons learnt from the past experience. As a range of evaluations has brought to light, previous campaigns did not succeed enough in this endeavour (Demos/Green Alliance, 2003; Darnton, 2004; Jackson, 2005). In fact, an extensive survey of small and medium-sized enterprises conducted in 2003 found that only 6% of respondents thought that they undertook activities that could be damaging to the environment and that only 18% could name environmental legislation unprompted. The same survey also found that while just over 50% of businesses acknowledged that good environmental practice can reduce operating costs, only 23% of respondents had implemented measures to reduce environmental damage (NetRegs, 2003).These results have clearly showed that while environmental impacts and legal obligations are extremely important for the strategy's success, the awareness about the relevance of these aspects among businesses has been quite low. A study regarding potential savings in the agricultural sector via improved environmental performance produced similar evidence, confirming a strong lack of awareness about opportunities, including economic ones, provided by sustainable development (DEFRA, 2008).

One more important elements of the renewed sustainable development strategy approved in 2005 has been the UK government's commitment to the reduction of the country's greenhouse gas emissions within a wider perspective of climate change and energy policies. In fact, the Climate Change Communications Initiative was launched, with funding of around £12 million over the period 2005–2008, with the objective of tackling public attitudes towards and understanding of climate change, stressing how each one can help reduce our personal contribution to climate change. Besides, climate change was indicated as a top priority for both the UK's G8 and European Union presidency in 2005.

A further update of the strategy took place in 2011, when the coalition government (HMG, 2010) published its document "Mainstreaming sustainable development – The Government's vision and what this means in practice" (DEFRA, 2011). This document has renewed the commitment to the core principles underpinning the strategy adopted in 2005 and highlighted the interconnections between the three pillars of SD – economic, social and environmental. The new strategy included a package of implementation measures for delivering the strategy through actions for Green Economy tackling climate change, protecting and enhancing the natural environment, improving fairness and well-being, and empowering local-level and tailor-made solutions. An approach for cross-sectoral sustainable development mainstreaming has been agreed upon, consisting in broad terms of ministerial leadership and oversight, leading by example, embedding sustainable development into policy, and transparent and independent scrutiny.

Accordingly, a number of cross-sectoral provisions have been further defined by the policy paper "Greening government commitments" (GGC) published by DEFRA, referring to the period 2011–2015. In particular, a range of new sustainable public procurement rules were introduced concerning the way of running buildings and purchasing goods and services at the central governmental level in such sectors as energy (e.g. New rules for procurers of energy-using goods under the Energy Efficiency Directive 2012/27/EU; timber (Timber Procurement Policy (TPP)), etc. The decision was taken that all departmental business plans should contain actions contributing to sustainable development and the DEFRA would take the leading responsibility for reviewing these plans in relation to sustainable development principles. The Minister for Government Policy will then hold departments to account through the quarterly business plan review process.

Moreover, the document announced the objective to develop real and measurable indicators to monitor sustainability performance across government and report results publicly. Therefore, independent monitoring of sustainability in government operations, procurement and policies by the Environmental Audit Committee and more frequent and up-to-date publishing of information and statistics were planned. An overview of GGC reporting requirements was attached to the document, introducing a set of criteria to be met by all central governmental bodies in order to enable monitoring and transparency of implementation. DEFRA in its turn committed to collect and publish statistical data built on a range of indicators of sustainable development, linking with other national and international initiatives. Among others, central government departments and agencies were required to use the green business strategy to comply with the GGC, and they were also expected to collect and publish information about the impacts of their supply chain.

The last revision of the strategy was competed in 2016 by the policy paper "Greening government commitments", setting out the actions that UK government departments and their agencies will take to reduce their impacts on the environment in the period between 2016 and 2020. This document defined targets for UK central government departments and their agencies, aiming at reducing their greenhouse gas emissions, the overall amount of waste, in particular to send to landfill, and water pollution. It reiterated the commitment for the central administrations to take into account sustainability in decision-making, as well as improve sustainable procurement and reporting. A set of reporting requirements have been established for the same period of 2016–2020, replacing the initial guidance that was attached to the previous strategy published in 2011.

3.2.2 Governance for sustainable development in the UK

The UK governance architecture for sustainable development has been characterised by a rather complex and strongly decentralised structure, with DEFRA playing a central role in overseeing sustainable development across central government since 2001. Besides defining general guiding principles in order to help in developing sustainable development tools and capabilities across Whitehall,

DEFRA has issued additional sustainable development guidance for departments on impact assessments and policy appraisal, and a cross-government sustainable development e-learning module with Civil Service Learning. All central government departments have committed to make sure that their own policies and activities contribute to sustainable development, and they review their progress towards sustainable development every year and report on it in their annual reports and accounts. Moreover, a Parliamentary Environmental Audit Committee (EAC) was established in the House of Commons towards the end of 1997, with the principle task of scrutinising and reporting on how EPI and sustainable development is implemented across government (Jordan, 2002). A Sustainable Development Commission acting as an independent advisory body to government and the devolved administrations on sustainable development was created in 2000, being assigned the responsibility of monitoring the governments' progress on sustainable development. Without going too much into detail on various administrative and organisational reforms undertaken in this field and the consequent redistribution of powers, it is worth mentioning that the activities of both bodies have been recognised as significant in opening up the working of the government to greater scrutiny and evaluation (Russel and Jordan, 2010: 162).

Since 2011, the ministerial leadership and oversight has been announced. Within this mechanism, the Environment Secretary sits on the key domestic policy cabinet committees, including the Economic Affairs Committee, to enforce the government's commitment to sustainability across policy-making. A Ministerial Steering Group oversees delivery of new Commitments for Greening Government's Operations and Procurement.

The UK Environment Agency has been among the most relevant actors in the implementation of the national policies and commitments, especially contributing to monitoring and overview of environmental aspects in various policy sectors, collecting environmental statistics, carrying out consultations and supporting projects. It has also engaged in partnership with other governmental bodies, such as DEFRA, the Department of Transport, Local Government and the Regions (DTLR), the Regional Government Offices; the Regional Development Agencies; industry and commerce; local authorities; non-government organisations in the environmental and social sectors; trusts; researchers, consultants and academia. Lastly, annual reports (Greening Government Commitments) on the progress of the strategy have been published regularly since 2015.

Besides the emphasis on policy coordination at central level, the UK Strategy for SD has been distinguished by a clearly multilevel nature. An extensive governance network for sustainable development has developed at the sub-state level, as the UK's devolution reforms have developed in parallel with the consolidation of the national and European policy discourse on sustainability. Thus, as literature suggests, the process of developing "common ideas" within the sustainability discourse in the UK has not been limited to an exchange of abstract ideas, but that hegemonisation has also involved an ongoing process of self-positioning between political actors (Hogwood, 2013).

In fact, strategies for sustainable development have been developed by all four devolved UK nations, evolving from the relatively narrow frame of environmental protection to a more complex and comprehensive framework. So, the Northern Ireland published its first Sustainable Development strategy in 2006 and a revised strategy called "Everyone's Involved" was approved in 2010. The associated Implementation Plan, "Focus on the Future", was published in 2011. The Scottish earliest commitment was formalised through its strategy published in 2005 (Scottish Executive, 2005), while in September 2011 the Scottish government published its Government Economic Strategy that reaffirmed its commitment to delivering increased sustainable economic growth, through Scotland's transition to a low-carbon economy.

The Welsh Sustainable Development Action Plan "Starting to Live Differently", was adopted in 2004 (WAG, 2004) by the National Assembly for Wales. This was then replaced in 2009, by "One Wales: One Planet", the Sustainable Development Scheme of the Welsh Assembly Government. The Welsh comprehensive Sustainable Development Charter and Environment Act were passed in 2016, covering a wide range of sustainability related issues from management of resources and risks, to climate change and green economy.

It has been highlighted (Hogwood, 2013) that in the UK, the outcome of the devolved efforts to carve a role for themselves in the multilevel governance of environmental and sustainability issues has been a continuously evolving network of channels of communication between regional, national and European policy makers, officials and experts. Overall, the devolved authorities were quite comfortable with a "stewardship" approach developed by the EU since 2001, which tended to draw together policy initiatives that in the past might have been sectorised under separate environmental headings such as air, water, soil, etc.

In this context, Scotland and Wales have shown particularly strong ambition in building their sustainable development and later on climate strategies designing emission reduction plans and support for vaster (e.g. Scottish wind power) and more innovative (e.g. Welsh tidal lagoons) renewable energy sectors compared to the national level. The reduction of substantial public investments in renewables, which has taken place during the last few years, along with tensions between the central government and devolved nations on such initiatives can hinder positive outcomes.

Along with the empowerment of nations, the UK cities have also acquired a stronger role in the sustainability agenda and expressed their commitment to it. In fact, a considerable number of cities have developed their local sustainable development agendas since the end of the 1990s by combining international strategic opportunities and the EU policy incentives. For example, some City Regions have secured new powers via City Deals and have prioritised low-carbon sectors through networks such as the Core Cities group and the C40 Cities Climate Leadership Group.

Finally, multiple networks involving the private sector and civil society have increasingly expanded, indicating their potential. Public and private finance initiatives in low-carbon sectors, for example, the Carbon Trust's Offshore Wind

Accelerator, have been successful at driving down cost to the extent that it is now cheaper than new nuclear and gas. Numerous low-carbon energy co-operatives and sustainable lifestyle projects have been promoted, although according to some evaluations (Gillard *et al.*, 2017) they have not been duly supported by the government. In contrast, it has been emphasised that these initiatives have been struggling to upscale their efforts or have any influence of policy because of unpredictable levels of financial support and restrictive framings of public participation. Instead, polycentric networks appear to possess an enormous potential for overcoming limits of the current climate policies, as they provide unique communication channels and economies of scale that drive innovation. Obviously enough, stronger support of public and governmental initiatives would be needed to boost and fully explore such potential.

Overall, the UK has made noteworthy efforts in promoting environmental sustainability in domestic policies and enhancing greater institutional coordination in this field by developing a national environmental policy integration system (Jordan and Schout, 2006). The UK has come the closest to having comprehensive national EPI framework by adopting a wide range of EPI instruments, including NEP, NSSD, sectoral strategies, reporting obligations, independent institutions, interdepartmental coordination, green cabinets, green budgeting and impact assessment.

However, criticism and concerns were expressed at a certain stage, emphasising a number of factors undermining the quality of the UK performance for sustainable development. These concerned, first of all, the heavy reliance on the support of the Prime Minister and the central coordinating bodies, in the absence of a legal or constitutional commitment to sustainable development or EPI (Jordan and Lenschow, 2008), which has been established largely as an administrative process (Russel and Jordan, 2010). Second, it has been suggested that SD was struggling to make headway against the dominance of traditional economic concerns in UK decision-making (Russel, 2007), with its progress being particularly hampered by inconsistency in the government's definition of SD and poor integration between the different administrative mechanisms, tools and processes to pursue SD. Third, some scholars have brought to light the fact that the UK Regulatory Impact Assessment (RIA) effectiveness for ensuring more integrated policies has been limited too, as many RIAs covered a narrow range of impacts, were conducted late in the policy process, had relatively closed consultation processes, etc. Closed policy communities and institutional processes have been mentioned as foremost among the main barriers hindering policy integration (Russel and Turnpenny, 2009). Despite these weaknesses, the UK has undoubtedly represented the most advanced contexts in the EU in terms of existing favourable preconditions for various public and private actors to develop pro-sustainability policy practices and behaviour by deploying opportunities offered by selected EU policy programmes.

To sum up, the two national contexts are at very different stages of the development of their sustainable development agendas, governance and policy instruments, thus providing for completely different conditions for the implementation of EU policy programmes, in particular those targeting sub-state and non-state actors. In this respect, the UK context seems to offer several advantages as it has already built a consolidated policy discourse and measures enhancing the integration of environmental objectives into sectoral policies. Remarkably, it has actually anticipated the shift of sustainable development approach based on EPI to the green economy policy narrative. In contrast, the Italian context appears much less equipped for sub-state authorities and enterprises to be actively involved in EU programmes, as a very few domestic initiatives have been implemented to enhance their motivation, knowledge and capacities in this field. Indeed, a lack of a comprehensive national strategy for sustainable development has only recently been recovered mainly in terms of the high-level political discourse, while concrete policies and governance settings allowing for translating the announced objectives into policy practices are still to be established.

References

Barr, S. (2008). *Environment and Society: Sustainability, Policy and Citizens*. Routledge: London.

Börzel, T.A., Hofmann, T. and Panke, D. (2012). Caving in or sitting it out? Longitudinal patterns of non-compliance in the European Union. *Journal of European Public Policy*, 19 (4), pp. 454–471.

Bulmer, S. and Burch, M. (2005). The Europeanization of UK government: From quiet revolution to explicit step-change? *Public Administration*, 83 (4), pp. 861–890.

Darnton, A. (2004). Driving public behaviours for sustainable lifestyles. *Report for Defra*, May. Available at: http://collections.europarchive.org/tna/20080530153425/www.sustainable-development.gov.uk/publications/pdf/desk-research2.pdf.

Demos/Green Alliance (2003). *Carrots, sticks and sermons: Influencing public behaviour for environmental goals*. Report produced for Defra, Version 4.0. Available at: www.demos.co.uk/files/CarrotsSticksSermons.pdf [Accessed 15 June 2018].

Department of Trade and Industry (DTI) (2003). *Our Energy Future: Creating a Low Carbon Economy*. London: HMSO.

Department for Environment, Food and Rural Affairs February (DEFRA) (2008). Understanding behaviours in a farming context. Discussion Paper. Available at: http://webarchive.nationalarchives.gov.uk/20130222210253/http:/www.defra.gov.uk/statistics/files/defra-stats-foodfarm-environ-obs-research-behavious-aceopaper-nov08.pdf.

DEFRA (2011). *The government's vision and what this means in practice*. Available at: https://assets.publishing.service.gov.uk/government/uploads/system/uploads/attachment_data/file/183409/mainstreaming-sustainable-development.pdf.

European Commission, (2016). Analysing the success drivers of EMAS in selected member states case study on Italy, http://ec.europa.eu/environment/emas/pdf/other/IT_EMAS-CaseStudy.pdf.

Gillard, R., Gouldson, A., Paavola, J. and Van Alstine, J. (2017). Can national policy blockages accelerate the development of polycentric governance? Evidence from climate change policy in the United Kingdom. *Global Environmental Change*, 45, pp.174–182.

Her Majesty's Government (HMG). (1999). *A Better Quality of Life: Strategy for Sustainable Development for the United Kingdom*. London: HMSO.

HMG (2005). *Securing the Future: Delivering the UK Sustainable Development Strategy*. London: HMSO.

HMG (2010). *The Coalition: Our Programme for Government*. London: HMSO. Available at: https://assets.publishing.service.gov.uk/government/uploads/system/uploads/attachment_data/file/83820/coalition_programme_for_government.pdf.

Hogwood, P. (2013). The UK's devolved authorities and the European sustainability discourse: Between identity and actor hierarchy. In: Barnes, P.M. and Hoerber, T.C. eds., *Sustainable Development and Governance in Europe: The Evolution of the Discourse on Sustainability*. London and New York: Routledge.

Jackson, T. (2005). *Motivating sustainable consumption. A review of evidence on consumer behaviour and behavioural change*. Report to the Sustainable Development Research Network sponsored by Defra. Available at: http://sustainablelifestyles.ac.uk/sites/default/files/motivating_sc_final.pdf.

Jordan, A. (2002). Efficient hardware and light green software: Environmental policy integration in the UK. In: Lenschow, A. ed., *Environmental Policy Integration: Greening Sectoral Policies in Europe*. London: Earthscan, pp. 35–56.

Jordan, A. and Lenschow, A. (2008). *Innovation in Environmental Policy? Integrating the Environment for Sustainability*. Cheltenham: Edward Elgar.

Jordan, A. and Schout, A., (2006). *The Coordination of the European Union. Exploring the Capacities of Networked Governance*. Oxford: Oxford University Press.

Jordan, A., Wurzel, R. and Zito, A. (eds.) (2003). *New Instruments of Environmental Governance*. London: Frank Cass.

Ministero dell'Ambiente e della Tutela del Territorio (MATT). (2002). *Strategia d'azione ambientale per lo sviluppo sostenibile in Italia*. Available at: www.minambiente.it/sites/default/files/archivio/allegati/sviluppo_sostenibile/strategia_svs_2002.pdf.

MATT (2008). *Piano d'azione per la sostenibilità ambientale dei consumi della pubblica amministrazione*. Available at: www.minambiente.it/pagina/piano-dazione-nazionale-sul-gpp.

MATT (2017). *Strategia Nazionale per lo Svilippo Sostenibile*. Available at: www.minambiente.it/sites/default/files/archivio_immagini/Galletti/Comunicati/snsvs_ottobre2017.pdf.

NetRegs (2003). *SME-nvironment: A survey to assess environmental behaviours among smaller UK businesses*. Available at: www.scribd.com/document/299091619/Netregs-2003.

Pizzimenti, E. (2008). Do Paradigms Matter? L'istituzionalizzazione dello sviluppo sostenibile in Italia (1992–2006). *Rivista Italiana di Politiche Pubbliche*, 3 (1), pp. 101–128.

Russel, D. (2007). The United Kingdom's sustainable development strategies: Leading the way or flattering to deceive? In: Steurer, R. and Martinuzzi, A. eds., *Special Issue: Sustainable Development Strategies in Europe: Taking Stock 20 years after the Brundtland Report. Environmental Policy and Governance*, 17 (3), pp. 189–200.

Russel, D. and Jordan, A. (2010). Environmental policy integration in the UK. In: Goria, A., Sgobbi, A. and Von Homeyer, I. eds., *Governance for the Environment: A Comparative Analysis of Environmental Policy Integration*. Cheltenham: Edward Elgar, pp. 157–179.

Russel, D. and Turnpenny, J. (2009). The politics of sustainable development in UK government: What role for integrated policy appraisal. *Environment and Planning C: Government and Policy*, 27 (2), pp. 340–354.

Scottish Executive (2005). *Choosing Our Future: Scotland's Sustainable Development Strategy*. Edinburgh: Scottish Executive.

Weale, A. (1997). The United Kingdom. In: Jänicke, M. and Weidner, H. eds., *National Environmental Policies*. Berlin: Springer, pp. 89–108.

Weale, A., Pridham, G., Cini, M., Konstadakopulos, D., Porter, M. and Flynn, B. (2000). *Environmental Governance in Europe*. Oxford: Oxford University Press.

Welsh Assembly Government (WAG) (2004). *Starting to Live Differently: The Sustainable Development Scheme of the National Assembly for Wales*. London: HMSO.

Wurzel, R.K.W., Zito, A.R. and Jordan, A.J. (2013). *Environmental Governance in Europe: A Comparative Analysis of New Environmental Policy Instruments*. Cheltenham: Edward Elgar.

Zito, A.R. and Egan, M. (1998). Environmental management standards, corporate strategies and policy networks. *Environmental Politics*, 7 (3), pp. 94–117.

4 Actions for sustainable urban development in cohesion policies

4.1 Sustainable development and SUD in the Italian structural funds programming

4.1.1 National strategy and governance: an overview

Quite in line with the overall low prioritisation of the agenda for sustainable development in domestic policies, the Italian main national programming document (National Strategic Framework of Reference – NSFR) for the period 2007–2013 has neither contained any specific linkage with the EU strategy for sustainable development nor referred to the NSDS (Ministero dello Sviluppo Economico, 2013). Thus, no comprehensive conceptual framework has been designed in order to embody this principle in the planned policy measures, although an ad-hoc paragraph has been included in the document in compliance with Articles 3 and 7 of the General SF Regulation and several disparate orientations towards sustainability can be traced in the document, especially with regard to the environmental domain.[1]

More specifically, a number of environmental threats, such as air and water pollution, forests, hydrogeological risks, CO_2 emissions and waste have been mentioned with regard to sustainability challenges. Accordingly, the NSFR has implicitly committed to implement the EPI principle through the following programming priorities: Priority 3 "Energy and Environment: sustainable and efficient use of natural resources" and Priority 6 "Networks and mobility". The social dimension of sustainability has been dealt with by Priority 4 "Social inclusion, services for quality of life and territorial attractiveness", while Priority 8 "Competitiveness and attractiveness of urban systems" aimed to comply with the EU guidance on the sustainable urban development mainstreaming and was allocated 5.8 billion euro entirely provided by the ERDF. To this end, a number of objectives mainly concerning urban regeneration, energy efficiency, sustainable mobility and health and cultural services have been identified within the framework of this priority, though largely overlapping with those included in the aforementioned Priorities 3, 4 and 6.

As for method, metropolitan cities and municipalities were in general supposed to be the main recipients of financial allocations under this priority, although the mechanism of identification of actual beneficiaries was delegated to National and Regional Managing Authorities that would define and implement operational programmes dealing with the said objectives. Regardless of the fact that the document contains many generic references to the past experience of implementation of innovative urban projects, no concrete examples or actions were reported. Moreover, the overlapping nature of policy objectives that could potentially be covered by different programming priorities and the lack of a comprehensive national urban strategy have been mentioned among the main factors that jeopardised, in particular, the implementation of interventions for SUD (Tortorella, 2015: 68–69). In fact, as empirical data on implemented projects shows, most interventions focused on the infrastructural operations, such as municipal parking, swimming pools, bicycle tracks, roads and buildings restructuring (around 80%), while actions for enhancing local entrepreneurship, health services or environmental infrastructures absorbed much lower financing. Likewise, the impact on urban governance has been considered limited too, as cities and municipalities were mainly just the project beneficiaries and were not involved in the programming process, except for Campania and Umbria Regions (ibid: 77).

Compared to this fragmented and somewhat confused framework, a number of innovations were introduced in the 2014–2020 programming period. The principle of policy integration has been mentioned as being among the core cross-cutting priorities of the main national programming document – the Partnership Agreement (PA). Accordingly, numerous references to the principle of sustainable development have been introduced in the document, although many of them lacked concrete operationalisation in terms of policy measures. In fact, the need to conceptualise the principle of policy integration as a tool for achieving sustainable development goals more clearly has been highlighted by and included in the PA ex ante evaluation. The main task of the latter was to spotlight possible incoherence or solve potential gaps existing in the draft programming document, which should be in its final version. Hence, the evaluation recommended improving provisions and measures enabling the implementation of the policy integration principle with specific regard to environment. It suggested adopting specific arrangements for enhancing policy coordination between interventions co-financed by different funds and improving complementarity of action at the national, regional and local levels.

The following four arrangements had to be accomplished to this end (PA, p. 145–147):

i. Developing a national strategic and operational guidance on the integrated approach;
ii. Implementing new EU instruments effectively for community-led local development, in particular with regard to EU Urban Agenda;
iii. Promoting inter-institution coordination or even unification of organisational units dealing with ERDF and European Social Fund (ESF) at regional level;
iv. Establishing specific policy and governance instruments in order to guarantee better integration and coordination between the centre and periphery, in

particular with regards to the management of regional and national operational programmes.

In response to this requirement, a specific section describing policy synergies and integration was included in each thematic section of the PA (DPS, 2014), but most provisions for policy integration introduced by the document have remained rather generic and hypothetical. For example, the necessity of guaranteeing the linkage between Thematic Objective (TO) 1 "Research and Development" and TO3 "Competitiveness of SMEs"; as well as between TO6 "Environmental protection", TO7 "Sustainable transport" and TO8 "Sustainable employment and mobility" has been recognised across the document. However, few concrete examples of transposing these desirable connections in the definition of policy interventions can be found in the final version of PA.[2] In some cases, the coordination gap has only been recovered through output indicators that attempted to measure a combined impact of actions from two or more policy sectors, without specifying their complementarity at the outset.

In general, references to the EPI principle appear more straightforward compared to the NSRF 2007–2013, but its operationalisation mainly relies on the already consolidated procedural instruments of environmental impact evaluation, such as Strategic Environmental Assessment and Environmental Impact Assessment. Moreover, the existing technical and expert structures of the respective Managing Authorities (MA), which normally deal with environmental protection, as well as the network of national and regional environmental agencies have been mentioned among the main pillars of the strategy's governance.

A section dedicated specifically to an integrated territorial approach has been included in the PA (DPS, 2014), delineating two main pathways: the national Urban Agenda and the National Strategy for the so-called inner (peripheral) areas. Both strategies committed to the Europe 2020 priorities, covering competiveness, environmental sustainability and social inclusion goals. The possibility of adopting specific local governance tools (CLLD and ITI) for the implementation of these strategies has also been introduced, leaving the decision about the feasibility of adopting these instruments to programme MA. As far as the agenda for SUD is concerned, a detailed and rather comprehensive analysis of challenges faced by Italian urban areas in terms of economic development, services, immigration, environment, etc. have been reported in the SWOT analysis dealing specifically with the territorial dimension.

The following three "development drivers" have been identified to guide the Italian Urban Agenda at national level, embracing the environmental, social and economic dimensions:

i. Redesign and modernisation of urban public services, including, in particular, sustainable mobility, energy efficiency, and information and communication technologies (TO2 and 4);
ii. Practices and projects for social inclusion of the most disadvantaged social groups and neighbourhoods, including, in particular, services for children

and elderly people, social housing and assistance to disadvantaged families (TO9);

iii. Strengthening the cities' capacity to support local segments of global production chains, including advanced and innovative services for enterprises (TO3).

The total amount of resources to be invested in interventions related to Urban Agenda amounted to EUR 1.412.276.095 or 6.52 % of the total ERDF funding assigned to Italy, thus being slightly above the 5% of mandatory ERDF spending for this priority. Additionally, a small amount of ESF – EUR 237.612.544 or 2.14%) has also been targeted to this priority.

However, a rather centralised approach has been adopted for the implementation of this Agenda. In fact, a National Operational Programme (Programma Operativo Nazionale) – NOP METRO, approved by the EU Commission on 14 July 2015, was designed with the strategic objective to strengthen the institutional and programming role of cities, as they play a central role in the definition of local investment strategies and in the management of local public services. The financing allocated for this programme (€892.933 million) has absorbed a substantial quota of budget reserved for Urban Agenda, to which a 34% national co-financing should be added.

The NOP's strategy has mainly focused on the first two drivers, while TO3 was supposed to be dealt with by Regional Operational Programmes (ROPs) that could identify a fourth "regional" driver, selecting in particular actions for TO5 "Climate and environmental risks" and TO6 "Environmental protection". Accordingly, as Table 4.1 shows, a bulk of SF spending for the Italian Urban Agenda had to be invested on TOs 2, 4 and 9, that focused respectively on sustainable mobility and energy efficiency in public buildings and lightening within the environmental pillar; and measures against poverty and social exclusion within the social one.

Two target categories of urban areas were identified at national level to implement the strategy. One group was composed by ten metropolitan cities defined by Law 56/2014 (the Delrio Law) – Rome, Bari, Bologna, Genova, Firenze, Milano, Napoli, Torino, Reggio Calabria and Venice, while the other group of cities that

Table 4.1 Priorities and financial allocations of NOP METRO 2014–2020

TO	*Title*	*Funding (million €)*	*%*	*EU Fund*
2	Digital agenda	151.982	17	ERDF
4	Sustainable urban services and urban mobility	318.288	35.6	ERDF
9	Services for social inclusion	217.193	24.3	ESF
9	Infrastructure for social Inclusion	169.219	19	ERDF
11	Technical assistance	35.249	4.1	ERDF
	Total	**891.931**	**100**	

Source: Author's elaboration on the NOP METRO

could benefit from the Programme was selected by the Special Status Regions[3] and included Cagliari, Catania, Messina and Palermo. The PA suggested that regional operational programmes should develop their strategies for sustainable urban development for all remaining regional and provincial capital cities, and design, where appropriate, complementary measures also for metropolitan cities covered by the NOP METRO.

Such a programme setting closely followed the path of domestic territorial governance reforms introduced by Law 56/2014 that promoted specific constitutional and administrative provisions concerning the creation of metropolitan cities and strengthening the role of cities and their unions in planning and development policies (Parlamento Italiano, 2014). Therefore, the governance framework designed by the NOP has established that municipal authorities of metropolitan cities covered by the programme would act as intermediate programming bodies – Urban Authorities (UA), within which City Mayors were supposed to play a particularly relevant role. In accordance with Article 7 (4) of the ERDF Regulation 1301/2013, UA were assigned the responsibility for selecting projects in respect of the principle of joint project management and shared strategic planning by the UA and the MA of the programme in the form of the National Agency for Territorial Cohesion.

The PA has also welcomed the establishment of partnerships and inter-municipal projects, emphasising in sections 3 and 4 that the EU provisions aiming to strengthen the role of cities in the current programming period were perfectly coherent with the direction of domestic policy reforms and could indeed contribute to achieve the following important results:

- Strengthening the part of city governments as they play a crucial role in local investment strategies; enhancing the inter-institutional dialogue and interactions in delivery of collective services;
- Territorial refinement of project instruments in order to achieve shared results;
- Better focused implementation of innovative actions established by the SF Regulations 2014–2020;
- Better coordination between ordinary policies and additional investments;
- Encouraging the consolidation of metropolitan cities and administrative reforms at local level;
- Ensuring citizens' and stakeholders' participation in the definition and implementation of investments.

It was decided that ROPs would define additional measures of SUD strategies, namely, the target territories within each region and the respective UA, or would at least identify the criteria for the selection of UA at regional level. Participatory practices and co-projecting methods were strongly recommended in order to guarantee the definition of the most appropriate operational measures for SUD. At the same time, complementarity and coordination were suggested to be crucial for designing interventions at both national and regional levels.

In sum, the main Italian programming document for the period 2014–2020 has incorporated a number of significant policy and governance innovations aimed at pursuing sustainable development objectives, particularly with regard to the urban dimension. The general policy priorities were clearly aligned with the Europe 2020 framework for smart, sustainable and inclusive growth. The financing was distributed among these three pillars in a rather balanced manner, with around 1/3 assigned to each.

As regards the SUD, concerns have been expressed for the fact that although the overall thematic focus of measures for sustainable urban development has been better defined compared to the 2007–2013 programming, a strong path-dependence of the programming can be observed. In fact, some scholars (Tortorella, 2015) suggest that the design of the new programming priorities appear to be little more than "window-dressing" and no substantial changes in terms of concrete interventions will follow. In fact, several policy measures included by the new PA fall in the same areas where interventions were already implemented during the past decade, including e-government, e-learning, sustainability in public services, urban mobility and energy efficiency. Besides, the outputs of many of the implemented projects were far from being a success. The bulk of financial resources was allocated to the southern regions of the country.

As far as governance instruments for sustainable urban development are concerned, the PA has established very general provisions, stating that policy integration at the local level will be guaranteed through the Community-Led Local Development (CLLD) and Integrated Territorial Investments (ITIs) instrument, which will enhance, where appropriate, the territorial dimension of development policies.

The task of horizontal coordination between different EU funds, as well as the definition of common criteria for the selection of CLLD were delegated to Regions, which were supposed to establish ad-hoc committees, bringing together the managing authorities of all EU funds concerned. No specific guidance on how the ITI instrument could be operationalised was provided, and regardless of the very relevant past experience of integrated territorial development projects in Italy (Magnatti *et al.*, 2009), which has frequently been mentioned in the document, no concrete linkages or specific provisions have been formulated to foster this potential in the new programming approach.

Instead, in continuity with the 2007–2013 programming period, regional MA were invited to create a dedicated axis for sustainable urban development in their ROPs. As Figure 4.1 shows, 11 regions have designed a specific axis dedicated to SUD, compared to 9 in the previous programming period, although the comprehensive amount of resources to be invested in SUD measures is expected to decreased by 3.5 billion during the current programming period of 2014–2020, compared to 5.8 invested in 2007–2013 (IFEL, 2015).

In sum, a number of tensions can be identified in the Italian agenda for SUD. First, the recommendation to invest a bulk of interventions on the two thematic drivers (modernisation of urban services and social inclusion), which, among others, contained a number of measures that have already been financed during the past programming period, appears to be somewhat in contradiction with the commitment to ensure a better territorial fine-tuning and complementarity of

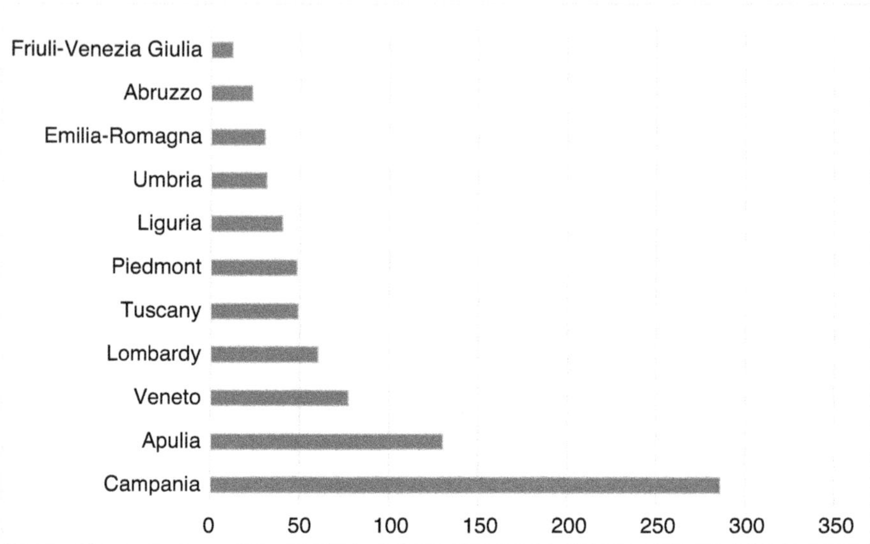

Figure 4.1 Financial allocations for SUD in ROP in the 2007–2013 programming period (EU and national co-financing, in million €)

Source: Author's elaboration on the data reported by IFEL (2015)

interventions announced by the same strategy. In fact, there has been apprehension regarding the risk of mismatch between the programming guidance at the national level and the practical implementation dynamics at the project level, which may arise again (Tortorella, 2015). Second, the territorial focus of the strategy on the metropolitan cities has been widely contested, as the majority of Italian cities are small and medium-size. Third, the quota of resources managed at the regional level in both more and less developed regions has been reduced by about 5% compared to the 2007–2013 programming. In these conditions, the margins of manoeuvre for regional authorities to develop more comprehensive territorially led SUD were significantly narrowed down, in terms of both the scope and size of their strategies for SUD. Lastly, the operational consistency of such a centralised approach has been contested too (Tortorella, 2015), taking into account the fact that the overall amount of 893 million euro was far from enough to effectively tackle development challenges of 14 cities, in eight of which basic transport and environmental infrastructures are lacking. Remarkably, the environmental dimension of sustainability was supposed to be addressed mainly by regional operational programmes as an additional priority, in the conditions of reduced financial resources.

Despite the fact that PA has put a lot of emphasis on such principles as partnership, cooperation and co-production, the governance architecture of the strategy has been strongly centralised, with the National Agency for Cohesion acting in the form of Managing Authority of the NOP and playing the chief role in the overall decision-making concerning the SF programming. Urban authorities identified by the NOP have been assigned mainly operational managerial functions disregarding the EU guidance, requiring an enhanced programming capacity at the city level.

Finally, while providing a detailed overview of statistical data on major development indicators, which is essential for justifying SF interventions, the PA appears to be poorly equipped for demonstrating the complementarity of the proposed measures with the ordinary domestic policies and programmes, as well as for showing the progress, where appropriate, compared to the past programming period. Although the importance of the integrated approach for sustainable urban development has been recalled throughout the document, no specific measures or guidance has been provided to enhance policy coordination in this field, except for the division of thematic objectives between the national and regional operational programmes.

Furthermore, although the PA 2014–2020 has explicitly recognised the relevance of eco-innovation and the greening of economy for increasing the competiveness and sustainable resource management, only a few fragmented policy measures have been envisaged in order to enable the integration of environmental goals into economic measures. In fact, the commitment to the principle of policy integration announced in the introductory part of the document appears to have been watered down, especially with regard to the specific objective of sustainable urban development. Importantly, a national strategy for sustainable urban development is still missing, although a special Interministerial Committee for Urban Policies (Comitato Interministeriale per le Politiche Urbane – CIPU) was established in 2012 under the presidency of the Council of Ministers with the specific task of coordinating urban policies implemented by relevant central administrations and enable dialogue between central and sub-state authorities in the context of economic growth, social inclusion and territorial cohesion.

In sum, two main trends can be traced in the scenario of usage of EU SF at the national level. It clearly comprises the ideational element, as several new policy ideas have been introduced in the Italian programming documents over the two periods in order to adjust them to the EU political priorities. At the same time, elements of strategic usage have been in place too, since there is plenty of evidence to show how the SF resources have been pragmatically employed to increase financial resources, for example, for infrastructural investments in southern regions, or political potential of metropolitan cities as a consequence of the domestic territorial governance reforms.

Against this background, very different patterns of usage have emerged at regional level

4.1.2 The case of Emilia-Romagna

The Emilia-Romagna Region has traditionally been among the best performing regions in the management of EU SF in Italy in terms of both the regularity of programming and spending, and thematic coherence with EU priorities (Fargion *et al.*, 2006).

As far as the more general perspective on sustainable development is concerned, the 2007–2013 regional programming documents (Regione Emilia-Romagna, 2007) have already contained numerous specific references to the EU priorities for sustainable development, as announced by the Gothenburg declaration (2001) and the subsequent Environmental Action Programme of 2002. Accordingly, the ROP has highlighted the need to accomplish an integrated approach to policy-making by integrating the environmental objectives into economic and social policies at the earliest possible stage. Therefore, the document commits to build its approach taking into account the seven main challenges of the revised EU strategy for SD (2005):

i. Climate change and clean energy – achieving the emission reduction targets;
ii. Sustainable transport – pollution reduction and road security;
iii. Sustainable consumption and production – implementing a regional plan for environmental technologies and ecological compatibility of products and processes;
iv. Conservation and management of natural resources – preventing the loss of biodiversity by 2010 and better management of natural resources (air, water, forests, etc.)
v. Public health, with particular attention to children;
vi. Social inclusion and migration;
vii. Global poverty and sustainable development.

In order to meet the above-mentioned challenges at the regional level, the ROP has formulated a number of specific provisions announcing coordination efforts with other regional policy instruments, such as Regional Environmental Action Plans and the Regional Energy Plan as well. Although the only priority devoted to energy and environmental qualifications (Axis 3) has specifically addressed the environment dimension of sustainability, the principle of strategic horizontal policy integration has been introduced among the main guiding principles of the programme and its meaning can be summarised as follows. The ROP aims to boost regional economy in the perspective of competitiveness and sustainability, aiming at the same time at enhancing cultural and natural potential of the region, especially in urban areas, by promoting not only infrastructural investments but also new sustainable models of resource management. Within this framework, an integrated approach is considered to be crucial for the achievement of the objective of sustainable territorial development, by bringing together such components as research and innovation, environmental protection, economic competiveness and cultural heritage. As a consequence, the various EU funds (ERDF, ESF, EAFRD and EMFF) should be managed in an integrated manner, helping develop synergies between different sectoral measures.

The establishment of the regional Environmental Authority in 2006 was particularly relevant in this sense, as it was assigned the task to check the compatibility of the planned interventions with the EU environmental legislation as well as to contribute to the integration of environmental concerns in all regional operational programmes co-financed by SF. The involvement of this Authority was ensured not only during the formulation phase, but also throughout its implementation as it has been included in the Programme's Steering Committee where all other relevant social and economic stakeholders were represented. The overall strategic objective of the ROP has been to better integrate the Region into the system of pan-European relations, increase investments (in particular foreign investments), develop ICT and sustainable mobility networks.

The 2014–2020 regional programming has developed in continuity with this approach, while further strengthening the focus on sustainability. While generally committing to the principle of sustainable development and the Europe 2020 Strategy objectives, it stated its priority for enhancing the regional Smart Specialisation Strategy (S3) underpinned by the principle of policy integration. Therefore, the overall objective of the new programming documents has been to enhance the innovation capacity and industrial transformation in the Region – defined as "regional innovation ecosystem" – by tackling at the same time the problems of environmental sustainability of products and productive processes, social inclusion and well-being, information and communication society. Accordingly, the axis for Research and Innovation (TO1), Competitiveness and attractiveness of the productive sector (TO3) and Low-carbon economy and production (TO4) have absorbed the greatest part of regional resources, as shown in Table 4.2.

The total amount of resources of the ROP is €481.895.272, of which 240.947.636 are covered by the ERDF co-financing. While minor investments have been allocated to the Axis 2 dedicated to ICT and digital agenda (6.2%), Axis 5 – artistic, cultural and environmental heritage (7.8%) and Axis 6 – attractive and participatory towns (6.2%) – 30.013.716 euros, of which 14.456.585 euros ERDF.

Table 4.2 Emilia-Romagna Regional Operational Programme 2014–2020 (ERDF + national co-financing)

TO	*Priority Axis*	*Funds (50% ERDF)*	*Share in total %*
1	Research and innovation	€ 140.568.58	29.2
2	ICT development and digital agenda implementation	€ 30.094.76	6.2
3	Production system competitiveness and attractiveness	€ 120.473.82	25.0
4	Promotion of the low-carbon economy in regions and in the production system	€ 104.379.05	21.7
5	Enhancement of artistic, cultural and environmental resources	€ 37.589.53	7.8
6	Attractive, participative towns	€ 30.013.72	6.2
7	Technical assistance	€ 18.775.81	3.9
	Total	**€ 481.895.272**	**100**

Source: Author's elaboration on the data reported by the ERDF Regional Operational Programme (2014–2020)

In this way, only one Priority Axis, "supporting the shift towards a low-carbon economy in all sectors" has directly addressed the dimension of environmental sustainability, attempting to build a number of cross-cutting references integrating the energy-environment-climate package with economic activities in the following areas of intervention:

- Encourage businesses to lower their energy consumption and to produce energy from renewable resources to support self-consumption, including by setting up ecologically equipped production areas;
- Promote lower energy consumption in buildings and public facilities, as well as the introduction of renewable energy production systems;
- Promote sustainable mobility in urban areas.

The ambition of the announced objectives has been aligned to the EU targets, including a reduction of energy consumption of production processes for industrial businesses and public buildings by 20%, increasing businesses' energy production from renewable resources by 20% and self-consumption by 25%. Importantly, these targets have not been established ad hoc for the SF programming but they were fixed by Regional Law 14/2014 for enhancing investments – Industry 4.0, and financially supported through the establishment of the multipurpose regional energy fund.

As for energy efficiency, a strong linkage with the voluntary action by local public administrations within the EU Covenant of Mayors has been highlighted, as around 300 out of 348 municipalities have joined the programme. Besides prioritising support for energy efficiency interventions in the municipalities that have already developed their SEAPs, they established a range of measures for sustainable urban mobility, as envisaged by the Regional Integrated Plan for Air Quality 2020 (Regione Emilia- Romagna, 2014a).

As far as the territorial dimension is concerned, a specific Axis, (6), has been designed in order to address territorial and urban development problems. More specifically, this Axis aims to implement integrated actions within the framework of the EU urban agenda with the objective of strengthening identity of urban areas, triggering participatory processes involving citizens and enterprises in strategic planning at the city level, and creating new opportunities for jobs and inclusion. Moreover, additional actions for SUD have been planned under thematic Axis 2 "ICT and Digital Agenda" and Axis 5 "Valorisation of cultural, artistic and environmental resources".

Nine urban areas around the cities of Bologna, Piacenza, Parma, Reggio Emilia, Modena, Ferrara, Forlì, Rimini and Cesena were selected for implementing urban regeneration projects, focusing on specific potential and assets of each of these areas. A great variety of areas of intervention has been identified at the local level depending on their specificities. Ferrara has chosen sustainable mobility and tourism, Modena – entertainment and artistic productions, Reggio Emilia – social innovation and welfare, and Rimini – innovative services to enjoy the city's cultural heritage. As far as the city of Bologna is concerned, actions for co-design of new collaborative and digital services for the urban community have been envisaged under this axis, in complementarity to those designed by the NOP METRO for which the city was eligible too.

The aforementioned towns were selected based on a double-fold criteria: the concentration of functional assets (demographic characteristics, research and education potential, mobility, environment and competiveness) and the availability of local public services, enabling them to perform as attractiveness poles for surrounding areas.

In sum, although the Emilia-Romagna Region has not elaborated an autonomous comprehensive document on sustainable development, a number of complementary regional plans has been developed in the first decade of the 2000s, laying down a solid ground for sustainability action and practices in various areas covered by the ROP ERDFs. These include the Strategic Document of Emilia-Romagna (Regione Emilia-Romagna, 2014c), the Regional Innovation Strategy for Smart Specialisation (Regione Emilia-Romagna, 2015b), the Regional Plan for Research Infrastructures (Regione Emilia-Romagna, 2014d), the Regional Digital Agenda (Regione Emilia-Romagna, 2011), the Regional Plan for investments, the Energy Plan, etc. These documents shape a comprehensive framework of regional action for sustainable economic growth based on research and innovation, and covering environmental and, to a lesser extent, social issues.

Remarkably, Emilia-Romagna is one of the few Italian regions that have started working on climate change mitigation and adaptation strategy. In 2015, the Regional Government approved a first pivotal document for developing this strategy (DDG 2200/20159), aiming to bring into a unique framework the various regional instruments enabling the achievement of sustainable development objectives. The following actions have been considered crucial in this sense:

- Developing regional plans and programmes for climate mitigation and adaptation;
- Defining monitoring indicators, which are already partly included in SEA and EIA procedure, in particular for SF programming;
- Creating additional measures for climate mitigation and adaptation in sectoral plans
- Extending the application of the EMAS regulation to entire industrial areas;
- Introducing participatory practices in order to enable the integration of adaptation and mitigation objectives into sectoral policies;
- Encouraging financial and economic instruments enhancing mitigation and adaptation, including EU programmes (e.g. LIFE);
- Guaranteeing coordination with local initiatives, in particular Sustainable Energy Plans (SEAPs) developed with the EU Covenant of Mayors.

Therefore, imperatives of sustainable development have been embedded in the Emilia-Romagna development policies since the end of the 1990s and a number of policy instruments have consolidated over the last decade developing in synergy with the EU discourse and policies on sustainability, in particular in the field of SF programming. In fact, a progressive widening of the scope of SD objectives has been traced in both regional sectoral polices and the EU SF programming in the Region, which increasingly embraced the dimensions of smart and sustainable growth, low-carbon economy and social inclusion.

The Region has used the EU strategically, with a clear long-term vision of how EU policy priorities can be integrated into regional planning documents and policies, and in what way they may help boost regional and local potential. Being conscious about regulatory and financial opportunities offered by the EU, the SF programming has also been used to legitimise previous political choices rather than getting familiarised with new policy ideas or practices. In fact, references to the Europe 2020 strategy are strongly embedded in the system of regional goals and priorities, and the Region has also managed to somewhat bypass the burden established by the PA in terms of prioritisation of thematic objectives.

The same is the case with the EU effort to strengthen the territorial dimension of development policies, which has been warmly appreciated and readily implemented by the Region, in particular in urban areas.

In fact, a representative of the Regional Managing Authority of the ERDF has stressed that the EU structural funds provide a very important strategic opportunity for regional development and, in particular, for sustainable urban development (Interview 1): "It is thanks to the EU guidance and instruments that we have developed a structured strategy for sustainable urban development. Although the financial resources were clearly limited but they still offer additional opportunities for these policies".

The environmental dimension of sustainability has progressively expanded from the objective of environmental protection to sustainable energy, clean and green business, and low-carbon economy.

As far as the governance dimension is concerned, a number of interdepartmental committees have been established in order to guarantee better coordination of ROP's measures with ordinary regional policies. Instead, the governance innovations introduced by Priority Axis 6 dedicated to SUD have clearly paved the way to the development of additional coordination instruments with the local level. Although measures for integrated urban development were not new to this context, the governance opportunities of the 2014–2020 programming have been effectively deployed to strengthen the role of towns in economic, environmental and social policies. In fact, the governance architecture established by Emilia-Romagna to implement its strategy for sustainable urban development has relied on a network of 10 the so-called Open LABs that were established in each of the ten selected towns, where the respective municipal administrations were assigned the function of Urban Authorities with the responsibility of defining operations to implement, in collaboration with local communities and stakeholders.

In this way, Open LABs have brought together private companies, local community, universities and research centres, public administrations and all other actors concerned, which could contribute to the definition and implementation of urban regeneration projects in the respective towns. These bodies were invited to settle their activities in the historical buildings subject to requalification, where the activities of LABs themselves would take place, and which would encourage social innovation initiatives boosting local potential and enhancing local identities. The LABs were entitled to receive the SF funding only during the launching phase and were expected to become self-financing within the next three years. A coordination board was established at the regional level in order to guarantee the overall coordination of actions for sustainable urban development financed from various thematic axes of the ROP.

Such governance settings have been considered an important opportunity for the Region allowing to fill in functional gaps that emerged in the structure of sub-regional governance as a consequence of territorial reforms and, in particular, after the so-called Delrio Law 56/2014, that has substantially redesigned the competences and functions of the intermediate provincial authorities playing an important role also in the management of EU structural funds.

Although Emilia-Romagna has not adopted CLLD or ITI tools, as it was suggested that this "would create unnecessary complexity and overlapping functions" (Interview 1), the Region has strongly relied on existing forms of participatory and negotiated programming at sub-regional level, which have consolidated in the regional programming during the past decades. Regardless of the fact that officially, Urban Authorities were supposed to only select interventions to be implemented, in reality they have actually been involved even in the definition of actions, closely collaborating with the MA in order to shape the programming priorities at the local level (Interview 1).

Moreover, a regional Consortium for innovation and technology transfer (ASTER) of Emilia-Romagna was established during the programming period 2007–2013, composed of the Emilia-Romagna regional government, the six universities and the national research centres located in the region (the National Research Council: CNR, the Italian National Agency for New Technologies, Energy and Sustainable Economic Development: ENEA, the National Institute for Nuclear Physics: INFN), the Regional Union of Chambers of Commerce, working in collaboration with regional business associations and innovation centres. The Consortium aims to build the Regional Innovation System (RIS) by launching shared actions and integrated projects for innovation and development of the territory and its business, enhancing research and innovation, qualified employment and well-being of its residents. It is strongly committed to making the Region innovative, competitive, inclusive and sustainable, creative and open to the world. ASTER works in collaboration with enterprises, universities, research centres and institutions for the development of the "innovation ecosystem" of the territory.

Overall, the Emilia-Romagna administration has appreciated the novelties introduced by EU urban agenda and the SF guidance for sustainable urban development, which is deemed to have created favourable conditions for valorisation of urban areas that would otherwise be problematic. Surprisingly, the operational obstacles, thematic limitations and delays at the national level have been considered the main problematic aspects of the strategy. The expectations of the Region about the ambition of EU resources and targets for sustainable urban development has been partly disappointed: "We expected more copious financing to be mandatory assigned to the objective of sustainable development, honestly, 5% is too little [. .]. Furthermore, the timing of EU guidance and details on territorial instruments did not fit programming needs" (Interview 1).

In sum, consistent with the past, Emilia-Romagna has assumed a pro-active approach in the SF programming, trying to anticipate policy changes at European level and searching for appropriate institutional and policy solutions that would enhance investment opportunities and strategic development of the sectors of regional economy, in compliance with EU programming regulations. Most thematic objectives promoted by the EU 2014–2020 structural programming were already comprised by the regional policy agenda, while the governance innovations introduced were strongly embedded in the regional tradition of integrated programming. Therefore, EU SF have strategically been deployed for enhancing specific regionally relevant policy measures, but they have also been used to legitimise several pre-existing policy and governance choices in economic development policies and planning.

4.1.3 The case of Veneto

Despite several similarities between the Veneto and Emilia-Romagna regional contexts in terms of the level of economic development, employment and the characteristics of productive system, their choices and strategies with regard to the EU agenda for sustainable development have noticeably diverged.

In fact, unlike Emilia-Romagna, Veneto, in general, has been rather reluctant to introduce policy and governance innovations promoted by the EU, mainly due to the political position of the Lega Nord, which is in majority in the regional government for over a decade by now. Over the last years, the Lega Nord has shifted from its previous political identity as a voice for Italy's north (Di Sotto, 2009) to placing hostility towards the policies and institutions of the European Union at the heart of its rhetoric (Brunazzo and Gilbert, 2017). Moreover, the regional policy style has traditionally been characterised by low propensity to adopt inclusive modes of decision-making, preferring short-term distributive policies (Messina, 2016). These features were quite in contrast with the programming approach of EU structural funds that have, for decades, been an unique tool for developing a long-term perspective for regional development policies, as well as for embracing sustainable development agenda therein (Pizzimenti, 2009). Though lack of policy integration and coordination were mentioned as foremost among the main critical aspects of traditional regional development policies in Veneto (Messina, 2016), a number of policy innovations have nonetheless been introduced in the regional policy structures, being largely supported by the regional public administration.

Against this backdrop, the ROP ERDF for the 2007–2013 programming period has diffusely referred to the concept of sustainable development, in particular in the EU context, and delineated a detailed scheme for ensuring the integration of environmental priorities into development policies, including, in particular, eco-innovation, waste management, renewable energy and the reduction of various sources of pollution. Moreover, EPI has been mentioned among the main cross-cutting principles of the ROP. Beyond more general references to the global and

European strategies for sustainable development, two specific thematic axes on energy (Axis 2) and environment and territorial valorisation (Axis 3) were introduced. However, the operationalisation and the monitoring system established by the ROP were poorly connected to the policy integration provisions listed by the Strategic Environmental Assessment (SEA) and it did not allow for the measurement of their actual progress in terms of reduction of negative impacts or increasing benefits of environmentally relevant policies. Not only were the indicators suggested for the various measures poorly focused on policy outputs related to implemented actions, but they also failed to foresee any kind of intermediate evaluation. The policy framework concerning interventions in urban areas was extremely vague too, without specifying either concrete policy measures or their relevance in the perspective of sustainable development, except for urban mobility and sustainable tourism. The green public procurement procedures applied to calls for proposals and tenders managed by the regional administration were considered the main operational tool for implementing the EPI principle. In sum, a number of ideational elements could be traced in the pattern of usage of the EU structural funds, although many of these transformations appeared to be rather symbolic in nature.

A qualitatively new phase opened shortly after the end of the 2007–2013 programming period. Significantly, the first comprehensive regional economic programming document for the period 2016–2018 was delivered (Regione Veneto, 2011b). While announcing the objective of guaranteeing a cross-sectoral coordination of actions and implementing an integrated approach to development policies as required by the Europe 2020 strategy, this document maintains sectoral divisions and a specific focus on financial aspects rather than on strategic planning. Remarkably, the document does not mention the principle of policy integration, though there are several references to the concept of sustainable development, in particular with regard to its environmental dimension. The latter has also been dealt with by many other regional plans, such as the regional law on the territorial government (Regione Veneto, 2004), the Water Protection Plan (Regione Veneto, 2009), the Regional action plan for mitigation of hydrological risk (Regione Veneto, 2011) and the Energy Plan (DGR 1820/2013).

The regional 2014–2020 programming of EU SF has built on the aforementioned documents that were explicitly referred to, in particular by ROP ERDF, indicating how strategic the EU financial support will be for the consolidation of the ongoing policy in various sectors, in order to bring the region close to the objective of smart, sustainable and inclusive growth.

For example, as far as competiveness is concerned, Regional Laws on Productive (L.R. 13/2014) and Commercial (L.R. 50/2012) Districts have been mentioned, highlighting the fact that the Veneto region provides a very favourable context and significant potential for boosting innovation and growth. In fact, Veneto is on the fourth place at the national level in the rate of innovation investments among private companies: it holds 36.4% compared to the national average of 31.5%. Surprisingly, the ROP does not contain references to the concept of sustainable economy, green economy or circular economy, although, like Emilia-Romagna, the region has elaborated its Smart Specialisation Strategy (RIS3) as a precondition for approval of its ROP by the EU Commission (Regione Veneto, 2015).

The environmental and social dimensions of sustainability have received a stronger emphasis in the document, compared to the economic pillar. With regard to the former, the ROP has specifically focused on environmental protection and risks, as well as on the energy efficiency objective in a wider perspective of climate change mitigation. Accordingly, two thematic axes have been designed in the programme: Axis 4 “Sustainable Energy and Environmental Quality” and Axis 5 “Seismic and Hydraulic Risks”, announcing linkages between the ROP strategy and measures established by some of the aforementioned regional plans.

Instead, thematic Axis 6 on Sustainable Urban Development has adopted a more comprehensive perspective embracing the environmental, social and economic dimensions. It has paid particular attention to the objective of social inclusion and citizens’ well-being, especially in terms of accessibility and quality of public services. The following three pillars of action have been identified – sustainable mobility (TO4), social inclusion (TO9) and digital agenda (TO2), taking into consideration the territorial needs on the one hand, and the national level guidance on the other. The total amount of financing for Axis 6, as Table 4.3 shows was EUR 77 million (12.8% of the total ROP ERDF).

The total budget of the programme is EUR 600.310.716, and it has been distributed among the aforementioned Priority Axes as below.

Hence, besides measures for economic recovery, stronger linkage between research and productive systems, broadband and digitalisation of public administrations, energy efficiency and environmental risk prevention, the ROP committed to improving the quality of life and sustainability in urban areas, paying particular attention to disadvantaged and marginal groups of population. The following vectors have been considered relevant for improving the quality of urban environment:

Table 4.3 Veneto ERDF Regional Operational Programme 2014–2020 (ERDF + national co-financing)

TO	*Priority Axis*	*Funds (50% ERDF)*	*Share in total %*
1	Research, development and innovation	€ 114.000.000	19.0
2	Digital agenda	€ 77.000.000	12.8
3	Production system Competitiveness	€ 170.739.776	28.4
4	Energy sustainability and environmental quality	€ 92.558.512	15.4
5	Seismic and hydro risks	€ 45.000.000	7.5
6	Sustainable urban development	€ 77.000.000	12.8
	Technical Assistance	€ 24.012.428	4.0
	Total	**€ 600.310.716**	**100**

Source: Author’s elaboration on the data reported by the ERDF Regional Operational Programme (2014–2020)

local public services – in particular, the local public transport – social housing, contributing to social and energy sustainability and integrated management of local public services.

The aforementioned actions targeted five provincial capital cities – Venice, Vicenza, Padua, Treviso and Verona – with their respective neighbourhoods, based on the OECD criteria for the identification of functional urban areas. Furthermore, a group of smaller municipalities (Mirano, Montebelluna, Castelfranco, Camposampiero, Cittadella, Monselice, Este, Isola della Scala, Legnano, Schio, Thiene e Bassano del Grappa) has been identified as a group of towns identifiable as "urban centres" eligible under the National strategy for inner areas that lack access to a package of basic local public services. In both cases, the final selection of beneficiary areas, as well as the definition of their Urban Authorities was to be carried out through a call for proposals: while in the former case a maximum of five cities could be selected, in the latter case only one. Obviously, a two-step process has reduced the time for programme implementation.

Evidently, the performance of the Veneto Region with regard to the sustainable development mainstreaming approach in the SF programming appear to differ from the Emilia-Romagna's case in a number of ways. While the latter has maintained the continuity of its political priorities that reflected the specificities of its context and legitimised a number of previous choices in the perspective of economic, environmental and social dimensions of sustainability, each of which has been clearly articulated by the ROP, the Veneto Region has shown less consolidated position, showing a mix of strategic and ideational usages. A number of new policy ideas have been included in the ROP following the EU and the national level guidance, but only a few of them have strategically been embedded into policy actions at the local level. The creation of programming and governance architecture for SUD has been somewhat cumbersome and its direction was unsure until a very late moment of definition of the programme (Regione Veneto, 2013).

As a chief officer of the Veneto MA has highlighted, EU regulations and political guidance on sustainable urban development have been considered fundamental for developing new policy ideas and measures at regional level, which would not have otherwise been introduced. He has stressed that "whereas in the programming period 2007–2013 there was a soft 'labelling' of actions for sustainable urban development across the operational programme, the new ERDF regulation provided a fundamental framework for establishing a coherent and comprehensive strategy" (Interview 2). Being fully aware about the practical difficulties of building and implementing a comprehensive agenda for sustainable urban development, the current regional administration sees the EU SF as an opportunity, not only in terms of additional financial resources, but also as a vehicle for dissemination of new policy perspectives. In fact, a number of internal organisational inconsistences and the lack of consensus, which originally jeopardised the formulation of the regional strategy especially with regard to the axis for SUD, have been largely overcome in the last years. A series of significant administrative changes followed, including the resignation of the head of the programming office, shortly before the ROP was submitted for approval to the European Commission. Between 2014 and 2015, ad hoc staff has been assigned the specific responsibility of catering to territorial strategies at the Department for Unitary Programming.

The obvious differences between the EU integrated and bottom-up approach and the Veneto traditionally top-down and sectoral strategy has made the process of policy change difficult and cumbersome, but the last developments have clearly showed that transformations can be channeled by agency despite of structural obstacles.

In this regard, the boundaries traced by the PA in terms of both thematic areas of intervention and territorial priorities have been seen even more critically than EU shortcomings, including the late publication of specific guidance on sustainable urban development, high complexity and costs of administrative procedures and the difficulty of adapting EU policy and governance models to the local conditions in a very short time span.

However, neither CLLD nor ITI tools have been adopted by the Veneto Region, mainly because of the MA's awareness about the lack of administrative and institutional capacity at the local level to run such instruments. Moreover, considering a relatively modest amount of EU funding available for the Region, the organisational costs of these instruments have been considered higher than their potential benefits for managing the funds. A specific axis for SUD within the operational programme has been considered a suitable and appropriate operation tool.

4.2 Sustainable development and SUD in the UK structural funds programming

4.2.1 National strategy and governance: an overview

As Chapter 3 has illustrated, the UK has committed to sustainability agenda since the early 1990s and its strategy for the usage of EU structural funds has firmly been embedded in this mainstream policy approach too. However, the UK National Strategic Reference Framework (NSRF), for the 2007–2013 programming period, has been strongly earmarked by a limited number of the "Lisbon" – related priorities, focusing its main investments on business innovation to support sustainable production and consumption, skills and employment, social and economic cohesion in local economies, including in urban and rural areas. Against the EU requirement to ensure that at least 60% of all expenditure under the Convergence objective and 75% of the expenditure under the Competitiveness and Employment objective support the Lisbon Agenda for jobs and growth, the UK NSRF increased the share of investment to the aforementioned priorities up to 73% in less developed areas and to 83.4% in more developed ones (European Commission, 2007).

The principle of sustainable development has been referred to as a horizontal priority and the NSRF has committed to develop integrated strategies for addressing environmental concerns, also taking into account the principles of gender equality, equal opportunities and non-discrimination and incorporating the needs of local communities. The document puts a strong emphasis on the necessity to ensure that effective partnership arrangements are built into the new programmes, including local authorities and private stakeholders.

In comparison to the overall funding assigned for Italy, the amount of financial resources allocated to the UK was considerably limited. For the 2007–2013 programming, it amounted to €10.6 billion of which €2.9 billion were allocated to the Convergence Objective, €7.0 billion went to the Regional Competitiveness and Employment Objective and €722 million were assigned to the European Territorial Cooperation Objective. Most of these resources (€4.5 billion) targeted research & development measures, aiming to promote innovation, research and knowledge transfer, with an additional €1.8 billion for encouraging entrepreneurship and supporting a thriving small and medium-sized enterprise (SME) sector. Environmental protection was the third important priority, including the objectives of the sustainable management of natural resources and combating the negative effects of climate change, with a budget of nearly €1.6 billion. Around €1.7 billion were invested in building a skilled and adaptable workforce, followed by measures for supporting ICT application and take-up (nearly €400 million) and investments in accessibility, with a focus on small-scale investments mainly in remote areas (€368 million).

A more focused approach has been announced in the main national programming document (Partnership Agreement) of the UK for the current 2014–2020 programing period. It has declared a strong commitment to sustainable development objectives, stating that all ESI Funds in the UK will include integrated strategies for addressing environmental, social and economic concerns, covering the following areas of action:

i. living within environmental limits;
ii. ensuring a strong, healthy and just society;
iii. achieving a sustainable economy;
iv. promoting good governance;
v. using sound science responsibly.

The environmental dimension of sustainability has been particularly emphasised and it was stressed that the delivery of the thematic objectives within each operational programme will include activity that directly supports the sustainable development objectives outlined in the Common Provisions Regulation, comprising environmental protection, resource efficiency, climate change mitigation and adaptation, biodiversity, disaster resilience, risk prevention and management.

However, as in the previous programming period, competitiveness and innovation have remained at the top of the UK investment priorities for EU Structural Funds. Yet, in the PA, the integration between economic and environmental dimensions has further been strengthened, developing in the direction of low-carbon economy.

The total financial allocation is approximately €11.8 billion for the ERDF and the ESF, including €206 million for the Youth Employment Initiative and €866 million for European Territorial Cooperation. An additional €5.18 billion will be devoted to the development of the agricultural sector and rural areas from the European Agricultural Fund for Rural Development (EAFRD), and some €243 million for the European Maritime and Fisheries Fund (EMFF).

As Table 4.4 shows, the PA resources have been almost equally distributed (1/3 each) between the three strategic pillars for smart, sustainable and inclusive growth, directing major resources (in billions of euro) to Thematic Objective (TO)3 (€2.4), TO6 – Environment and Resources Efficiency (€4.1) and TO10 – Better Education and Training (€2.1) and TO8 – Employment and Mobility (€2.0).

Such prioritisation of objectives is coherent with the EU strategy and the SF thematic guidance, but the document highlights that the country has already been directing considerable domestic resources to address Europe 2020 objectives as set out by the National Reform Programmes (HMG, 2014a). Additionally, a number of other domestic policy programmes have been implemented even before

Table 4.4 UK-EU Partnership Agreement 2014–2020: thematic objectives and the respective financial allocations

TO	*Priority Axis*	*Funds*	*Share in total %*
1	Strengthening research, technological development and innovation	€ 1.581.678.70	9.8
2	Enhancing access to, and use and quality of ICT	€ 266.878.70	1.6
3	Enhancing the competitiveness of SMEs, of the agricultural sector (for the EAFRD) and of the fishery and aquaculture sector (for the EMFF)	€ 2.403.748.08	14.8
4	Supporting the shift towards a low-carbon economy in all sectors	€ 1.427.264.29	8.8
5	Promoting climate change adaptation, risk prevention and management	€ 364.269.32	2.2
6	Preserving and protecting environment and promoting resource efficiency	€ 4.138.909.14	25.6
7	Promoting sustainable transport and removing bottlenecks in key network infrastructures	€ 163.870.72	1.0
8	Promoting sustainable and quality employment and supporting labour mobility	€ 1.990.029.18	12.3
9	Promoting social inclusion, combating poverty and any discrimination	€ 1.292.505.57	8.0
10	Investing in education, training and vocational training for skills and lifelong learning	€ 2.127.332.18	13.1
11	Enhancing institutional capacity of public authorities and stakeholders and efficient public administration	€ 0.00	0.0
	Technical Assistance	€ 434.891.81	2.7
	Total	**€ 16.191.377.67**	**100**

Source: Author's elaboration on the data reported by the UK-EU PA (2014–2020)

the start of the new programming period, largely sharing policy goals with the EU Agenda for smart, sustainable and inclusive growth, which could be clearly strengthened through the additional EU funding. More specifically, the New Industrial Strategy (2012a), the Superfast Broadband Programme, the UK Plan for Growth (HMG, 2011) can be mentioned with regard to the economic dimension, while the UK National Energy Efficiency Action Plan and National Renewable Energy Action Plan for the United Kingdom (HMG, 2012b) as well as the UK Prioritised Action Framework for Natura 2000 have been relevant for the environmental component. As far as the social inclusion is concerned, a few national initiatives have been undertaken, such as Action Plan "Women and the economy" (published in 2013) or the voluntary initiative "Think Act Report" (TAR) that helped companies to improve gender equality in their workforces, particularly in relation to recruitment, retention and promotion. The reduction of youth and women unemployment, as well as promoting social inclusion and combating poverty have been among the main priorities. In most of the aforementioned programmes, the private sector was expected to invest to the same extent that it would in commercially viable areas, with the public sector making up the funding gap where the costs exceed expected revenues.

As far as governance arrangements are concerned, the PA's structure itself reflected a strongly decentralised pattern of implementation and broad competences of the devolved administrations of Northern Ireland, Scotland and Wales on a wide range of policy issues, including economic development and environment. In fact, while the devolution settlements are reasonably similar in relation to many matters connected with ESI Funds, the delivery of SF differs significantly across the UK nations, in terms of both strategic objectives and governance settings. Accordingly, the first chapter of the PA identifies common challenges and sets out a range of shared principles and priorities for the ESI Funds for the UK as a whole, followed by specific national chapters that have been prepared by the respective devolved administrations, setting out how each nation will focus on the UK funding priorities in the context of the specific challenges it faces. Coordination between the central and the devolved administrations has been guaranteed through a range of both formal and informal agreements, including in particular a Memorandum of Understanding signed in 2012 (HMG, 2012c), laying down the core principles of interaction between the administrations, including communication, consultation, cooperation and implementation of EU obligations (PA, Part 1–2, p. 3). This strategy develops in the conditions of a long-term story of tensions between the centre and the devolved administrations, which has taken the form of cooperative regionalism (Bulmer *et al.*, 2006: 89; Cole and Palmer, 2011: 20), although being largely constrained by the dependence of the devolved administration from the centre. Instead, competences in the social dimension are fragmented, as employment legislation covers the whole country and the UK government is also responsible for a number of welfare programmes. Responsibility for such provision in Northern Ireland is devolved, and analogous programmes are in place. Further education and vocational training is devolved and England, Wales, Scotland and Northern Ireland have each developed programmes for professional training and school to job transition.

Thus, specific arrangements for coordination between the ESI Funds and other funding instruments have been set out in details in the national chapters of the PA, while the promotion of equality and sustainable development have been mentioned among the UK's horizontal policy objectives. There are several provisions illustrating how the principle of cross-sectoral policy integration will be implemented in substantive terms, with particular regard to coordination between different funds and sectoral policy measures. For example, with regard to the objective of "smart growth", the PA has stressed the need to align all ESI Funds and integrate actions across different thematic objectives for achieving the goal of skills development. This is due to the fact that sectors which were traditionally helped through EAFRD or EMFF, such as land management, food and drink, forestry, aquaculture and fisheries offer quality opportunities for vocational placements as much as sectors traditionally supported through ERDF, such as innovation or renewable energy. Whilst EAFRD and EMFF will not directly contribute to this thematic objective, the skills requirements in rural and coastal areas can form part of the regional skills plans (e.g. in Scotland). Regarding the objectives of "sustainable growth", the PA highlights, based on SWOT analysis, that a cross-sectoral action of ESI Funds should be undertaken to contribute towards the shift to a low-carbon economy in the UK, aiming to develop infrastructures, support low-carbon transport solutions particularly in urban areas, encourage technological innovation, promote energy efficiency, and encourage demand for low-carbon goods and services.

Thus, the pattern of policy integration has developed beyond the EPI principle, increasingly involving the social dimension, although the former principle has remained at the core of recent policy measures for reducing, reusing and recycling, decarbonisation of the economy and resource efficiency.

The relevance of integration between different territorial levels has been recognised too, highlighting that the transfer of powers to the Devolved Administrations will allow for differentiated and integrated approaches in each nation of the UK, taking into account their specific territorial characteristics. The feasibility of application of the territorial development instruments CLLD and ITIs across the UK has been recalled by the PA, but the decision on whether these instruments should be actually activated was delegated to the devolved administrations. As a consequence, the CLLD tool has been adopted in England, Scotland, Wales and Northern Ireland for delivering EAFRD and EMFF, where it had already been applied to implement parts of these funds in the programming period 2007–2013. England is the only UK nation that decided to use CLLD to deliver parts of the ERDF and the ESF.

Importantly, the architecture of the territorial governance in the UK has changed over the last decade. In 2010, the While Paper "Local growth: realising every place's potential" (HMG, 2010) announced the replacement of nine Regional Development Agencies (RDA) that had been chief actors for local economic development policies as well as for managing SF for decades, by the system of 39 Local Enterprise Partnerships (LEPs) (Ward and Hardy, 2013). Based on voluntary partnership between local authorities and businesses, the mission of LEPs has been to bring together key local players, including universities, the voluntary and community sector and social and environmental partners, to take a strategic view on how best to deliver growth and jobs in their economic areas.

As far as the objective of SUD is concerned, the PA has committed to use ESI Funds for a range of integrated actions across cities in the UK in order to strengthen the cities' role in economic development based on the experience of the previous programming period (e.g. JESSICA Initiative) and building on domestic policy initiatives. In line with the provisions of Article 7 of the ERDF Regulation, Cities and Core City Regions were supposed to exercise significant influence within the various delivery structures across the UK as part of the design of the ERDF programmes, with the financial allocation of 5.4%. In fact, actions for integrated SUD have been included in the operational programmes of England, Scotland and Wales co-financed by the ERDF, although different programming approaches have been applied.

The implementation of these provisions has developed in the conditions of further territorial reforms (HMG, 2016) that established new institutional basis for devolving powers and resources to urban areas under the following three models: Growth Deals – providing for short to medium-term funding for business and employment skill support in local areas; City Deals – enabling capital investments at city and city-region level in medium-long term; and Devolution Deals – covering city regions and sub-regions providing for funding for public services in long-term. Some of these instruments applied to England and Wales only, while others, like City Deals, to the UK as a whole. A new Cities and Local Growth Unit was set up in 2014 as a joint unit between two UK government departments (Department for Communities and Local Government and the Department for Business, Energy and Industrial Strategy) and HM Treasury with the aim of creating a single team for local economic growth policy (EPRC, 2016).

In sum, the UK framework for the 2014–2020 EU SF programming has provided ample margins for the devolved authorities to play a pro-active role and engage with the EU agenda for sustainable development by defining their own priorities in this field, choosing whether and how to use the new territorial governance instruments (CLLD and ITI) and to what extent to strengthen the territorial dimension of development policies.

In addition, a substantial rescaling of programming units has taken place: the ERDF and ESF programming package has been organised into six operational programmes (West Wales and the Valleys, East Wales, Scotland, Northern Ireland, England, Gibraltar) compared to 22 programmes implemented in the 2007–2013 programming period.

4.2.2 The case of England

In keeping with the provisions of the 2007–2013 NSRF document and the PA for the 2014–2020 programming period, the England ERDF programme, with the overall financial allocation of 3.628.260.303 euro, contains a number of references to the principle of sustainable development and the related measures.

However, a rather narrow conceptualisation of this principle arises from the programme that puts a strong emphasis on the traditional economic and social orientations of development policies. From this standpoint, it develops in continuity with the approach that prevailed for most smaller regional operational programmes implemented in the 2007–2013 programming period, which mainly focused on competitiveness, employment and the economic development dimension. Thus, despite announcing its commitment to the EU strategy for growth and jobs, the programme contains limited direct references to sustainable development objectives, except for those reported in the mandatory section defining sustainable development as a horizontal priority and the one concerning sustainable urban development. In fact, it highlights the relevance of integrated local community-led development strategies as an appropriate tool for meeting diversified development needs across less developed, in-transition and more developed areas of the country.

Building on a number of national strategic documents, such as the Plan for Growth (DBIS, 2011a), the National Innovation and Research Strategy for Growth (DBIS, 2011b), as well as on the English Smart Specialisation strategy, the Programme draws significant attention, also in financial terms (see Table 4.5), to TO1, TO2 and TO3 to competitiveness and digital infrastructure. In the same way, even for TO 4, 5, 6, 7 that naturally contain, more directly, the reference to the environmental dimension of sustainability, programme priorities privilege the economic component.

Table 4.5 England ERDF Operational Programme 2014–2020: thematic objectives and respective allocations

	Priority Axis	*Funds*	*Share in total %*
1	Promoting Research and Innovation	€793.269.792	21.7
2	Enhancing Access to, and use and quality of ICT	€110.841.953	3.0
3	Enhancing the competitiveness of SMEs	€1.578.585.03	43.3
4	Supporting the shift towards a low-carbon economy in all sectors	€748.057.523	20.5
5	Promoting climate change adaptation, risk prevention and management	€86.661.198	2.4
6	Preserving and protecting environment and promoting resource efficiency	€90.442.443	2.5
7	Sustainable transport in Cornwall and the Isles of Scilly	€57.925.547	1.6
8	Promoting social inclusion and combatting poverty and discrimination	€38.343.701	1.1
	Technical assistance	€145.130.411	4.0
	Total	**€3.649.257.601**	**100**

Source: Author's elaboration on the data reported by the ERDF Regional Operational Programme (2014–2020)

Hence, Priority 4 aims to enhance the shift towards a low-carbon economy in all sectors, referring in particular to the production and distribution of energy derived from renewable sources; promoting energy efficiency and renewable energy use in enterprises, private and public building. Priorities 5 and 6 that target environmental protection, resource efficiency, climate adaptation and risk prevention, mainly focus on measures promoting innovative technologies to reduce waste, water and air pollution, as well as investments in green and blue infrastructure and actions that "support the provision of ecosystem services on which businesses and communities depend to increase local natural capital and support sustainable economic growth" (DCLG, 2015: 150). Priority 7 aims to promote sustainable transport, developing and improving environmentally friendly (including low-noise) and low-carbon transport system. In sum, all priorities targeting the environmental dimension of sustainability are strongly unpinned by the economic rational. Priority 9 aims at promoting social inclusion, combating poverty and any discrimination, without ever mentioning the social dimension of suitability. Although the principle of policy integration was explicitly recalled with regard to energy and transport interventions, no specific provisions on how various measures should integrate this principle have been formulated.

As far as SUD is concerned, the programme has dedicated to this objective 8.67% of the ERDF under Art. 7(2) of ERDF Regulation. It has introduced both EU instruments for enhancing the territorial governance – CLLD and ITI – in order to deliver focused and integrated interventions. It has been specified that CLLD will promote localised partnerships of public, private and civil society sectors at the city level. Hence, England ERFD programme goes beyond the EU Guidance requiring to apply the CLLD approach to ERDF interventions under TO9 (social inclusion), by adding other investment priorities to be managed according to this method, in particular as far as the objective of SME competitiveness and entrepreneurship are concerned. The programme has established that integrated actions for SUD should be designed by the intermediate authorities identified in the Core City Regions, in line with Article 7 (4) ERDF Regulation and Articles 123 (6) and 125 (3) (a) Common Provisions Regulation.

Therefore, Urban Authorities have been assigned the responsibility for the selection of operations, with London designated as an Intermediate Body with a broader range of tasks delegated in line with Article 123 (7), reflecting its relative size and existing Intermediate Body status.

Accordingly, the MA has invited Core City Regions to submit strategies for integrated urban actions, combining a minimum of two thematic objectives listed below and describing how proposed activities would be complemented by other major investments envisaged over the lifetime of the Programme within urban areas concerned:

TO1: Strengthening Research, Technological Development and Innovation;
TO3: Enhancing the Competitiveness of SMEs;
TO4: Supporting the Shift towards a Low Carbon Economy in all sectors;

TO5: Promoting Climate Change Adaptation, Risk Prevention and Management;

TO6: Preserving and Protecting the Environment and Promoting Resource Efficiency.

Overall, the proposed strategies were required to provide interlinked actions aimed at securing a lasting improvement in the economic, environmental, climate, social and demographic conditions of the urban area concerned, and to describe how the existing LEPs will be involved in the implementation of the strategy.

The following nine cities, mentioned in Table 4.6, were selected for developing local strategies for sustainable urban development with the following financial allocations.

Moreover, a totally territorial axis has been designed by the programme for sustainable transport in Cornwall and the Isles of Scilly (C&iOS), which benefit from an Integrated Territorial Investment (ITI) to ensure the implementation and delivery of a targeted programme of investment for the territory by combining the ERDF and the ESF.

Overall, England's approach to the SF programming seems to show several elements confirming the legitimising scenario of SF usage as regards both the model of cross-sectoral policy integration and the pattern of the strategy territorialisation. It shows a clearly green business-oriented conceptualisation of smart, sustainable and inclusive growth, and is firmly embedded in the national economic development policy architecture supported by LEPs.

No specific provisions for integrating sustainable development objectives into local strategies have been introduced, the entire responsibility of this being delegated to the respective UA. No coordination arrangements have been designed

Table 4.6 English cities selected for developing local strategies for sustainable development and respective allocation

City	*Allocation (million €)*
Birmingham	12.7
Bristol	3.3
Leeds	19.9
Liverpool	12.8
Manchester	22.2
Newcastle	15.9
Nottingham	12.1
Sheffield	10.5
London	204.9
Total	314.3

Source: Author's elaboration on the data reported by the ERDF Regional Operational Programme (2014–2020)

between the central and local authorities thereby preventing the complementarity of action across all other programme priority axes.

A strong additional nature of actions, compared to ordinary domestic policies, is found to be prevalent throughout the document, motivated by the overall limited amount of EU funding assigned to the country. As the programme itself explains, "the ERDF represents a very small proportion of public funding available in England to support growth, let alone private finance. The strategy therefore focuses on areas where ERDF can have greatest marginal impact when combined with national investment" (DCLG, 2015: 1). At the same time, the Programme highlights that 2014–2020 ERDF funds will be strategically deployed together with national resources to target market failures that constrain growth, emphasising that "without ERDF these investments would either not take place or not take place to the same scale and timeframes".

As already mentioned, this unique ERDF programme for England has substituted nine smaller scale (regional) programmes for the Competitiveness objective and one for the Convergence objective implemented during the programming period 2007–2013. Such choice has been viewed as a strong centralisation trend, accompanied at the same time by the fragmentation of territorial development institutions (EPRC, 2016). In addition to concerns expressed with regard to limited resources and functional consistency of LEPs (Ward and Hardy, 2013), the issue of doubtful accountability of LEPs has been raised by the document itself, specifying that "LEPs are typically not accountable, formally constituted bodies: they are partnerships providing a strategic steer and oversight". Such a claim is striking, considering that, as the document further states, these bodies are supposed to play "a central role in developing local European Structural and Investment Fund strategies that reveal the economic needs and challenges of specific areas and provide intelligence that helps inform the choice of thematic objective, investment priority and indicative actions within this Programme" (DCLG, 2015: 7).

The second important issue concerns the distribution of EU funding across the nation. While aggregating all interventions within a single operational programme, important differentiations have been made in the amount of funding available for different regions based on the level of their social and economic development. However, some decisions taken by Whitehall in this regard have been heavily contested by the regions. In 2014 nine local authorities (four in funding for England, South Yorkshire and five in Liverpool city region) challenged the coalition government's regional allocation of EU structural funds for 2014–2020 in the High Court. The local authorities argued that UK Ministers had used a flawed methodology to calculate national funding allocations for English LEP areas, which would see South Yorkshire and Merseyside receive significantly less money than the European Commission had intended. The High Court ruled against the government and the Court's judgement confirmed that the government's funding allocations for South Yorkshire and Merseyside were both over €90m less than the EU intended. The government subsequently appealed the ruling and in February 2015 the Supreme Court overturned it to uphold the government's original funding allocations and confirm ministers' discretionary powers to allocate EU structural funding (Hunt *et al.*, 2016).

4.2.3 The case of Scotland

Previous studies have suggested that since the very outset of the devolution process, Scotland has assumed a more pro-active role in relations with the EU level compared to Wales and Northern Ireland, being aware about the need to demonstrate added value to governance within their territories (Hogwood, 2013). In fact, such EU ideas as inclusivity, transparency and participation were intensely used to distinguish the Scottish approach from more traditional top-down style of Whitehall.

As policy applications of the concept of sustainability grew, Scotland has widely promoted experiments in the application of environmental sustainability to new policy areas cutting across traditionally defined sectors. The Scottish Sustainable Development Strategy (SSDS) was approved in 2005 (Scottish Government, 2005), while in 2009 Scotland passed its Climate Change Act, which was considered to be one of the world's most ambitious legislative initiatives. This occurred after the Scottish National Party came to power in 2007, demanding greater control over Scotland's EU policy. Remarkably, the Scottish Executive was the first UK authority to pass legislation associated with the EU Water Framework Directive (60/2000/CE), providing the guidance for other nations as well as for the DEFRA itself.

The SSDS has established the following four main priorities that substantially framed all subsequent policy schemes:

i. Sustainable consumption and production: achieving more with less by reducing the inefficient use of resources, considering the impact of products and materials across their whole lifecycle and encouraging people to take into account the social and environmental consequences of their purchasing choices;
ii. Climate change and energy use: securing a profound change in the way in which energy is generated and used and reducing greenhouse gas emissions;
iii. Natural resource protection and environmental enhancement: protecting natural resources by developing a better understanding of environmental limits and actively improving the quality of the environment;
iv. Sustainable communities: creating communities that embody the principles of sustainable development locally.

More key environmental sustainability statements of policy have been formulated by the Green Jobs Strategy (2005), the Scottish Biodiversity Strategy (2004) and the Scottish Regeneration Policy Statement of the Scottish Government (2006). The latter highlighted the fact that improvements could only be achieved through an integrated policy approach going beyond investment in the physical infrastructure of the areas concerned. Moreover, the importance of partnership was emphasised, recognising that in places where projects and activities were developed through a networked, inter-agency approach, project quality appeared to be driven up (Scottish Government, 2006: 48).

Lastly, specific instruments for sustainable development mainstreaming (including SEA and EIA) have become a mandatory legislative requirement for new policy initiatives, including the obligation for all projects to demonstrate how they intend to address this cross-cutting theme and ensuring that minimum standards are met as a condition of awards.

The aforementioned priorities have been largely integrated into the Scottish regional SF programming since the 2000–2006 period, when environmental sustainability was introduced as a key horizontal theme and the approach to sustainable development was taken forward substantially, considering its embeddedness in wider policy-making as one of the legacy aims of the Programme.

In the 2007–2013 programming period, the Regional Competiveness Programme in Lowlands & Uplands Scotland (Scottish Government, 2009), covering more developed areas and been allocated €375.958 million of ERDF co-financing, has established three essential cross-cutting priorities:

- The sustainable growth of the Scottish economy in a way that does not compromise the environmental resources of future generations;
- The inclusion of as much as Scottish society as possible in the achievement and benefits of that growth, through equal opportunities and social inclusion actions; and
- The conservation of Scotland's environmental assets in pursuing sustainable development.

Commitments announced by the programme have developed in line with the four SSDS priorities, shaping the programme objectives as follows. Sustainable consumption was reflected in a commitment to funding and encouraging greater "greening" of enterprises and compelling projects to consider the consequences of their procuring choices. The active support of renewables took forward the commitment to climate change and energy use. Natural and environment resource protection was pursued by supporting projects that gave such objectives strong economic development grounding in making full sustainable economic use of environmental assets. Lastly, sustainable communities were promoted with the aim to support urban regeneration within the framework of sustainable economic development.

A series of actions have been defined to specifically support the environmental dimension of sustainability under the various thematic priorities (Scottish Government, 2009):

Priority 1 – research and innovation

- Support the sustainable commercial use of renewable technologies with the aim of promoting the development of a thriving new energy sector that would bring together economic development and climate change goals.

- Encourage the "greening" of enterprises through improved resource efficiency, including environmental and carbon-use audits, more environmentally sustainable production systems and business processes and plans for energy and resource efficiency.
- Support new firm start-ups, with requirement for adoption of baseline environmental processes, considering that the potential for a cultural change in environmental sustainability is more likely to develop with new rather than existing enterprises, particularly where energy and resource efficiency processes are mainstreamed into their practices from the beginning.

Priority 2 – enterprise growth

- Support improvement of the renewable energy research capacity of the region by enhancing the centre of research expertise within the University of the Highlands and Islands (UHI) and its network.
- Promoting "green" tourism projects aimed at enhancing the value of the natural assets of the region, maintaining the quality of the landscape environment and the steps required to ensure its sustainable preservation.

Priority 3 – urban regeneration

- Enhancing community sustainability through funding of small-scale infrastructure developments for enterprises that comply with sustainable development goals, for example through the application of environmental building standards.
- Encouraging transport infrastructural projects to ensure that environmental sustainability has been fully taken into account in project design, not least in maintaining the quality and biodiversity of the region's natural environment.
- Supporting activities aimed at raising environmental awareness in communities and enterprises.
- Supporting small-scale renewables in local energy generation, which will contribute to the local dimension of the wider Scottish sustainable development agenda.

Besides, based on the Scottish Index of Multiple Deprivation (SIMD), a number of priority areas for urban regeneration support were identified at local level, which were affected by high levels of social exclusion, unemployment, low levels of educational attainment, poor health, lack of local services and low income and other indicators of poverty. Community regeneration measures mainly included initiatives for social housing, health assistance, educational programmes and indigenous enterprise development.

In the same way, the other programme Highlands & Islands Scotland (H&IS), covering less developed areas, which obtained €121.862 million ERDF co-financing under the EU Convergence objective, was strongly underpinned by the principle of policy integration. It has put particular emphasis on the dimension of community sustainability, addressing such problems as regeneration of disadvantaged neighbourhoods through better employability, improved quality of life and health conditions.

The programme stated that these objectives could only be achieved through an integrated policy approach going beyond investments in physical infrastructure of these areas, highlighting that "the economic, social, physical and environmental aspects of regeneration require an integrated approach which 'joins up' planning and delivery across these aspects, so that change is mutually reinforcing" (Scottish Government, 2008, p. 52). At the same time, the programme committed to the principle of partnership, stressing that no sole organisation would be able to deliver ambitious outcomes. Therefore, the Community Planning Partnerships (CPPs) were established through Regeneration Outcome Agreements – one for each Local Authority area – to take forward these strategies by setting out how the relevant partners at local level intend to combine their activities to achieve regeneration outcomes. The CPPs brought together the key partners involved in local regeneration including the local authority, voluntary sector organisations, local health boards and other relevant bodies.

One of the core directions of the programme has been the "greening" of economy and the effort for the Highlands and Islands to "seize the business opportunities and advantages arising from sustainable development with a view to creating a vibrant, low-carbon economy and the country being a location for green enterprise". Therefore, a combination of measures was formulated in order to support "economic opportunities arising from a commitment to environment sustainability – such as renewable technologies and economic efficiencies arising from waste recycling – as well as more general information-raising and skills improvements in mainstreaming environmental issues into economic activity" (Scottish Government, 2008).

In fact, the dimension of sustainable growth was at the core of the Highlands & Islands programming 2007–2013, aimed at meeting three main challenges:

i. Enhancing business competitiveness, commercialisation and innovation;
ii. Enhancing key drivers of regional and sectoral sustainable growth;
iii. Enhancing sustainable growth of peripheral and fragile areas.

However, a wider vision for the Highlands & Islands development embracing the economic, environmental and social dimensions was clearly defined, aspiring for "prosperous, inclusive and self-sustaining communities, where the unique cultures, traditions and environments are enhanced and the region makes a distinctive contribution to Scotland, the UK and the EU competitiveness through supporting people, place and prosperity" (H&I, p. 60).

The urban dimension of interventions for sustainable development has been clearly traced throughout the documents, including water and waste management, reduction of CO_2 emissions and land use, although it did not design a specific axis for it.

Overall, the 2007–2013 approach to sustainability as a horizontal programming priority has shown a high consistently with the EU Lisbon Strategy for growth and jobs, which earmarked the SF programming spending, while also paying significant attention to the environmental dimension.

As in the case of England, the two operational programmes were merged into a unique document in the 2014–2020 programming period, with the total ERDF allocation being 476.788.331 million of euros for the whole period , as Table 4.7 shows.

The new programme has confirmed its commitments to sustainability goals, highlighting the need to take advantage of EU funding for achieving structural reforms. These reforms are needed to enhance sustainable economic growth that would not otherwise take place, or not to the same scale and timeframes.

By highlighting the effort to create alignment between all EU Funds deployed in Scotland, the 2014–2020 ERDF programme focuses on the following priorities (Scottish Government 2014b):

TO1: Strengthening research, technological development and innovation;
TO2: Enhancing access to, and use and quality of information and communication technologies (ICT);
TO3: Enhancing the competitiveness of small and medium-sized enterprises (SMEs);
TO4: Supporting the shift towards a low-carbon economy in all sectors;
TO6: Preserving and protecting the environment and promoting resource efficiency.

In general, the programme has emphasised that effective coordination and greater integration of actions across the ESI funds and with other EU and national funding is fundamental in providing a more strategic approach to meeting the common aims and objectives.

Table 4.7 Scotland ERDF Operational Programme 2014–2020

TO	*Priority Axis*	*Funds*	*Share in total %*
1	Strengthening research, technological development and innovation	€111.500.000.00	23.28
2	Enhancing access to, and use and quality of information and communication technologies	€25.000.000.00	5.22
3	Enhancing the competitiveness of SMEs, of the agricultural sector (for the EAFRD) and of the fishery and aquaculture sector (for the EMFF)	€154.581.000.00	32.28
4	Supporting the shift towards a low-carbon economy in all sectors	€124.851.563.00	26.07
5	Preserving and protecting environment and promoting resource efficiency	€53.445.772.00	11.16
	Technical Assistance	€9.535.768.00	1.99
	Total	**€478.914.103.00**	**100**

Source: Author's elaboration on the data reported by the ERDF Regional Operational Programme (2014–2020)

Therefore, it has stated that planning for the 2014–2020 programmes will be focused on identifying and supporting better connections between these objectives, and on creating mutually reinforcing links between funding programmes rather than adding new and separate streams. Hence, the programme has committed to promote a holistic and integrated approach to development, support management and maintenance of green and blue corridors (such as wildlife corridors or improvements to urban waterways) in and between urban areas, to improve environmental quality and access to green space. The development of the infrastructures has been closely connected to local employability and social inclusion measures, aiming to provide people with training, volunteering and work opportunities in transforming their own communities. Sustainable urban development objectives have been at the core of the strategy.

The principle of policy integration has been clearly conceptualised by the programme along with three criteria: *integration*, for example where policy aims at target groups for investment are shared; effective *demarcation*, recognising the correct role for each fund either by type of area, by activity or by project scale; and *complementarity* based on the recognition of the very specialist role of some funds (e.g. precise environmental focus or urban focus, or the scale of skills delivery, etc.). Accordingly, the Ppogramme suggested that delivery arrangements and mechanisms should focus on a thematic rather than a fund/sectoral approach in order to enable policy alignment.

In addition, a number of important governance innovations have been introduced. Unusually, instead of designing programme priorities, the Scottish ERDF Programme has been organised into 11 Strategic Thematic Interventions, repressing packages of measures of significant scale and defined scope, which will be managed and co-financed by Lead Partners (LP). Such a design aimed at ensuring that funds would be invested into key growth areas, where they could generate maximum impact, including the following: Business Competitiveness, Developing Scotland's Workforce, Employability, Green Infrastructure, Innovation, Low-Carbon Infrastructure Transition Fund, Low-Carbon Travel & Transport, Resource Efficient Circular Economy, Smart Cities, Social Inclusion & Poverty Reduction, Youth Employment Initiative. Multiple references to the concept of sustainable development have been embodied in the actions envisaged within the aforementioned areas, comprising sustainable and quality employment, eco-innovation, energy efficiency and low-carbon transport, smart mobility, social inclusion, etc.

The LP were expected to play a crucial role in maximising the impact and ensuring that the SF recourses could be effectively and efficiently used. They have been selected from among Scottish government policy directorates, agencies and local authorities, who already manage domestic funding in the same policy area and thus, possess the relevant administrative experience and capacity to manage and match large-scale funds. More specifically, the following responsibilities were assigned to LP:

i. Publicising SIE funds through mechanisms such as challenge funds or procurement exercises, so individual organisations or delivery bodies can apply for financial support;

ii. Working effectively with the Managing Authority to ensure that funds are awarded only to projects eligible under European Structural and Investment Fund regulations;
iii. Fulfilling administrative responsibilities including compliance with audit requirements, and ensuring that there is a clear document trail demonstrating that funds are used in accordance with the required standards.

This mechanism also considered the ability of LP to provide match funding alongside EU funds and create a single point of contact for smaller organisations submitting funding applications. Such kind of operational support has been crucial for the Programme Managing Authority that holds the overall responsibility for the programme implementation, management and monitoring, financial management and controls; selection of projects for funding and reporting on targets.

As far as the objective of SUD is concerned, the specific Thematic Intervention Smart Cities has intended to promote the following strands of action:

i. Reduce C CO_2 emissions through the innovative use of ICT;
ii. Alleviate traffic congestion through smart mobility planning;
iii. Increase citizen engagement through the increased use of mobile technology and social media;
iv. Reduce energy use through smart metering and smart grids;
v. Promote better care through new telecare and telehealth technology services.

The Scottish Alliance (SA) has been identified as the LP for this SI, bringing together its seven member local authorities: Aberdeen, Dundee, Edinburgh, Glasgow, Inverness, Perth and Stirling, in partnership with the Scottish government. The SA network was launched independent of EU programming with the objective of enhancing the development of joint projects across the seven cities to make them internationally competitive and collectively becoming an engine of growth for Scotland. The SA governance architecture is underpinned by the smart city approach, driven by the principles of collaboration and engagement, openness, innovation, sustainability and resource efficiency (Urban Foresight, 2016).

Notwithstanding the existence of the SAT and other consolidated forms of local partnership, neither has the Scottish ERDF Programme designed a specific axis for SUD, nor has it adopted the territorial governance tools (CLLD and ITI) for managing interventions targeting urban areas, as according to the Scottish MA this would require a level of disaggregation of the programme to an intermediate body, and would separate innovation and environmental activity too rigidly, from other activities under the programme. However, the Scottish ERDF Programme has identified a range of measures for promoting SUD, aligned with the spirit of the EU regulations and respecting the national UK guidance, in particular under the thematic objective of Smart Cities and Green Infrastructure. The comprehensive funding for these strands of activity together amount to an equivalent of 7.3% of the ERDF Programme, or €35 million.

The analysis above shows that Scotland has been very pro-active in incorporating sustainability objectives in its regional development policies. Since the early years of EU strategy in this field, it has strongly promoted the principle of policy integration by first introducing environmental sustainability as one of the horizontal themes and then increasingly extending this principle on social issues. All projects financed by the programme were expected to demonstrate their contribution to the respect of sustainable development objectives at both application and delivery stages (Interview 3). There have been limited changes in this sense in the Scottish ERDF programming from 2007–2013 to 2014–2020 period, except for a few innovations concerning the urban dimension, as it invested less in infrastructures, refurbishment, site servicing, etc. Indeed, as has been pointed out in an interview to MA, a number of aspects that appeared in the EU urban agenda in 2016 had already been incorporated in the Scottish ERDF operational programme for the period 2014–2020 (Interview 3). These take into account the Commission's ambitions for sustainable urban development through enabling infrastructure and piloting "smart city" technology and approaches, alongside the need to address environmental challenges including noise, air and water quality, and habitat and wildlife preservation. As the same interview (3) has explained, there was no need to apply CLLD or ITI instruments to enhance the local participation in the implementation of the programme, as the innovative governance architecture of the Scottish Alliance and other existing domestic instruments, such as City Deals, Business Gateway network, SE and HIE, Scottish Govt/TS/SNH/ZWS were used to deliver the ERDF programme. It has been stressed that the Scottish MA has a long-term experience in working with Community Planning Partnerships bringing together local government, third sector and other stakeholders in delivering projects (still used in ESF but not appropriate to this ERDF programme). The relevance of the existing local partnerships has been considered very high and therefore, the current operational programme has been designed around existing local structures so as to complement the links between the regional (Scottish) and local level. Many efforts have been made in the past to build such enduring local partnership, including the Joint Programme Monitoring Committee and Highlands and Islands Territorial Committee, as well as smaller groups for inclusive, smart and sustainable stakeholders. The Committees meet bi-annually and the groups every quarter. The MA has led partner events twice or thrice a year and periodically launches a review on implementation in order to understand where changes were required. All lead partners fed into this process that appears to work rather successfully in both the formulation and implementation of ERDF (Interview 3). Although the EU guidance on sustainability has been perceived as extremely relevant, no substantial changes are expected to happen in the regional development approach as there is a strong commitment of the Scottish government to this objective.

Therefore, strategic and legitimating scenario has dominated in the usage of the ERDF in Scotland. The Scottish programme is strongly aligned with the evolving EU priorities and, indeed, seems to have anticipated a number of programming elements, considering that the SF Regulations were published with a significant delay. The EU funds are perceived as an important source of additional financial resources and networks, and they are pragmatically channelled to those areas that can boost territorial potential.

Notes

1 The Italian plan for the programming period 2007–2013 was assigned 22.9 billion of euro from EU structural funds, with a higher quota of resources directed to the so-called "Convergence" or less developed Regions. The Convergence Objective concerns regions characterised by low levels of GDP and employment, where GDP per head is less than 75% of the EU average as it stood between 2000 and 2002. It applies to 99 regions representing 35% of the EU-27 population and aims to promote conditions conducive to growth and ones which lead to real-time convergence in the least-developed Member States and regions. The Regional Competitiveness and Employment Objective is applicable to the rest of the EU, or to 172 regions, representing 65% of the EU-27 population. It aims to enhance the competitiveness and attractiveness of regions, as well as boost their employment levels. It should be noted that the rural development and fisheries policy are separate and do not form part of this aforementioned total.

2 The following Thematic Objectives (TO) for the EU Structural and Investment Funds interventions have been defined to translate the Europe 2020 priorities into regional policies: 1) Strengthening research, technological development and innovation, 2) Enhancing access to, and use and quality of information and communication technologies (ICT), 3) Enhancing the competitiveness of small and medium-sized enterprises (SMEs), 4) Supporting the shift towards a low-carbon economy in all sectors, 5) Promoting climate change adaptation, risk prevention and management, 6) Preserving and protecting the environment and promoting resource efficiency, 7) Promoting sustainable transport and removing bottlenecks in key network infrastructures, 8) Promoting sustainable and quality employment and supporting labour mobility, 9) Promoting social inclusion, combating poverty and any discrimination, 10) Investing in education, training and vocational training for skills and lifelong learning, 11) Enhancing institutional capacity of public authorities and stakeholders and efficient public administration.

3 In Italy there are fifteen Regions with ordinary status (Regioni a statuto ordinario): Piemonte, Lombardia, Veneto, Liguria, Emilia-Romagna, Toscana, Umbria, Marche, Lazio, Abruzzo, Molise, Campania, Puglia, Basilicata and Calabria and five Regions – Friuli-Venezia Giulia, Sardegna, Sicilia, Trentino-Alto Adige/Südtirol and the Valle d'Aosta/Vallée d'Aoste holding a special autonomy (Regioni autonome a statuto speciale), due to their relevant geographic and/or cultural specific features

References

Brunazzo, M. and Gilbert, M. (2017). Insurgents against Brussels: Euroscepticism and the right-wing populist turn of the Lega Nord since 2013. *Journal of Modern Italian Studies*, 22 (5), pp. 624–641.

Bulmer, S., Burch, M., Hogwood, P. and Scott, A. (2006). UK devolution and the European Union: A tale of cooperative asymmetry. *Publius: The Journal of Federalism*, 36 (1), pp. 75–93.

Capozza, I. and Garrone, G. (2007). Italy: Towards Responsibility-Sharing in Environmental Protection. In A. Breton, G. Brosio, S. Dalmazzone and Garrone, G. eds., *Environmental Governance and Desentralisation*. Cheltenham: Edward Elgar Publishing Limited.

Cole, A. and Palmer, R. (2011). Europeanising devolution: Wales and the European Union. *British Politics*, 6 (3), pp. 379–396.

Department for Communities and Local Government (DCLG) (2015). *European regional development fund England Operational Programme 2014 to 2020*. Available at: www.gov.uk/government/publications/draft-european-regional-development-fund-operational-programme-2014-to-2020.

Department for Environment, Food and Rural Affairs February (DEFRA) 2011. *The Government's vision and what this means in practice*. Available at: https://assets.publishing.service.gov.uk/government/uploads/system/uploads/attachment_data/file/183409/mainstreaming-sustainable-development.pdf.

Department for Business Innovation and Skills (DBIS) (2011a). *The Plan for Growth*. Available at: https://www.gov.uk/government/publications/plan-for-growth-5.

DBIS (2011b). *Innovation and Research Strategy for Growth*. Available at: https://www.gov.uk/government/publications/innovation-and-research-strategy-for-growth-2.

Diamantini I. (1996). *National Report. Regional Sustainable Development. Italy*. Department of Civil and Environmental Engineering Press. Trento: Università di Trento.

Dipartimento per le politiche di sviluppo e coesione (DPS) (2014). *Accordo di Partenariato 2014–2020*. Available at: www.dps.gov.it.

Di Sotto, N. (2009). *Dalla periferia all'Europa. I partiti etnoregionalisti e l'Unione Europea*. Soveria Mannelli: Rubbettino.

European Commission (2007). *Cohesion policy in the United Kingdom 2007–2013*. Country Fiche. Available at: http://ec.europa.eu/regional_policy/archive/atlas2007/fiche/uk_en.pdf.

European Policies Research Centre (2016). Negotiating Development? Contracts, Agreements and Deals in the Governance of Regional Policy in Europe. *EoRPA Policy Briefing*. University of Strathclyde.

Fargion, V., Morlino, L. and Profeti, S. (2006). *Europeizzazione e rappresentanza territoriale. Il caso italiano*. Bologna: Il Mulino.

Forno, F. and Graziano, P. (2011). *Il consumo critico*. Bologna: Il Mulino.

Giuliani, M.(1998). Decidere per l'ambiente. Attori, processi, politiche. Milano: Servizi editori.

Gillard, R., Gouldson, A., Paavola, J. and Van Alstine, J. (2017). Can national policy blockages accelerate the development of polycentric governance? Evidence from climate change policy in the United Kingdom. *Global Environmental Change*, 45, pp. 174–182.

HM Government (2010). *While paper local growth: Realising every place's potential*. Available at: www.gov.uk/government/publications/local-growth-realising-every-places-potential-hc-7961 [Accessed 11 June 2018].

HMG (2011). *The plan for growth*. Available at: www.gov.uk/government/publications/plan-for-growth-5.

HMG (2012a). *The industrial strategy*. Available at: www.gov.uk/government/policies/industrial-strategy.

HMG (2012b). National renewable energy action plan for the United Kingdom. Available at: https://ec.europa.eu/energy/en/topics/renewable-energy/national-action-plans.

HMG (2012c). Devolution: Memorandum of understanding and supplementary agreements. Available at: www.gov.uk/government/publications/devolution-memorandum-of-understanding-and-supplementary-agreement.

HMG (2014a). *Europe 2020: UK National Reform Programme 2014*. Available at: www.gov.uk.

HMG (2014b). United Kingdom Partnership Agreement Part 1 (Sections 1 and 2). 15 October. Available at: www.gov.uk/government/uploads/system/uploads/attachment_data/file/368808/bis-14-1179-united-kingdom-partnership-agreement-part-one.pdf.

HMG (2016). *Cities and Local Government Devolution Act 2016*. Available at: www.legislation.gov.uk/ukpga/2016/1/contents/enacted [Accessed 11 June 2018].

Hogwood, P. (2013). The UK's devolved authorities and the European sustainability discourse: Between identity and actor hierarchy. In: Barnes, P.M. and Hoerber, T.C. eds., *Sustainable Development and Governance in Europe: The Evolution of the Discourse on Sustainability*. London and New York: Routledge.

IFEL (2015). La dimensione territoriale nelle politiche di coesione. Stato d'attuazione e ruolo dei Comuni nel Quadro Strategico Nazionale 2007-2013. Roma: Studi e Ricerche IFEL.

Lewanski, R. (1997). *Governance l'ambiente*. Bologna: Il Mulino.

Magnatti, P., Ramella, F., Trigilia, C. and Viesti, G. (2009). *Patti territoriali. Lezioni per lo sviluppo*. Bologna: Il Mulino.

Messina, P. (ed.) (2016). *Politiche e istituzioni per lo sviluppo del territorio. Il caso del Veneto*. Padova: Padova University Press.

Ministero dello sviluppo economico (2013). *Quadro strategico nazionale per la politica regionale di sviluppo 2007–2013*. Available at: www.agenziacoesione.gov.it/opencms/export/sites/dps/it/documentazione/politiche_e_attivita/QSN/QSN2007-2013_giu_07.pdf.

Parlamento Italiano, Italian Parliament, Delrio Law (Legge 7 aprile 2014 n.56,"Disposizioni sulle Città metropolitane, sulle Province, sulle unioni e fusioni di comuni"), GU Serie Generale n.81 del 07–04–2014.

Pizzimenti, E. (2009). "Do Paradigms Matter?" L'istituzionalizzazione dello sviluppo sostenibile in Italia (1992–2006). *Rivista Italiana di Politiche Pubbliche*, 3 (1), pp. 101–128.

Regione Emilia-Romagna (2007). PROGRAMMA OPERATIVO REGIONALE 2007–2013 FONDO EUROPEO DI SVILUPPO REGIONALE OBIETTIVO COMPETITIVITÀ REGIONALE E OCCUPAZIONE. Available at: https://fesr.regione.emilia-romagna.it/por-fesr/programmazione-precedente.

Regione Emilia-Romagna (2011). Piano Telematico dell'Emilia-Romagna 2011–2013: un nuovo paradigma per l'innovazione. Available at: http://digitale.regione.emilia-romagna.it/cos-e-agenda-digitale/percorso/percorso-fino-qui

Regione Emilia-Romagna (2014a). Il Piano Aria Integrato Regionale (PAIR2020), deliberazione n. 115 dell'11 aprile 2017 l'Assemblea Legislativa. Available at: http://ambiente.regione.emilia-romagna.it/aria-rumore-elettrosmog/temi/pair2020.

Regione Emilia-Romagna (2014b). Il Programma operativo del Fondo europeo di sviluppo regionale. Available at: http://fesr.regione.emilia-romagna.it/por-fesr/Por-fesr.

Regione Emilia-Romagna (2014c). Documento strategico regionale dell'Emilia-Romagna per la programmazione dei fondi strutturali e di investimento europei (SIE) 2014–2020. Strategia, approccio territoriale, priorità e strumenti di attuazione, Deliberazione del Consiglio Regionale 167/2014. Available at: http://formazionelavoro.regione.emilia-romagna.it/sito-fse/POR-2014-2020/allegati/DEL_2014_167_v2.pdf/view.

Regione Emilia-Romagna (2014d). Piano Regionale per le Infrastrutture di Ricerca in Emilia–Romagna. Available at: https://fesr.regione.emilia-romagna.it/por-fesr/documenti/programma/pianoregionaleinfrastrutturericerca.pdf.

Regione Emilia-Romagna (2015a). POR FESR Emilia Romagna 2014–2020, Asse 6 Città attrattive e partecipate. Linee Guida per la definizione della strategia di sviluppo urbano sostenibile delle città, Decisione C(2015) 928. Available at: https://fesr.regione.emilia-romagna.it/por-fesr/documenti/asse-6/documenti-asse-6-1.

Regione Emilia-Romagna (2015b). *Research and Innovation Strategy for Smart Specialisation*. Available at: http://fesr.regione.emilia-romagna.it/s3.

Regione Veneto (2004). Norme per il governo del territorio e in materia di paesaggio, Legge Regionale 23 Aprile 2004, N. 11 (BUR N. 45/2004). Available at: www.Consiglioveneto.It/Crvportal/Leggi/2004/04lr0011.Html.

Regione Veneto (2009). Piano di tutela delle acque. Norme tecniche di attuazione. Allegato A3 alla Deliberazione del Consiglio Regionale n. 107 del 5/11/2009 e successive modifiche e integrazioni. Available at: www.regione.veneto.it/web/ambiente-e-territorio/tutela-risorsa-idrica.

Regione Veneto (2011a). Piano delle azioni e degli interventi di mitigazione del rischio idraulico e geologico. Deliberazione della giunta regionale n. 1643 del 11 ottobre 2011. Available at: https://bur.regione.veneto.it/BurvServices/pubblica/DettaglioDgr.aspx?id=235593.

Regione Veneto (2011b). DOCUMENTO DI ECONOMIA E FINANZA REGIONALE (DEFR) 2016–2018, Segreteria Generale della Programmazione Sezione Programmazione Unitaria 2014/2020. Available at: www.regione.veneto.it/web/programmazione/defr.

Regione Veneto (2013). Città e territorio. Linee strategiche per la preparazione del POR FESR della Regione Veneto, Direzione Programmazione, Position paper presentato al tavolo di partenariato, Vicenza il 4 dicembre.

Regione Veneto (2015). *Smart Specialisation Strategy Della Regione Del Veneto*. Available at: www.regione.veneto.it/web/attivita-produttive/Smart-Specialisation-Strategy.

Ronchi, E. Colucci, P. (2011). *Vento a favore. Verso una proposta condivisa per l'ambiente, oltre gli schieramenti politici*. Milano: Edizioni Ambiente.

Scottish Government (2004). Scotland's Biodiversity: It's in Your Hands – A strategy for the conservation and enhancement of biodiversity in Scotland. Available at: https://www.gov.scot/Publications/2004/05/19366/37239.

Scottish Government (2005). Scottish Sustainable Development Strategy. Available at: https://www.gov.scot/Publications/2005/06/1693437/34516.

Scottish Government (2008). Highlands and Islands Scotland. European Regional Development Fund 2007-2013: Structural Funds Operational Programme. Available at: https://www.gov.scot/Publications/2008/07/29142448/0.

Scottish Government (2009). *Lowlands and Uplands Scotland ERDF* Operational Programme 2007-2013. Available at: https://www.gov.scot/resource/doc/313256/0099254.pdf.

Scottish Government (2014a), Operational Programme under the 'Investment for Growth and Jobs' goal. Available at: https://beta.gov.scot/publications/esif-operational-programmes-2014-2020/.

Scottish Government (2014b). *Department for Business, Enterprise and Regulatory Reform (BERR) (2007)*. Available at: http://ec.europa.eu/regional_policy/archive/atlas2007/fiche/uk_en.pdf.

Tortorella, V. (2015). *Politica di coesione e questione urbana. Programmi e strumenti di finanziamento per lo sviluppo delle città*. Roma: Carocci.

Urban Foresight (2016). *Blueprint for Smart Cities in Scotland*. Available at: https://www.scottishcities.org.uk/site/assets/files/1232/smart_cities_scotland_blueprint_web.pdf.

Ward, M. and Hardy, S. (eds.) (2013). *Where Next for Local Enterprise Partnerships?* London: The Smith Institute.

5 Local action for sustainable energy

The EU Covenant of Mayors

5.1 The CoM implementation in Italy

5.1.1 National strategy for sustainable energy and the EU Covenant of Mayors in Italy. A country overview

Italy has developed its national strategy for sustainable energy rather late by approving three subsequent versions of its National Energy Strategy (NES) in 2008, 2013 and 2017. Aiming to comply with the EU Climate and Energy Package and the related EU legislative provisions, these strategies have progressively heightened the ambition of target and widened the scope of measures, being framed by three main objectives: reducing emissions from ETS (European Trading System) and non-ETS, increasing energy production from renewable sources and reducing energy consumption from traditional sources (MSE and MATTM, 2017). The last version of the NES presents the first comprehensive nation-wide scheme for action underpinned by three mutually complementary components: competitiveness, security and environment. Hence, a number of macro policy measures have been identified at the national level in order to fulfil a more competitive, sustainable and secure national energy system through interventions in the following fields: reduction of the energy price; improving energy efficiency and developing competitive gas market; improving energy security and reducing the dependence on external supply of energy; promoting sustainable economy through the development of energy sector and comprehensive governance reform. Compared to the previous version of the strategy (2013), the objective of decarbonisation of economy has been introduced in view of new commitments deriving from COP21 and the EU Roadmap 2050, as well as the challenges put forward by the Industry 4.0 agenda. Moreover, a range of specific quantitative targets to be achieved by 2030 have been defined, covering the following fields: energy efficiency (10 Mtep al 2030), renewable energy production (28%); electricity production 55%; transport 21%; stopping energy production from carbon; doubling investments in research and development for clean energy; expanding sustainable mobility; reducing dependence on energy export from 76% to 64%.

As far as the governance of the strategy is concerned, unlike its previous versions, the current strategy emphasises the objective of cross-sectoral policy integration and calls for better coordination among Central Administrations, Regions, Research Institutions and the National Energy Authority. Therefore, an Interministerial Coordination Board has been established, composed by the Ministry of Economic Development, the Ministry of Environment, the Ministry of Transport and regional representatives, with a possibility of involving local authorities and other stakeholders on ad hoc basis. Remarkably, there is no specific reference to the role and contribution of local authorities to the implementation of the strategy, nor have these authorities been involved in the public consultation procedure conducted within the framework of its formulation (MSE and MATTM, 2017).

Beyond the NES, the Italian government approved the National Action Plan for Renewable Energy in 2010 transposing the EU Directive 2009/28/CE and the National Action Plan for energy efficiency, which was adopted in 2007 in order to transpose the EU Directive 2006/32/CE and revised twice in 2011 and in 2014. The last revision was due to the adoption of Directive 2012/27/CE on energy efficiency, which was transposed by Legislative Decree 102/2014 and then modified and integrated in 2016 (L.D. 141/2016). These provisions have introduced a range of measures, including information and education, targeting public administrations, private companies and citizens, although economic incentives (e.g. reduction of taxes) have been reduced. Although the local level has been indicated as the most appropriate one for implementing interventions for energy efficiency and renewable energy, neither any specific instruments for local authorities have been created, nor has any reference to the EU Covenant of Mayors been made in the aforementioned national plans and legislative provisions.

Interestingly, numerous initiatives targeting local level have been implemented in Italy since 2005, such as awards, small funding schemes, low-scale projects, in order to increase the awareness of local public authorities and private companies about the relevance and potential of sustainable energy in various sectors, including energy production, waste, building and construction, etc. (Lumicisi, 2013).

The only national law requiring specific regional and local action in the field of energy efficiency and energy use dates back to 1991 (Law 10/1991) and establishes that regions and provinces identify appropriate geographic areas for planning interventions for efficient energy use, including renewables, while municipalities with more than 50.000 inhabitants envisage a specific plan for renewables in their town planning. To sum up, the territorial dimension of energy and climate policy governance has been almost totally overlooked in the Italian national strategy and no specific policy instruments for local authorities were developed in order to enhance the local action for energy saving and efficiency.

Against this backdrop, as Figure 5.1 shows, Italian municipalities have shown an extremely high interest towards the EU Covenant of Mayors. As of December 2017, 3.276 municipalities of the total population of 7.978 were members of the programme, most of whom had joined the programme between 2010 and 2013 (Figure 5.1).

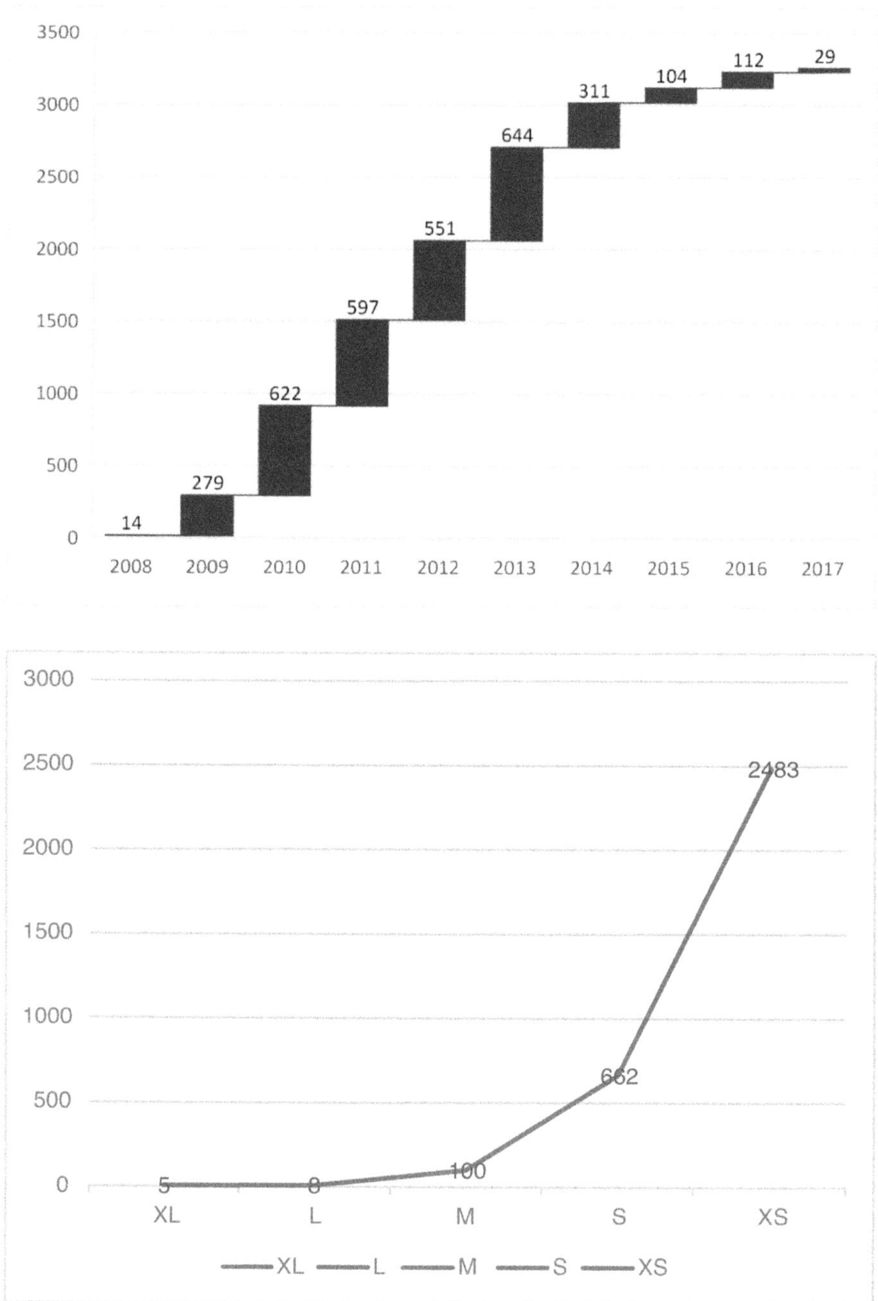

Figure 5.1 Membership of Italian municipalities in the Covenant of Mayors by year of adhesion and population

Note: Municipalities by population size: XL > 500.000; L 250.000 ≤ 500.000; M 50.000 ≤ 250.000; S 10.000 ≤ 50.000; XS population ≤ 10.000.

Source: Author's elaboration on the data available from the website of CoM www.covenantofmayors.eu/index_en.html as of June 2017.

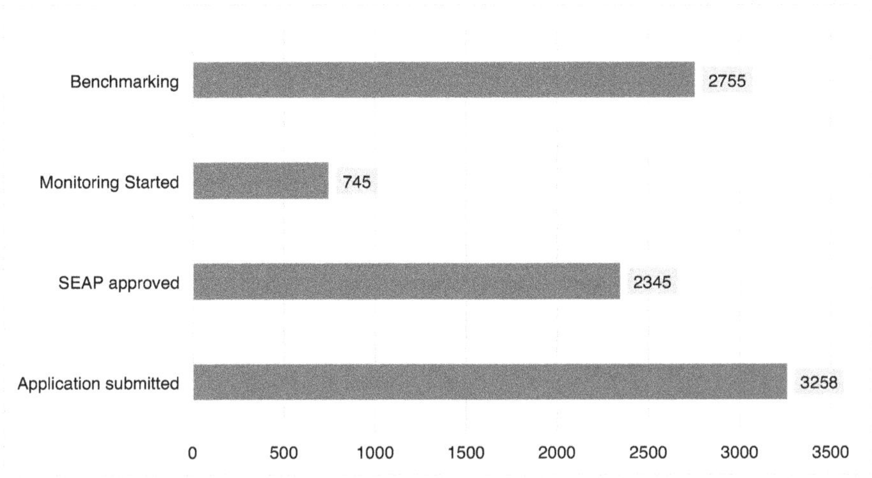

Figure 5.2 Progress of SEAPs implementation in Italy

Source: Author's elaboration on the data available from the website of CoM: www.covenantofmayors.eu/index_en.htmlas of June 2017

Such a high number of participating municipalities covers around 65% of the country's population and notably, most of them (76%) are small or very small, with the number of inhabitants between 5.000 and 10.000 (see Figure 5.1). There are only 100 medium-sized cities (50.000–250.000), 8 large (250.000–500.000) and 5 very large (more than 500.000) (Figure 5.1).

However, despite a remarkable interest towards the programme among Italian municipalities, the overall degree of commitment to the CoM does not appear to be high. The data reported in Figure 5.2 shows that around one-third of those who applied for membership did not submit their SEAP and less than 30% of approved SEAPs performed monitoring.

Moreover, a very different pattern of the territorial distribution of participating municipalities can be observed across the country. The collected data (see Figure 5.3) shows that Lombardy, that has the highest number of municipalities in the country, holds the leading position with 917 of its 1.523 municipalities. Other regions follow with significantly lower shares of CoM members, accounting for around 52% of participating municipalities from the Northern, 20% from the Central and 28% from the Southern macro-areas. It seems reasonable to suggest that these different dynamics of participation in the CoM may be related to historical differences observed between these macro-areas in terms of socio-economic development, political culture and civil traditions (Bagnasco, 1977; Putnam *et al.*, 1993; Trigilia, 2012), although the existence of such a division from the point of view of dominating political culture based on electoral majorities has recently been doubted (Diamanti, 2009).

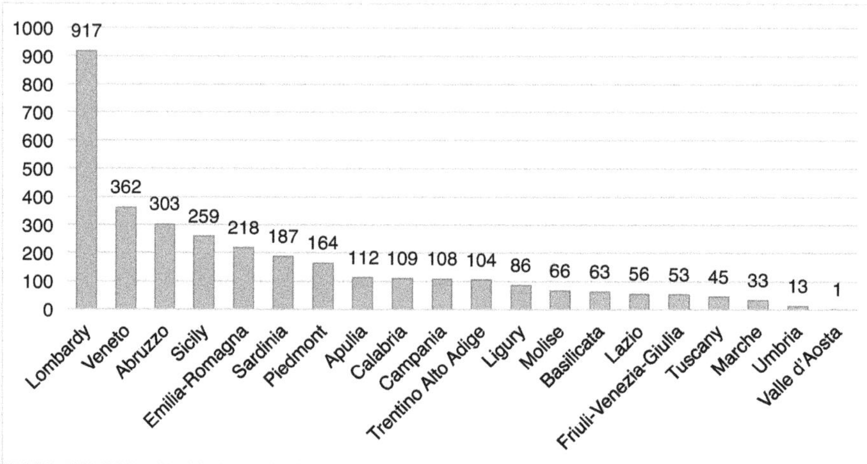

Figure 5.3 Territorial distribution of participating municipalities by region

Source: Author's elaboration on the data available from the website of CoM: www.covenantofmayors.eu/index_en.html as of April 2017

Such territorial distribution does not seem to be determined either by the size or the population of regions, but rather by the degree to which various territorial actors including regions, provinces and various private entities (foundations, local banks, energy agencies) have committed to the CoM in their quality of "territorial coordinators" in the case of territorial bodies and the so-called "supporters" for all other entities. In fact, a strong concentration at the level of provinces can be observed (e.g. Genova, Modena, Verona, Bologna, Pescara, Chieti, Foggia, Lecce, etc.) as a consequence of specific networking and coordination activities carried out in order to promote the CoM and activities related to the preparation and implementation of local SEAPs. In the same way, numerous private consultancies and agencies have provided highly qualified assistance to local authorities in their effort to perform energy accounting, the preparation of local BEIs and SEAPs' actions. In particular, the Energy Service Companies (ESCos) have become widely diffused through the national territory, offering specific expertise and financial support to municipalities, in particular through the energy manager, along with developing local plans for the reduction of energy consumption, the reduction of energy wastes and the installation of systems and machines with higher efficiency and performances.

As far as the overall ownership of Italian municipalities of the CoM goals and targets is concerned, as Figure 5.4 shows, most of them committed to the 2020 Climate and Energy package mitigation objectives only (94%), while only 2% settled the adaptation objective without increasing the 20% target of emission reduction. Only 3% of municipalities that joined the CoM after the upgrade of the programme into Mayor Adapt Initiative in 2015, introducing the adaptation

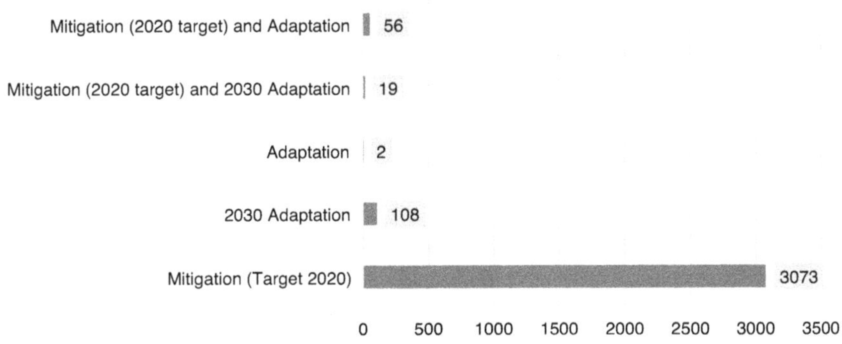

Figure 5.4 Commitment to CoM's targets by Italian signatories

Source: Author's elaboration on the data available on the website of CoM: www.covenantofmayors.eu/index_en.html, April 2017

objective and the 30% reduction target, have included the adaptation objective in their plans to be achieved by 2030. It is worth mentioning that the SEAP's targets are not fixed but can be updated whenever a municipality is willing to do so (Figure 5.4).

A more detailed analysis of a sample of 500 municipalities selected based on a balanced representation of cities of different sizes from all regions provides further useful insights on the degree of local authorities' commitment to the initiative. Hence, 27% of municipalities have established the target of reduction by 20%, 62% of municipalities between 21% and 30%, while 9% of local authorities committed to more than 30% of CO_2 reduction. Interestingly, as Figure 5.5 shows, municipalities from the central and southern regions were more ambitious compared to their northern counterparts (Figure 5.5).

With regard to timing, the data collected for the same sample of 500 municipalities shows that around 34% of municipalities have taken around one year to submit their plans and 45% have taken between two and three years. This is also a rather important indicator of political commitment to the initiative, as the recommend time for submitting SEAPs has been around 1–2 years. The data reported by Figure 5.6 shows that the speed of submission was higher in the north of the country, with 50% of municipalities complying with the one-year deadline, while more than a half of the municipalities in the central (60%) and southern (59%) regions (Figure 5.6) took around two to three years to submit their plans.

However, a particularly fast submission of SEAP might also mean that a municipality had previously developed similar strategies and thus less effort was required for streamlining its strategy into the SEAP format, compared to producing it from scratch. In fact, a number of Interviews (5, 6, 15) conducted for this research have suggested that local administrations tended to be pragmatic rather than ambitious

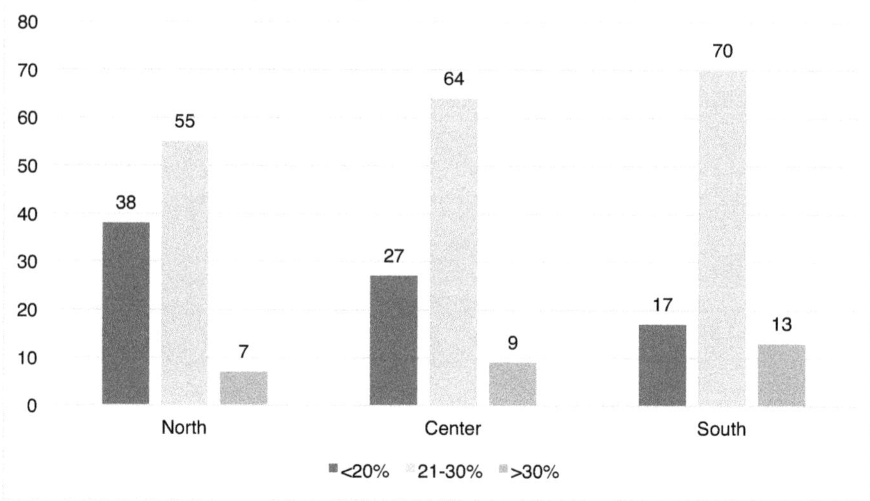

Figure 5.5 Emission reduction targets by macro-area

Source: Author's elaboration on the data available from the website of CoM: www.covenantofmayors.eu/index_en.html as of April 2017

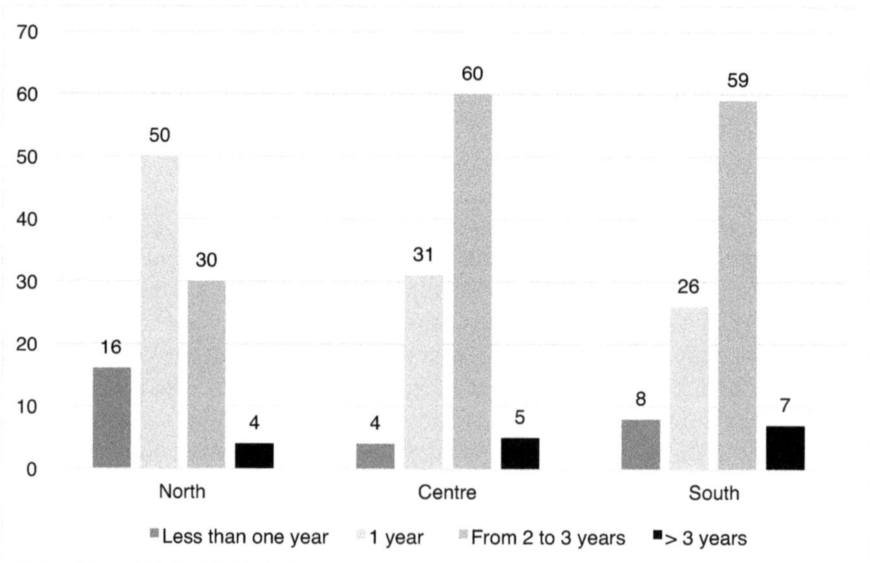

Figure 5.6 Timing of SEAP submission by macro-area

Source: Author's elaboration on the data available from the website of CoM: www.covenantofmayors.eu/index_en.html as of April 2017

in defining their commitments and targets, so as to be sure about the feasibility of their achievement in due time. At the same time, a lack of previous knowledge, and of financial and human resources has been highlighted among the main difficulties of participation in the CoM.

Despite several obstacles, Italian municipalities have been rather actively performing in establishing and completing the monitoring procedure, which is also an important indicator of seriousness of commitment and learning, particularly in the case of Italy, as no national or regional methodologies were developed in the country before the CoM. Approximately one-fourth of participating municipalities (23%) have completed at least a first stage monitoring, which is supposed to be carried out within two years from the start of implementation of the plan, while only 6% have performed complete monitoring, meaning a comprehensive evaluation of the strategy progress and the revision of BEI. For 15% of municipalities, this activity is in progress. These figures are in line with the EU average, while the interviews conducted for this research highlight an important learning effort of the municipalities in order to establish and fine-tune this procedure. While recognising the relevance of the monitoring instrument, most of them state to have needed external assistance of experts for putting the methodology suggested by the CoMO into practice (Interviews 7, 14, 15, 16). Therefore, a lack of resources (financial and human) has been reported as one of the main obstacles to complying with this CoM activity, while the internal instrumental learning related to this instruments within municipalities appears to be limited.

The territorial breakdown of the data on monitoring, as shown in Figure 5.7, indicates that the highest number of SEAPs (90%) that have not even started

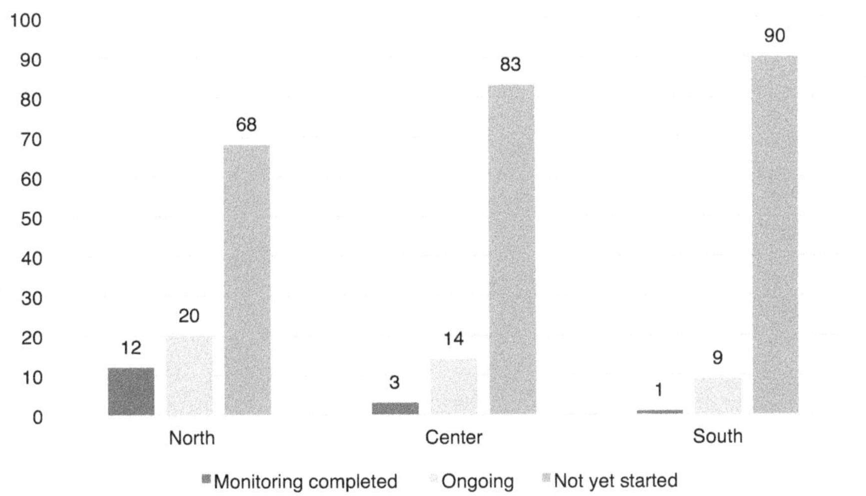

Figure 5.7 Progress of SEAP monitoring in Italy

Source: Author's elaboration on the data available from the CoM website www.covenantofmayors.eu/index_en.html as of April 2017

monitoring is concentrated in the south of the country, while the highest percentage of those who have initiated or already completed this activity has been registered in the north (22%).

Finally, as far as benchmarking in concerned, according to the data collected for 500 municipalities reported in Figure 5.8, northen regions have been home to around 42% of municipalities which developed benchmarks, while the central and southern regions accounted for 33% and 23%respectively. Overall, Italy shows the highest number of shared benchmarks, accounting for approximately 50% of all benchmarks collected by the CoM (Figure 5.8).

Thus, the pattern of usage described earlier indicates a mix of cognitive and strategic elements. Against a very high general interest regarding the programme, Italian municipalities have shown considerable effort on policy innovation and learning implied by the alignment to EU goals and emission reduction targets as well as by various CoM activities including, in particular, monitoring and benchmarking. Most of the performed activities were completely new to the Italian context and the participation in the CoM have contributed to considerably reshape local sustainable energy strategies and governance, based on new policy ideas and specific methodologies and guidance.

However, it is too early to claim for the ultimate success of this initiative, as the whole process can be considered completed only once the monitoring procedure envisaged by the programme has been in place and duly fulfilled by its participants. This activity has so far been progressing rather slowly, and major political

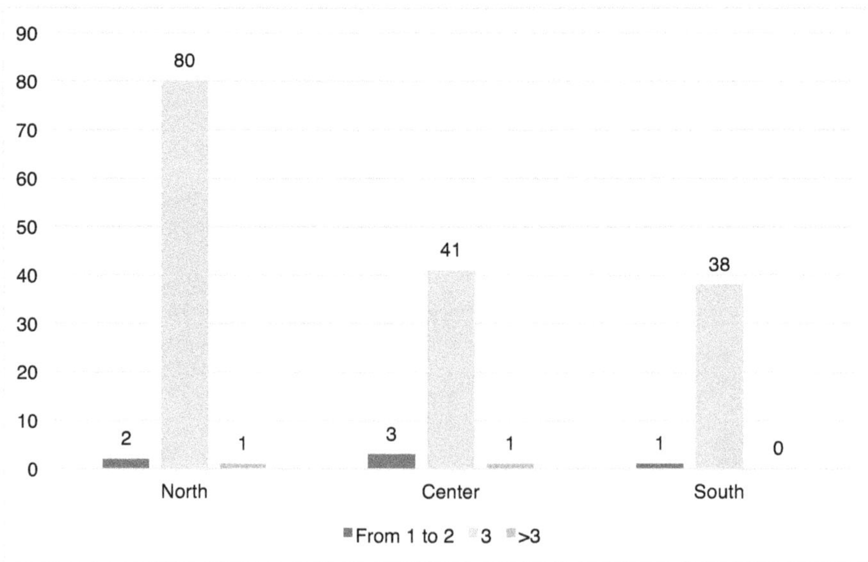

Figure 5.8 Number of benchmarks shared by Italian municipalities by macro-area

Source: Author's elaboration on the data available from the CoM website www.covenantofmayors.eu/index_en.html as of April 2017

and technical efforts will be required in the long run to guarantee its complete implementation.

The following in-depth analysis of two city cases offers further interesting insights on the implementation trajectory of the CoM in the country, providing a more nuanced view of motivations for participating in the programme and the challenges it entails.

5.1.2 The case of Bologna

The City of Bologna was among the first cities to apply for the CoM membership in 2008. It is the capital city of the Emilia-Romagna Region and with its 388.567 inhabitants, it is the seventh largest city in Italy, by population. The metropolitan area of Bologna covers 55 bordering municipalities with a total population of 1.009.210.

Bologna has historically been characterised by a pro-active local policy-making style, paying particular attention to EU initiatives and programmes. In fact, Bologna was among the first cities to develop a carbon dioxide reduction plan through the "Urban CO_2 Reduction" project financed under the EU URBAN Community Initiative Programme in the 1994–1999 regional policy programming period. In 1995, the Bologna local council approved its carbon dioxide reduction strategy, following a detailed energy study – Bologna Energy Study (BEST). The strategy fixed the target of a 16% reduction (compared to 1990 level) by 2005 and introduced interventions in the following sectors: efficiency in energy use and distribution, urban transport system, recycling, increase in vegetation, renewable energy use and incentives for reducing energy consumption. Although no systematic monitoring of this strategy was conducted, noteworthy governance actions have been undertaken in its support, including the creation of a new Bologna Agency for Energy and Sustainable Development, a new ambitious local transport plan, a variety of energy conservation projects, development of renewables, etc. (Beatly, 2000: 282).

The first Local Energy Plan (LEP) was approved in 1999, in compliance with the provisions of national Law 10/1991. The LEP was updated in 2007 and shortly after that, in December 2008, the city of Bologna applied for the CoM. Its participation in the initiative was perceived as an important opportunity for improving local sustainable energy strategy and developing wider networks on European level in this field (Interview 5). However, due to the alternation in the local government political majority, followed by political crisis and one-year receivership in 2010, Bologna was able to submit its SEAP only four years after its application for CoM membership.

Thus, the city renewed its commitment to the CoM in 2011 by submitting the local SEAP (Comune di Bologna, 2012) and it pragmatically developed its strategic action in the field of sustainable energy subsequently, despite subsequent changes in the political composition of municipal council. The continuity and consistency of action was ensured thanks especially to the establishment of a dedicated technical office in 2011, which conducted a systematic activity with the purpose of improving and developing actions envisaged by the LEP, which laid down the basis for the SEAP's measures with a noteworthy support from the JRC.

Hence, although some seminal policy ideas were available at local level, it took time and effort to translate it into a full-fledged strategy by improving at the same time the related policy measures and instruments. External experts and ad hoc staff have been hired for delivering some of these task.

The municipality has established the target of 20% CO_2 reduction, which in the words of an interviewee was "perhaps not ambitious enough, but certainly feasible and realistic, taking into account the starting conditions and resources available" (Interview 4). The SEAP covered the following five macro-areas: residential buildings, services, transport, agriculture and industry. The first three areas have been responsible for the highest levels of emissions with 35%, 28% and 20% respectively, while the implementation of SEAPs measures has naturally required from the municipality to develop a strong coordination role, along with the capacity to develop structures and partnerships with the local economic and social stakeholders. A formal partnership agreement was signed in 2012, defining mutual commitments and responsibilities of the municipality and all public and private stakeholders concerned in the implementation and promotion of the SEAP. However, it should be noted that the national legislative framework is poorly equipped for formalising and facilitating such kind of partnerships.

The municipality of Bologna has been one of the few Italian municipalities to have presented a full monitoring report (Comune di Bologna, 2015), which has been perceived to be a very useful and important instrument for fine-tuning SEAPs and further activities and carrying out evaluation of implemented actions (Interview 5), although external consultancy support was still required for completing this activity. Data collected for this report shows that a consistent level of reduction of emissions has been achieved by SEAP's measures, reaching the average of around 41% of the 2020 objective, achieved as a consequence of reduction by 53% in the transport sector; 43% in productive sector; 28% in public lighting, 11% in public buildings, etc. The City registered an increase of 88% of local electric energy production. As a consequence, the overall target of reduction has been updated to 21.3% by 2020, and a number of best practices have been identified at the municipal level, including such measures as a plan for energy efficiency of the popular housing in the Corticella area; a bike speed-way, a large solar panel installation for agri-food centre of Bologna, a LED lighting system in the City Hall and in the airport.

Although the municipality of Bologna has not upgraded its commitment to the Mayor Adapt adaptation objectives and new targets to be achieved by 2030, it has prepared and is currently implementing a local plan for climate adaptation within the framework of the project Blue-AP that got financing under LIFE + Programme in 2013. This plan is likely to be used by the city for transforming its SEAP into Sustainable Energy and Climate Action Plans (SECAPs) in the forthcoming years, as some first steps have already been envisaged in the municipal Urban Planning in 2018. It has been recognised, however, that the existing measures are not ambitious enough to achieve the 40% reduction target by 2030, as a radical transformation of production and consumption styles would be required for that (Interview 5).

Beyond these policy innovations, several distinct governance settings have been introduced in order to support the SEAP activities since its very origin. An interdepartmental coordination board has been created for delivering and monitoring the effectiveness of its policy measures, involving civil servants from different sectoral departments relevant to the SEAP. Moreover, an ad hoc participatory process has been designed around the preparation of SEAP, which then evolved in a permanent consultation forum aiming to engage social and economic stakeholders and the public in the process of revision of SEAP measures so as to increase political consensus around the strategy, improve policy measures and identify appropriate areas for the creation of public-private partnerships. The consultation process during the preparation phase was organised in eight meetings, involving around 160 stakeholders, which developed within three thematic focus groups: energy efficiency and saving in residential buildings, renewable energy production, and measures for industrial and service sectors. A cooperation agreement was signed between the municipality and stakeholders, establishing shared objectives, roles, responsibilities and modes of collaboration for the SEAP implementation and monitoring. Furthermore, a wide-scale communication campaign has been launched, including the creation of a dedicated website (www.paes.bo.it) containing exhaustive information on the plan and its implementation; an email for submitting comments and suggestions; a newsletter and social media channels, etc. In 2015, a festival of energy was organised, followed by the creation of a one-stop shop for citizens and a wide-scale communication campaign for schools.

In addition, the municipality has initiated intensive networking activities on the local arena involving public and private actors. It has first relied on the external support of the Energy Service Company (ESCo) “Del Sole” for both preparation and implementation of the local SEAP, which has been providing consultancy and assistance in energy saving and efficiency since 2011. Later, the first supra-local agency for Energy and Sustainable Development was established in May 2016, bringing together municipalities of the Metropolitan City of Bologna with the objective of providing local authorities with consultancy and assistance on energy and environmental sustainability issues, operating at national and European levels. In fact, a specific funding chapter for 230 million of euros has been envisaged in the ERDF Regional Operation Programme of Emilia-Romagna, analysed in Chapter 5, in order to support measures for energy requalification of public buildings (schools, sport centres, etc.) in that area, which should normally be targeted by SEAP interventions. The experience of public participation, as well as the interaction with social and economic stakeholders has been considered one of the main factors that greatly contributed to increase the feasibility of SEAP measures, as they closely target local communities (e.g. buildings owners) and, therefore, necessitate their awareness and willingness to undertake appropriate actions (Interview 5).

Overall, at the level of local administration, the CoM has been perceived as a useful and highly relevant tool for developing local sustainable energy strategy and identifying its instruments and targets. It has been particularly appreciated for its input as far as the design of monitoring mechanism is concerned, although the lack of resources (qualified staff and financing) has been considered to be a substantial obstacle to its effective implementation (Interview 5). By deploying substantive and operational guidance provided by the programme, the municipality has introduced significant policy and governance innovations in the field of sustainable energy, particularly in a cross-sectoral integrated policy approach, monitoring, horizontal institutional coordination and participatory practices. The administrative and political leadership, together with the traditional inclusive policy-making style of the municipality has facilitated its smooth participation and adjustment to the CoM, ensuring a progressive learning and increasing ownership of the strategy by the city.

Likewise, EU financial resources have been effectively attracted for supporting SEAP-related actions or local energy policies in general, including interventions under the ROP ERDF of the Emilia-Romagna Region or pilot cooperation projects within the framework of the URBACT or LIFE programmes. Interviews have highlighted that collaborative partnerships that developed through the CoM have contributed to increase in the participation of the municipality in new external cooperation networks.

To sum up, the scenario of strategic usage has mainly characterised the case of Bologna, although some elements of learning through the CoM policy and methodological guidance have also been observed in its case. Overall, the municipality has purposefully and pragmatically deployed the CoM and other related EU resources in order to improve its policies for sustainable energy and start building its climate policy agenda based on strategic local partnerships and solid cooperative networks at the EU level.

5.1.3 The case of Padua

Padua is a medium-sized city in the Veneto Region with a population of around 210.000 inhabitants. The municipality signed up to the CoM in 2010 and submitted its SEAP in one year in 2011 (Padua City Council, 2010), committing to reduce its CO_2 emissions by 21% compared to what it was in 2005. Such a smooth and quick progress has been made possible mainly due to the then local council's immediate interest and strong political commitment to sustainable energy issues, which quickly evolved in the application for participation in the CoM.

In fact, similar to Bologna, Padua has been among the few Italian cities to approve its Municipal Energy Plan in 1999, in compliance with Law 10/1991, and then the local Energy Efficiency Plan in 2005. As a consequence of approval of an Operational Energy Plan in 2009, the town enlarged the scope of action and started paying constant attention to climate change and wider environmental impacts on the city.

Importantly, the local SEAP has been prepared building on activities implemented within the framework of the project LAKs (Local Accountability for Kyoto Goals) that was developed and financed by EU LIFE+ programme. The project aimed to explore the cities' potential and develop synergies in order to contribute to the achievement of the Kyoto goals and of the Energy Package 20/20/20 targets established by the European Commission in 2008, and brought together four cities (Reggio Emilia and Padua (Italy), Girona (Spain) and Bydgoszcz (Poland)). More specifically, the objective was to develop policy instruments allowing the municipal authorities to enhance the achievement of emission reduction targets by 2020, monitor the level of emissions and the progress of established measures. Furthermore, project activities aimed at increasing the accountability and transparency of local policy-making through involving citizens into decision-making on energy issues. A manual providing the partner municipalities with a guidance on how to build and implement climate mitigation and adaptation policies, including the development of BEIs, was among the main deliverables of the project.

Interestingly, the preparation and implementation of SEAP has been strongly coordinated with the local Agenda 21 activities. The SEAP has focused on the following sectors of intervention:

i. Increasing renewable energy production and consumption;
ii. Improving the energy efficiency of public and private buildings;
iii. Sustainable mobility and smart services;
iv. Low-carbon economy;
v. Climate resilience and adaptation.

A financial plan for 400 million euros has been approved, which includes public funding as well as private investments.

The implementation of the SEAP has not brought about any organisational restructuring in the municipality, as a horizontal coordination working group was created within the internal coordination mechanism of the local Agenda 21, operating in a wider environmental sustainability perspective and led by the Department of environment and territory. In the same way, the consolidated network of local partnership that was established around the Agenda 21 process has been involved in the organisation of participatory process for the preparation and implementation of the SEAP, as well as in the procedure of its monitoring in 2013.

Therefore, dedicated working groups were established to coordinate activities on four levels:

i. All sectoral municipal offices dealing with energy performance;
ii. Enterprises managing local public services (waste, water, lighting);
iii. Other public bodies (hospitals, territorial agency for residential buildings) that may allow promotion and integration of the local energy strategy;
iv. Social and economic stakeholders involved in the Agenda 21 process, including universities.

In addition, the municipality of Padua has been extremely pro-active in obtaining EU funding for developing measures relevant for the implementation of its SEAP. A number of projects has been submitted and financed over the last decade, such as, for example, the project Padua FIT (2013–2017) financed by the EU Programme Intelligent Energy Europe, which has the objective of increasing energy efficiency of private residential buildings in the city. The major effort of the project is, therefore, to increase awareness, collective action and private investments into restructuring of buildings characterised by low levels of energy efficiency. In this project, the municipal administration has primarily played a mediating role between local communities and ESCOs, encouraging information about environmental and economic benefits of reconstruction, collaborative interaction within local communities, transparency and high quality technical expertise.

Between 2011 and 2013 the city of Padua participated in the project Covenant CapaCITY aimed at strengthening the capacity of local authorities to promote energy and climate action through planning and monitoring. The project was financed by the programme Intelligent Energy Europe and involved municipalities from fifteen European countries, for training, capacity building activities, interactive learning and exchange between municipalities, allowing them to develop or improve local SEAPs.

In 2014, the first full monitoring report was published by the municipality, providing a detailed overview of the main achievements and shortcomings of the plan, and carrying out a revision of the BEI as of 2013. It provided the direct positive impact of implemented policy measure on the quality of the city environment, in particular through the measures for smart mobility and services.

Although the municipality of Padova has not yet committed to the Mayors Adopt Initiative, it joined the project "EU Cities ADAPT", promoted by the DG Clima of the European Commission, which offers support to those cities that undertake the process of formulation and implementation of climate adaptation strategies, offering them the opportunity to get in touch and interact with other cities, following the same experience.

The scenario of participation in the CoM has been characterised by extensive strategic and cognitive usages, as a range of EU resources have been intensely used by the municipality. The fact that there were no direct financial instruments supporting the CoM were seen as clear weakness, although EU funding has been obtained for developing and upgrading the local SEAP. The possibility to interact with and learn from other municipalities (even Italian one) has been particularly appreciated, as no other coordination or learning tools were available at regional and national levels (Interview 6). The relevance of technical and methodological instruments acquired, thanks to the participation in the CoM, has been assessed as very high. Furthermore, besides being an effective tool for developing new policy instruments, improving energy efficiency and saving at the local level, SEAP has been considered a "valuable instrument for encouraging cultural transformations in the local community towards a major environmental sustainability" (Interview 7). Finally, the involvement of private actors has been considered to be fundamental for the SEAP's success, not only because of significant economic leverage that private investments may bring to its implementation but also for increasing the awareness about the economic potential and environmental risks, in particular in the industrial sector, which amounts to around 30% of total CO_2 emissions.

However, interviews also highlight the fact that despite the required inter-institutional coordination, the implementation of the SEAP actually remains mainly within the scope of activities of the energy department, and other offices often perceive it as additional and inappropriate workload (Interview 6, 7).

5.2 The implementation of the CoM in the UK

5.2.1 National strategy for sustainable energy and the EU Covenant of Mayors in the UK. A country overview

The UK has one of the longest records of sustainable energy policies in the EU. After having introduced its Climate Change Programme in 2000, the UK has promoted a wide range of policy instruments encouraging energy efficiency, emission reductions, renewable energy production (Bowen and Rydge, 2011), such as, among others, the Climate Change Levy (CCE, 2001); the Energy Efficiency Commitment (DEFRA, 2002); the Code for Sustainable Homes (DCLC 2007) and Community Energy Savings Programme (DECC 2009).

Along with long-standing commitment to the sustainable energy agenda, the UK has also been characterised by a very intense experience of city networking for climate change (Kern, 2010). The Nottingham Declaration – aiming to enhance local voluntary commitment to tackling climate change – was first launched in 2000 by a conference gathering around 200 representatives of local authorities, and was upgraded in 2005 at the Second National Councils' Climate Conference in Nottingham as a consequence of voluntary commitment of around 100 municipalities to the objectives reported in the document. The goal to achieve 200 signatories by December 2006 was successfully reached, while in 2017 the number of signatories was close to 300.

Since its origins, the Nottingham Declaration has enjoyed a high profile in local and central government where it has been seen as a successful initiative that played an important part in encouraging local government to take ownership of the task of reducing carbon emissions and tackling climate change. Moreover, the initiative has been supported by a wider partnership of various local and governmental bodies, as well as non-governmental agencies, including among others, the Improvement and Development Agency for Local Government (I&DeA) Local Government Association (LGA), Environment Agency, the Carbon Trust and the Energy Saving Trust (Gearty, 2007). Neither any specific measures or obligations have been introduced by the Declaration, not has any kind of monitoring or evaluation been established. Therefore, the commitment to develop a strategic plan for reducing carbon emissions could be easily disregarded by signatories, meaning that the impact of the initiative was potentially largely symbolic. Significantly, the Climate Change Bill was adopted in 2007 imposing legally binding targets for the reduction of CO_2 emissions by at least 50 per cent by 2050. Local authorities have been strongly affected by these national regulations as they steered local climate action by specific assessment indicators on emissions (Kern, 2010).

Against this background, it is somewhat surprising that UK local authorities have not shown much enthusiasm about the EU CoM that appears to share the spirit of the Nottingham Declaration, instead only adding a soft mechanism of mutual coordination, monitoring and accountability.

Hence, only 36 UK municipalities applied for the CoM membership, 34 submitted their SEAPs and only 18 SEAPs were approved by the COMO. As Figure 5.9 shows, despite such a low number of cities participating in the initiative, the CoM has been rather relevant in terms of population coverage (29%). The biggest cities in the UK have joined the programme, including London, Birmingham, Manchester, Cornwall, Glasgow, etc., shortly after the launch of the initiative in 2008 and 2009, though only a few other local authorities followed them in the subsequent years (Figure 5.9).

As for geographic distribution, the biggest share of local SEAP come from England, four from Scotland (Aberdeen, Edinburgh, Dumfries, Glasgow), one from Wales (Cardiff) and none from Northern Ireland. Besides, only eighteen of the submitted plans have been approved by the EU Commission as of January 2017, while the remaining fourteen are still in pending status. Two municipalities – Greater Manchester and Stirling – have not yet submitted their plans.

As Figure 5.10 shows, the ambition of UK local strategies' targets in terms of emission reduction has been much higher compared to their Italian counterparts. Fifteen of them have established a target between 21% and 30%, while eleven cities targeted more than 30% reduction. Five cities, including Birmingham, Edinburgh, Glasgow, Leicester and Newcastle have also joined the Mayor Adapt Initiative, committing to the adaptation objective and increasing the mandatory levels of CO_2 reduction to 30% (Figure 5.10).

The level of ownership of and commitment to the programme has also been confirmed by a rather a smooth and quick progress of those who applied for the initiative: 23 of them submitted their SEAPs within one year, nine of them took around two years, and it took between four and six years for the remaining four local authorities. However, as already mentioned with regard to the Italian case, it seems feasible to suggest that the speedy submission of SEAPs might have been possible due to the fact that most UK local authorities participating in the CoM had already developed their sustainable energy plans before joining the CoM. Notably, the framework of commitments agreed by the Nottingham Declaration has been quite close to the CoM pattern. Consequently, little efforts were required to adopt local strategies developed for the former initiative, to the requirements of the latter.

By the same token, as Figure 5.11 illustrates, the share of municipalities that started or completed the monitoring procedure has been rather high: half of those who had their SEAP approved performed monitoring (9) and six of them completed a full monitoring report by carrying out a comprehensive review of their strategy, including the BEI. As interviews conducted for this research explain, the CoM monitoring procedure has been welcomed by UK local authorities and it

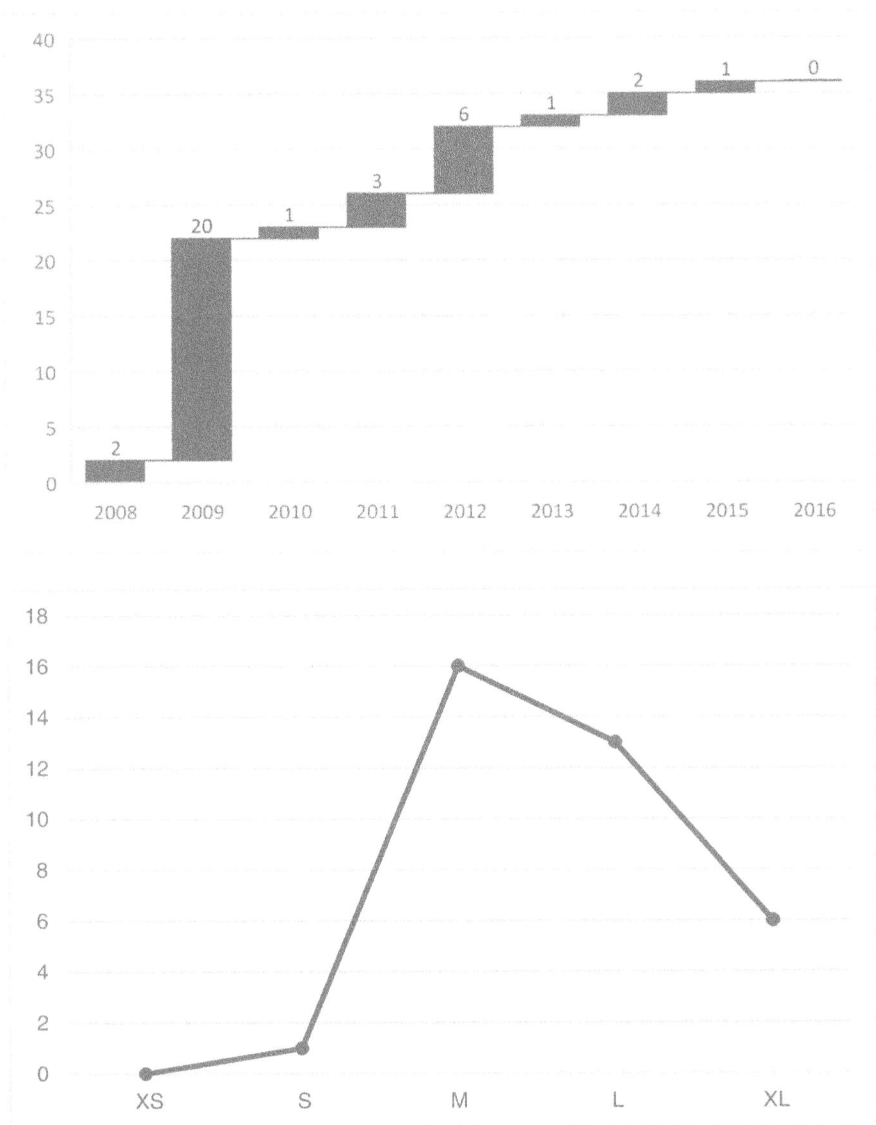

Figure 5.9 Membership of UK local authorities in the Covenant of Mayors by year of adhesion and size

Source: Author's elaboration on the data available from the website of CoM: www.covenantofmayors.eu/index_en.html as of June 2017

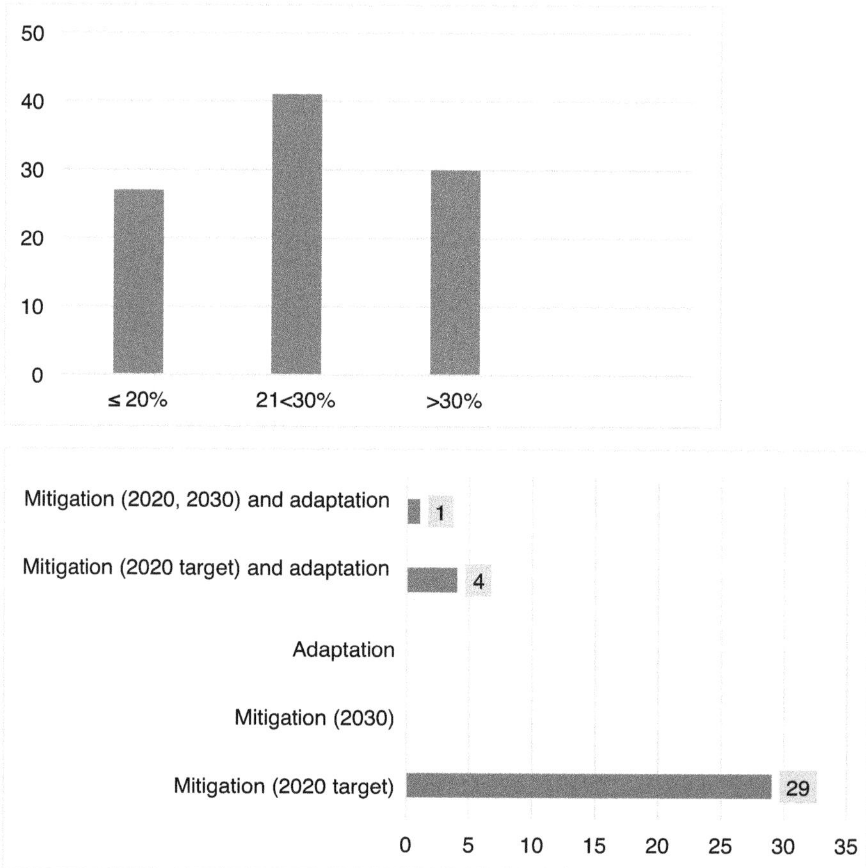

Figure 5.10 Commitment to CoM's objectives and emission reduction targets by UK signatories

Source: Author's elaboration on the data available from the CoM's website www.covenantofmayors.eu/index_en.html as of June 2017

should have been strengthened in order to make binding the monitoring responsibility. However, in contrast to Italy, the learning effect of this CoM activity has been considered limited and indeed, a risk of additional and useless workload has been mentioned, as mandatory monitoring obligations were introduced at the national level long before (Interviews 10, 12, 13). Likewise, UK municipalities have been actively involved in benchmarking by sharing 24 benchmarks for only 18 operating SEAPs (Figure 5.11).

Therefore, the legitimating scenario of usage appears to have prevailed in the country, as most of the UK signatories joined the network at the earliest stage, building upon their existing strategies for sustainable urban development.

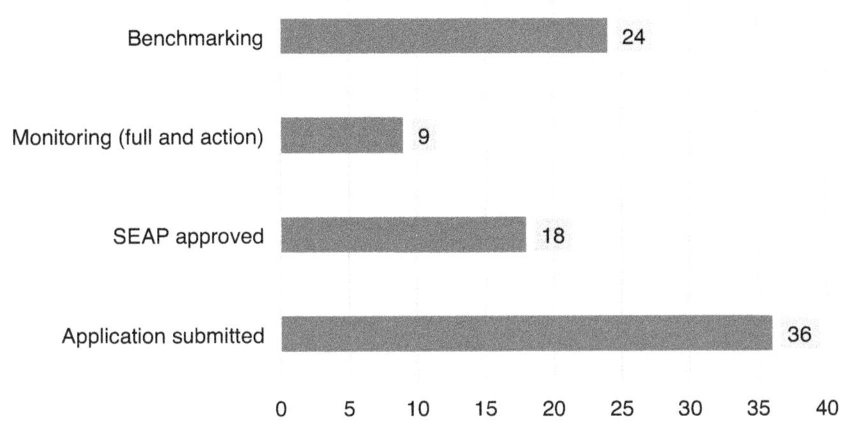

Figure 5.11 Progress of SEAPs implementation in the UK

Source: Author's elaboration on the data available from the website of the CoM: website www.covenantofmayors.eu/index_en.html as of June 2017

Interviews suggest that the double-fold objective to increase cities' international visibility and promote their image as a reliable partner in the field of sustainable energy policies at the EU level has been one of the main reasons of joining the initiative (Interviews 10–13). At the same time, the interviewees have expressed their opinions, according to which, a very low general interest towards the initiative was mainly due to the substantial overlap of the CoM with the domestic policy agenda and local initiatives set up by the Nottingham Declaration. UK local authorities saw little added value in developing the CoM activities as, among others, this entailed little more than symbolic action that nonetheless required additional workload, costs and staff. Furthermore, it has been emphasised that among the main obstacles to the diffusion of the CoM in the UK was in the name of the programme, as in most UK cities the position of mayor is a ceremonial one with no real decision-making power. So the title of the initiative itself did not evoke much enthusiasm on the part of local governments from the start. Moreover, a further explanation of the low relevance of the cognitive dimension in the case of the UK might lie in the fact that during the last decade the national government took a number of successful steps to promote adaptation and develop the capacity of local authorities, along with other public and private sector organisations, to use climate science for adaptation planning and decision-making (Porter *et al.*, 2014).

However, the evidence of strategic usage of the CoM has been collected too. This took into account, in particular but not exclusively, local authorities with elected mayors, such as Greater Manchester or Bristol, which have deployed the programme to increase their international networks aiming at obtaining EU funding (e.g. the ELENA facility, and Horizon 2020) or for developing strategic cooperation with other cities at the EU level in wider urban development agendas.

Interestingly, since the subsequent downgrading of UK renewable energy policies, the CoM is also perceived as a tool that helps keeping low-carbon issues high on local political agendas (Interviews 9,12). Moreover, experts warn that most of the 43% reduction compared to the 1990 baseline has been mainly due to the excellent progress in reducing emissions from electricity generation, while reductions in other sectors have stalled and the UK has no policies in place to meet more than half of the carbon emission cuts required by law by 2030 (CCC, 2018). In this context, the perspective of Brexit triggers concerns among local authorities, as some EU-linked climate policies and financing targeting sectors in which the level of pollution has continued to grow, such as transport or buildings, will expire. It has been stated that effective new strategies and policies are urgently needed to ensure emissions continue to fall in line with the previously agreed commitments (Interviews 12, 13).

The following in-depth analysis of two local strategies provides some more insights about the modes of usage, success and failures of the CoM in the UK.

5.2.2 The case of Glasgow

The Glasgow City Council was among the first UK cities to apply for the CoM membership in 2009 and it submitted its SEAP in 2011. Glasgow is Scotland's largest city with a population of around 580,000 – with the wider urban conurbation having a population of 1.2 million.

Over the last decades, the city has been implementing a large-scale strategy of transformation of its economy, including the regeneration of former industrial and port areas within the framework of the Scottish government's carbon emission targets, which has recently established the objective of achieving 42% reduction by 2020 (against a 1990 baseline) and 80% by 2050.

The original local SEAP set a target of 20% for the reduction of CO_2 emissions by 2020 across the city, which was subsequently increased to 30%, outlining a long-term low-carbon strategy. Within the framework of this strategy, the City Council itself has set a target of reducing CO_2 emissions from its own activities by 30% by 2020 as a contribution to a 40% reduction for the city as a whole. The overall ambition has been to make Glasgow one of Europe's most sustainable cities and in 2015 the City signed the Mayors Adopt initiative and appropriately upgraded its local strategy.

The original local SEAP was deeply embedded in national (UK Climate Act, 2008) and, in particular, Scottish (Scottish Climate Act, 2009) sustainable energy policy agenda and identifies more than 30 interconnected actions for energy demand reduction, efficiency and renewable energy covering buildings; transport; local electricity production; local district heating; land use planning and working with citizens and stakeholders in order to involve business and create a supportive public policy environment. It provided a comprehensive integrated strategy covering energy systems, energy management, waste, transportation, and behavioural change, within which a strong connection between environmental, economic and social dimensions were clearly discernable. The SEAP was part of a wider strategy, intended to "deliver major investment; create long-term jobs; help tackle fuel poverty; support the development of new clean energy sector in the city; create new revenue streams for the public sector and communities; improve air quality; and help regenerate communities. We will help transform Glasgow's image – making it a better place to live, work, and invest" (Glasgow City Council, 2010: 28).

The City of Glasgow has also delivered a full monitoring report and the SEAP has been substantially revised between 2012 and 2014, based on the activities conducted within the framework of the Step-Up project funded under the EU Seventh Framework Programme. This project aimed at enhancing local SEAP capacity to tackle all three Europe 2020 "20% targets" (reduction of emissions, energy efficiency and renewable energy production) through creating a coherent and easy-to-use model for energy planning, with learning drawn from the partner cities' existing experience of integrated energy planning, disseminating and replicating this approach through a learning network, to other ambitious cities across Europe. The contribution of the project to the revision of the SEAP has been fundamental: "We have been able to enhance our SEAP to the point where it has become a much more focused and less aspirational document" (Interview 8).

As a result, an enhanced SEAP – Glasgow's Energy and Carbon Masterplan (ECMP) 2014–2020 has been drawn, providing a holistic and coordinated strategy for actions and projects across the city to meet the target of reducing Glasgow's carbon dioxide emissions by 30% by 2020 from 2006 levels (Glasgow City Council, 2015). The new plan builds on a range of local strategic documents and initiatives, including among others, the council's Strategic Plan 2012–2017, the Local Development Plan, Glasgow Resilience Strategy and the Sustainable Glasgow Initiative, and aims to improve energy savings, increase energy efficiency, promote renewables and reduce emissions, while at the same time reducing fuel poverty, delivering jobs, regenerating communities, and building a more energy-secure city. Actions mainly focus on municipal and non-municipal buildings (residential and tertiary), public lighting, transport and industry, with particular attention to smart grid connections.

As for organisational structure, a newly formed City Energy and Carbon team and the existing Carbon Management team focusing on the Council's own activities has been in charge of supporting the delivery of the ECMP. Some of the staff have been working on city-wide carbon reduction from the EU funded STEP-UP project and some on the Council's carbon management programme. In the earlier period, specific functions were added to the tasks of the existing energy or environmental officers. An increasingly collaborative and cooperative approach across these work areas within the context of the Sustainable Glasgow Initiative is expected to allow ensuring that the legacy of the implemented projects is carried forward.

Finally, two surveys implemented during the preparation of the plan to collect citizens' (500) and stakeholders' (125) have shown wide public support for the energy and sustainability agenda. Given a limited involvement of the local communities in the previous SEAP, a number of measures have been designed by ECMP with the purpose of engaging community support through delivering direct benefits and involvement to communities, including the creation of a fund to facilitate local smaller scale community based renewable energy projects; training and jobs linked to projects; giving communities direct involvement in local projects; improving the local environment as an integral part of implementing projects (Glasgow City Council, 2015).

As far as financing is concerned, a number of public and private sources of funding has been identified, including in particular EU funding through the Scottish ERDF programme, as well as financing obtained through participation in competitive bids under EU direct thematic programmes, such as ELENA (European Local Energy Assistance Fund), LIFE and Horizon 2020. No surprise that the prospect of Brexit triggers concerns in the local administration about the possibility of continuing to rely on additional funding available from the EU, which has been extremely helpful for developing of a series of fundamental aspect of the local low-carbon strategy. A high strategic value of participation in EU programmes based on transnational partnership has also been highlighted, as they offer an exceptional opportunity to exchange knowledge and borrow experience from others (Interview 8).

Moreover, the renewed SEAP activities have been firmly embedded in the mechanism of horizontal coordination for low-carbon agenda between cities established by the Scottish Cities Alliance. The Alliance was created in 2011 with the objective to enhance economic development and boost capital investments for the flagship project "Scotland's 8th City – The Smart City", securing £10 million of European funding from the Scottish ERDF operational programme. Low-carbon and sustainable energy have been among the core priorities of the Alliance, including in particular energy efficiency retrofit, low-carbon heat, urban renewables, integrated energy systems and the circular economy.

As interviews (9, 10) highlight, although the ex-ante coordination between these different instruments is not always guaranteed and can be further improved, there has been a clear political guidance towards converging objectives at the local level, in which environmental sustainability is somewhat taken for granted as an established horizontal priority, being ensured by a long-term application of environmental impact assessments (EIA and SEA). A stronger emphasis on the social dimensions of sustainability has recently emerged, while the economic priorities are deeply embedded in the low-carbon agenda (Interview 9). Local investment instruments, such as Glasgow City Deal established in 2014 with the objective of funding innovation, business growth and employment at the local level, are also coordinated with the above priorities.

> Hence, although the CoM has been viewed as a useful reference point at EU scale for the city sustainable energy strategy, it has been mainly used to legitimise the already existing policy objectives and strategies, with lots of actions undertaken outside the CoM.
>
> (Interview 8)

As interviews highlight, the CoM framework has not been directly relevant for innovation and learning, as most of its instruments including data collection, monitoring, etc., had already been developed before within the framework of the UK and Scottish policy initiatives without involving any kind of external expertise, except for collaborative initiative with the University of Strathclyde. The motivation to participate in the CoM has been mainly related to the opportunity of acquiring a greater international visibility and the possibility of taking part in specific projects funded by the EU (Step-UP, etc.), which can contribute in bringing valuable improvements in the local low-carbon strategy and its instruments, including a well-structured investment scheme. In this sense, participation in the CoM has been strategic.

> The city links are becoming significant for us, more and more important that we reach out to other European cities, even if our nation is no longer member of the European Union . . . Glasgow wants to continue to be an international city for Europe and further still, we want also to be able to benefit from the discussion with our peer cities, many of which are also competitive cities, so it comes to global investment decisions. The CoM allows us to keep ourselves up there.
>
> (Interview 8)

The Scottish strategy for sustainable development and low-carbon function is considered to be a fundamental reference point, ensuring also the continuity and a long-term framework of objectives and targets for local authorities

> unlike the pattern in England, where sudden changes in government or sudden changes in the cabinet, ministers within the same government, can significantly disrupt the planning for low carbon, renewable energy agendas. That seems in Scotland not to be the case, we have a high degree of continuity, which is a strength of our government [. . .] there strong political contents.
>
> (Interview 8).

Thus, a mix of legitimising and strategic usage has characterised the implementation of the CoM in the case of Glasgow, based on a solid political commitment and considerable technical-administrative capacity that have ensured a strong ownership and a strategic use of additional resources for enhancing the local action for climate change.

5.2.3 The case of Poole

Borough of Poole applied for the CoM membership in 2012 and its SEAP was submitted and approved by the COMO soon after, in 2013. It is a relatively small town with around 158.835 inhabitants located in Dorset County on the South West Coast of England.

Its participation in the CoM builds on a long-term commitment to climate change agenda and its SEAP has originally established the 30% reduction target. In fact, the local council signed the Nottingham Declaration on Climate Change back in 2006, committing to significantly reduce carbon emissions. As an interview explains (Interview 11),

> one result of this commitment was the decision to take part in the Carbon Trust's Local Authority Carbon Management Programme. Participating in the programme ensured that the council took planned and practical steps to reduce its own impact on our changing climate. When the decision to join the CoM was taken, the town was coming to the end of our Carbon Management Plan, which was run from 2009 to 2013.

In that time, the local area was demanding the Council to reduce emissions and the opportunity of the CoM was taken to update the strategy. The current local SEAP grounds on a range of local plans, including the Local Transport Plan, Waste Management Strategy, Poole Sustainable Community Strategy and other strategic documents regarding the larger area made of Bournemouth, Dorset and Poole, concerning public health, well-being and energy efficiency (Borough of Poole, 2013: 6).

Thus, building on the emissions data collected within the framework of the National Indicator (NI), 186 data published by the Department for Energy and Climate Change, a new local model has been developed according to the CoM criteria, being guided by the idea that "low carbon is moving from being a cost centre to a net revenue generator" (Borough of Poole, 2013: 5), which employs not only public funding, but also attracts considerable private sector investment through standardised finance and delivery models.

At the same time, it has been emphasised that although lots of initiatives, frameworks and funding programmes have been launched by the UK government, including the last UK government Low-Carbon Goal, they do not seem to have provided specific insights for developing local sustainable energy strategies, whereas "the CoM has given that leverage to fulfil the local demand" (Interview 11).

The ambitious target of 30% has been set up by the SEAP 2014–2020, taking into account that they already implemented projects that were expected to reduce emissions by 32% by 2020. Buildings, equipment, facilities, industry, as well as transport have been identified as the main areas of intervention.

A Management Board chaired by the Borough's Carbon Reduction Manager has been established for implementing the local SEAP 2014–2020, which consists of the portfolio holder, the chairs of the economy and environment overview and scrutiny committee, the chairs of the action groups, a strategic director, the head of transportation services, a Transition Town representative, a NHS representative and a faith groups representative.

Moreover, collaborative working with local businesses and community organisations has been at the core of the delivery mechanism of this strategy. Besides enhancing coordination among different officers within the municipality, the Poole Environment Partnership (PEP) has been developed in order to ensure its effective implementation (Borough of Poole, 2016). The PEP is a form of Private-Public-Partnership, aiming to create delivery structures and implement projects by drawing on the experience and resources of the private sector at the local level, as well as to build effective mechanisms for collaboration, partnerships and funding with other local areas across the conurbation.

The PEP has acted as a Programme Board with the responsibility for the overall supervision of the development and delivery of projects, and monitoring progress towards the established SEAP targets. It has been organised into four themed action groups identified in accordance with the main priorities of action of the SEAP: Business, Domestic, Transport and Public Sector. These groups meet two or three times a year in order to ensure the continuity of action. The main rationale behind the locally implemented projects has been to engage appropriately with local businesses and communities' demands enhancing thereby their capacity for pro-sustainability action. The core underlying pillar of the SEAP activities has been the municipal leadership developing in strong partnership with the business sector, research bodies and local community.

The CoM guidance was closely followed in order to enact this local partnership, helping to bring local actors closer together:

> the very fact that I'm speaking to environmental groups about local problems [. .], we've got businesses that are interested in transport, working with the transport offices, businesses that are looking for a growth in the low carbon, they have to talk to myself on the economic development.
>
> (Interview 11)

As far as monitoring is concerned, Poole has not completed the procedure yet, although assessment of all implemented measures has been regularly performed, tracking the progress achieved against targets and considering costs. The monitoring mechanism of the CoM is perceived to be an important instrument for tracing the progress, but the local authority has stated that major resources would be needed to implement it properly (Interview 11).

Therefore, a certain learning effect can be observed in the case of Poole, taking also in consideration its participation in the benchmarking mechanism and some CoM events. Among the three benchmarks indicated by the town, one has been considered particularly relevant – Green PEA. It is a free business accreditation scheme for Green Positive Environmental Actions, which was promoted by a business action group with the objective of providing free energy efficiency and cost saving advice to businesses. The programme currently involves 75 business members across the Poole and Christchurch & East Dorset conurbation and has won a number of national awards (Borough of Poole, 2016).

Furthermore, the experience of participating in a Horizon 2020 bid has also been considered a very useful experience, as it taught how to build low-carbon clusters across Europe, instead of focusing action across the nation or at the local level only. In regard to this, Brexit is viewed as a serious concern, as it will cut not only funding but also the possibility to develop facilitated cooperation projects.

Overall, the participation in the CoM has been assessed as extremely beneficial for strengthening local collaborative networks and partnerships between the local Council and businesses within the framework of the local strategy for renewable energy. It has been also useful for engaging, informing and making citizens aware, and also understanding "exactly what the feeling out there is for renewable energies and what is the most appropriate technology for improving". The achievements of project activities have also been largely appreciated: "If you look at the achievement report, you will see it's far a wide scope of projects that have been undertaken, and it enlarged the range of funding opportunities available that came up and which we successfully completed" (Interview 11).

Moreover, the participation in the CoM paved the way to the membership in the Compact of Mayors, which is seen as strategic in view of a merge of Poole, Bournemouth and Christchurch, as decided by local councils. Both political commitment and administrative leadership have been mentioned among the most relevant factors of joining and successful participation in the CoM. In the case of Poole, in fact, there has been a strong prioritisation of the initiative on the part of the city energy manager along with significant political commitment:

> If we want the Carbon message to be heard at the right table, we need an ambassador. . . . You need initially to get the support to get the leader and the Mayor to start off. So you need to be a strong applicant for that. It is equally important, it makes an incredible difference when you're holding an event and you are able to say on the agenda that the event will open crowd or there will be some awards presentations by the Mayor or by the senior politician. It just gets people love this and it's raising the status of the event. So probably it's equally important, both before and after.
>
> (Interview 11)

At the same time, the lack of resources and especially of dedicated administrative staff allowing the administration to deal with properly with such a complex agenda has been mentioned among the main obstacles to the successful implementation of the CoM.

An important symbolic meaning has been attached to the CoM too, as it has been perceived as a very important tool for increasing the visibility of local authorities' contribution to climate policies. The programme has also been considered essential for raising awareness about strategic opportunities of networking for learning and fund raising for sustainable energy policies, institutionally and individually speaking:

> the implementation of the local plan has harnessed the local partnership [. . . .] for me personally, when working with European colleagues, I've become more and more aware of the network of opportunities, funding, etc. that's available. When I first started this programme, I was working on the office, trying to work out the Council energy bills
>
> (Interview 11).

Interestingly, a trip to Brussels for attending CoM meetings appeared much more problematic in the eyes of the Poole administration to justify than investing resources in fulfilling obligations deriving from participation in the CoM. Overall, the participation in the CoM have been perceived as an important opportunity to enhance the achievement of municipality's objectives in the field of sustainable energy.

To sum up, the findings of this chapter bring the evidence of very mixed patterns of usage of the CoM by local authorities. While elements of strategic usage have been traced in all four cases, the ideational dimension has been more relevant in some cases compared to others or with regard to some specific CoM's activities. For example, the so-called instrumental learning on how to redesign instruments for carrying out the policy has focused in some cases on methodological instruments, like the design of SEAP itself, while in others, as in the case of networking, has been fully deployed and strongly appreciated by all local authorities. In the same way, the degree of commitment and ownership does not seem to be determined by the context conditions but rather appear to be depending on the level of motivation: in fact, political and administrative leadership has been mentioned by all local authorities among the main factors determining the decision to join and successfully perform in the CoM. The availability of similar previous strategies has proved helpful for a smoother adaptation to the CoM, without, however, leading automatically to the legitimising usage, as the case of Glasgow has shown: the city has systematically invested in the revision of its strategy regardless of the fact that an already solid plan of action existed at the local level with the adoption of its first SEAP. There are at least two relevant questions to be addressed by further research: why did so many cities decide not to join and why many of those that join use this programme in a merely symbolic manner, that is, without implementing monitoring or participation in benchmarking, etc.

References

Bagnasco, A. (1977). *Tre Italie. La probematica dello sviluppo italiano*. Bologna: Il Mulino.

Beatly, T. (2000). *Green Urbanism: Learning from European Cities*. Canada: Island Press.

Borough of Poole (2013). Environment Partnership Sustainable Energy Action Plan 2014–2020. Available at: http://mycovenant.eumayors.eu/docs/seap/4874_1389275887.pdf.

Borough of Poole (2016). Carbon Reduction Achievement Report 'How the Council Saved Money from 2009 to 2016 (*Oh and managed to save the planet too . . .*). Master Report. Borough of Poole.Bowen, A. and Rydge, J. (2011). Climate Change Policies in the United Kingdom. Centre for Climate Change Economics and Policy. Grantham Research Institute on Climate Change and the Environment Economics Department Working Papers, No. 886. Available at: www.lse.ac.uk/GranthamInstitute/wp-content/uploads/2014/03/PP_climate-change-policy-uk.pdf.

Committee on Climate Change (CCC) (2018). Reducing UK emissions: 2018 Progress Report to Parliament. Available at: www.theccc.org.uk/publication/reducing-uk-emissions-2018-progress-report-to-parliament/.

Comune di Bologna (2012). Il piano di azione per l'energia sostenibile. Available at: www.comune.bologna.it/media/files/paes_12maggio2012_approvato_1.pdf.

Comune di Bologna (2015). PIANO D'AZIONE PER L'ENERGIA SOSTENIBILE Monitoraggio PAES: aggiornamento dell'inventario delle emissioni. Available at: www.comune.bologna.it/media/files/monitoraggio_inventari_paes__2013.pdf.

Department for Business, Innovations and Skills (2015). *Mapping local comparative advantage in the UK*. Available at: www.gov.uk/government/uploads/system/uploads/

attachment_data/file/546999/bis-15-344-mapping-local-comparative-advantages-in-innovation-framework-and-indicators.pdf.

The Commissioners of Customs and Excise (CCE) (2001). The *Climate Change Levy Regulations*. Available at: http://www.legislation.gov.uk/uksi/2001/838/made

Department Communities and Local Government (DCLD) (2007). *The code for sustainable homes. A step-change in sustainable home building practice*. Reviewed in 2010. Available at: https://www.gov.uk/government/publications/code-for-sustainable-homes-technical-guidance.

Department for Environment, Food and Rural Affairs February (DEFRA) (2002). *Energy efficiency commitment*. Available at: https://www.ofgem.gov.uk/ofgem-publications/58749/9520-eecjan05-pdf.

Department of Energy and Climate Change (DECC) (2009). *Community energy savings programme (CESP)*. Available at: http://webarchive.nationalarchives.gov.uk/20111205110845/https://www.decc.gov.uk/en/content/cms/funding/funding_ops/cesp/cesp.aspx.

Diamanti, I. (2009). *Mappe dall'Italia politica. Bianco, rosso, verde, azzurro . . . e tricolore*. Bologna: Il Mulino.

Gearty, M. (2007). The Nottingham Declaration Symbols, Strategy and Confidence. A Learning history. Issue VWS – Workshop Nr. 2 in a series of learning histories on the subject of "Innovation for Carbon Reduction" in or connected with Local Authorities. Available at: http://people.bath.ac.uk/mnspwr/doc_theses_links/pdf/dt_mg_APPDXGNott_case_issue_vws_A5.pdf.

Glasgow City Council (2010). *Strategic plan 2012 to 2017*. Available at: www.glasgow.gov.uk/CHttpHandler.ashx?id=14572&p=0.

Glasgow City Council (2015). *Energy and Carbon Masterplan*. Available at: https://www.stepupsmartcities.eu/ToolsandInspiration/EnergyPlanning/SEAPEnhancement/GlasgowEnhancedSEAP/tabid/4205/Default.aspx.

Kern, K. (2010). Climate governance in the EU multi-level system: The role of cities, Paper prepared for presentation at the Fifth Pan-European Conference of EU Politics, University Fernando Pessoa and Faculty of Economics of Porto University, Porto (Portugal), http://www.jhubc.it/ecpr-porto/virtualpaperroom/147.pdf.

Lumicisi, A. (2013). *Le città come protagonisti della green economy*. Milano: Edizioni Ambiente.

Ministero dello Sviluppo Economico (MSE), Ministero dell'Ambiente, della tutela del territorio e del mare (MATTM) (2017). *Strategia Energetica Nazionale*. Available at: www.sviluppoeconomico.gov.it/images/stories/documenti/testo_della_StrategiaEnergeticaNazionale_2017.pdf.

The New Nottingham Declaration on Climate Change. Available at: www.local.gov.uk [Accessed 19 February 2018].

Padua City Council (2010). Piano di Azione per l'Energia Sostenibile del Comune di Padova. Available at: www.padovanet.it/sites/default/files/attachment/C_1_Allegati_15960_Allegato.pdf.

Porter, J.J., Demeritt, D. and Dessai, S. (2014). The right stuff? Informing adaptation to climate change in British local government. Paper No 76, Sustainability Research Institute, University of Leeds.

Putnam, R.D., Leonardi, R. and Nanetti, Y. (1993). *Making Democracy Work: Civic Traditions in Modern Italy*. New Jersey: Princeton University Press.

Trigilia, C. (2012). *Non c'è Nord senza Sud. Perché la crescita dell'Italia si decide nel Mezzogiorno*. Bologna: Il Mulino.

6 Technological innovation for environment

The Eco-Innovation Programme

6.1 The case of Italy

6.1.1 Domestic context: eco-innovation policies and performance

Although a number of improvements have been observed over the last several years, Italy still appears to fall short of offering favourable conditions for eco-innovation compared to many other EU countries. According to the EU eco-innovation scoreboard, which maps countries' performance against a range of indicators capturing different dimensions of eco-innovation activities in terms of preconditions and outputs, Italy was ranked 7th in EU28 in 2016, performing below average in a number of dimensions, in particular in those concerning regulatory and financial support to enterprises. It has therefore been classified among the so-called "moderate innovators", preceded by a group of lead innovators and followers. However, the country has moved forward significantly, compared to the recent past, as it was at one of the lowest positions among the EU-15 member states between 2011 and 2014, staying below the EU average index for almost all indicators.

A few policy measures taken at the national level have been considered relevant for ensuring the already undertaken progress and future improvements. For example, a new programme for the development and consolidation of national technological clusters has been relaunched in 2016 with the purpose of updating the system of clusters approved in 2012, covering a wide range of areas relevant to eco-innovation and identified in coherence with the thematic objectives of the Horizon 2020 programme. The four new technological clusters (Made in Italy, Blue Growth, Energy and Cultural Heritage) are aligned with the National Research Programme 2015–2020 approved in 2016. Furthermore, specific programmes have been developed for expanding broadband infrastructure at the national level, promoting energy efficiency in SMEs, and encouraging innovative start-ups (D.L. 179/2012). Moreover, the National Plan for Industry 4.0 was launched in 2016, containing specific measures for enhancing technological improvement and digitalisation of production. A number of smaller action programmes, such as *EuroTransBio* for biotechnologies or *Breakthrough Energy Ventures* for green energy, have been promoted to support investments in green technologies and to enhance networking between companies. Importantly, a number of policy initiatives have been developed relying on the financial support and policy guidance of EU programmes including, in particular, Smart Specialisation Strategies (S3) implemented with the assistance of EU structural funding (National Operational Programme "Enterprises and Competitiveness") and projects financed by the so-called "Junker Plan". However, regardless of these improvements, the domestic context is still perceived by enterprises as rather problematic for investments in technological innovations in productive sector, mainly due to the lack of accessible risk financing, scarce human resources and persistent bureaucratic obstacles (Ambrosetti Club, 2017).

A closer look at the main components of the eco-innovation scoreboard at the time of implementation of the EU Eco-Innovation Programme provides a number of further helpful insights for understanding the interplay of factors determining the attitude of private companies to EU thematic programmes in this field.

Hence, between 2008 and 2009, when the first two calls for proposal for the Eco-Innovation Programme were launched, the Italian context showed rather a negative position in terms of eco-innovation inputs, including investments (financial resources, human resources, technical resources), public spending and regulatory aspects, such as the stringency of environmental legislation, which are intended to provide an initiative for eco-innovation activities in companies, research organisations, and other institutions. Italy scored 50 and thus, remained far below the EU average (100 points), performing worse than most EU-15 countries except for Greece and bypassed by Slovenia and Czech Republic from the group of CEE countries that joined the EU between 2004 and 2007.

Based on national statistics, the total number of R&D personnel and researchers accounted for roughly 1.24 % of the total labour force in 2006, below the EU average of 1.43%. As background information, it will be pertinent to note that a significant number of Italian researchers moved abroad, and a few measures that were meant to gather them back did not succeed (Eco-Innovation Observatory, 2010a). Furthermore, governmental allocations for R&D in environmental and energy sectors amounted to around 0.07% of the country's GDP in 2008 against the overall target of 3.5% established by the Lisbon Agenda. The Italian performance was particularly poor as regards the total value of green early stage investments, as Italy scored 11 against the EU average of 65. This could only partly be justified by the domestic industrial structure mainly composed of small and medium enterprises (SMEs) and family businesses, whose capacity of undertaking R&D projects was limited compared to big firms. A much more relevant barrier in this sense was a limited access to credit and a lack of flexible instrument for financial engineering (seed funding, risk-capital, etc.) in the domestic financial market. According to some data collected at the national level, in 2013, 39% of SME applications for financing were refused by at least three different banks (Fondazione per lo Sviluppo Sostenibile, 2017).

With regard to resource efficiency, the data provided by the Community Innovation Survey (Eurostat, 2009) shows a very modest performance with only 13% of firms that reduced material consumption per unit of output through innovations in 2000–2008 against the EU average of above 24% and 16.5% which reduced energy consumption – the EU average was above 27%. Moreover, productive activities suffered from a lack of organisational capacities within companies and financial public incentives supported a more sustainable production. The national waste legislation and its interpretation by regulators has been mentioned among additional constraint factors for effective reuse of secondary raw materials inside production processes (Eco-Innovation Observatory, 2010a).

Remarkably, despite such unfavourable conditions, the efforts of Italian public and private entities towards developing new or improved products and services, changing business models and other eco-innovation activities have increased over time and even exceeded the EU average. Over the last decade, the country has been characterised by a noticeable growth in eco-innovation and circular economy development, in particular in such sectors as textile, mineral oil, packaging, construction and waste, and its enterprises have significantly reduced material input per unit output (Eco-Innovation Observatory, 2014). Furthermore, Italy has shown one of the highest numbers of ISO 14001 registered organisations at the world level scoring much above the EU average. The number of Italian organisations that have obtained EMAS certificates has been significantly higher than EU average (1058 in 2014), as well as the number of enterprises that have joined the EU Ecolabel licences (331 out of 1000 licences awarded in the EU in 2010 went to Italian enterprises). The EMAS certification has also been extensively implemented by public administrations. It has been suggested that one of the possible reasons explaining such activism has been a widespread perception that EMAS certification would warrant more effective and leaner communication with environmental regulators, whereas environmental legislation has been normally perceived by companies, especially by SMEs, as one of the major constraints to business (Observatory of European SMEs, Flash Eurobarometer no.196).

However, the performance of the country in terms of eco-innovation outputs showing the extent to which knowledge outputs generated by businesses and researchers relate to eco-innovation, the number of eco-innovation patents and eco-innovation related publications has been significantly lower than the EU average: Italy scored 44 against 70 of EU average on the former indicator and 118 against 136 on the latter. At the same time, Italy has been in leading positions in terms of media coverage of eco-innovation related issues.

Although remaining below the EU average, Italy has progressively improved its performance in terms of socio-economic outcomes of eco-innovation activities by increasing the level of employment in and export of products from eco-industries. Finally, the performance of Italy in terms of environmental outcomes has been rather successful and obtained relatively high scores over the last three years (2013–2017) for material productivity (around 178 above the EU average (100)) and for energy productivity (137 above 100). It performed poorly as far as emissions intensity (69 against 100 EU average) and water productivity (80 against 100 EU average) are concerned. Based on 2010 data collected through ISTAT, more than 44.3% of companies have invested in reducing their environmental impact and improving the efficient use of natural resources.

In the context of a generally low priority given to research and innovation policies in the environmental field, no specific wide-scale policies or programmes were developed by Italy to promote eco-innovation before 2010. The first pilot National Programme on Environmental and Carbon Footprint was launched by the Ministry for the Environment, Land and Sea in 2011 with a three-fold objective: increase the competitiveness of Italian companies considering the relevance of "green" requisites of products in the market, rethinking the design and management of industrial production and distribution of products, and creating a new awareness for consumers to encourage increasingly responsible choices and good practices. The programme also aimed to enhance investments for sustainability among small and medium-size enterprises, as well as to test and promote different methodologies on the environmental impact assessment of production, distribution and consumption patterns. More specifically, by launching two calls for expression of interest between 2011 and 2013, the programme has offered specific expert support to companies that voluntarily committed to reduce their environmental footprint by increasing product life cycle and limiting carbon emissions and water use in the production of goods and services. The approach promoted by the programme covered the whole cycle, including the identification of appropriate technologies for the reduction of environmental footprint of productive processes and products, as well as the support to their market uptake and commercialisation.

The feasibility studies and the assistance covered by the programme had to be performed in close collaboration with the companies, in order to develop methodologies and evaluation systems of environmental performance, taking into account the differences of each economic sector, in order to harmonise and make them replicable on a wider scale. Around 200 companies joined the programme over the two years of its implementation, with carbon footprint analysis produced for more than 250 products (MATTM, 2013).

Besides, the National Revolving Fund for Green Jobs was established by the national "Growth Decree" D.L. 83/2012 (Art. 57) with the purpose of facilitating private and public investments in the green economy (innovative renewables, energy efficiency, eco-innovative processes, services and products etc.) but also in sectors related to the safety of the territory from hydrogeological and seismic risks. The first call was closed in May 2013 with 70 projects to be "co-financed" through loans with a subsidised interest rate of 0.5% for 6 years, mobilising 150 million of public and 100 million of private resources, as well as 200 long-term and 900 temporary jobs or jobs created from spin-offs (youth employment is a boundary requirement to receive the loans). SMEs represented 75% of the programme beneficiaries.

In sum, the attention to actions for eco-innovation has been rather low in the political agenda of the country, quite in line with a more general low prioritisation and ownership of sustainable development issues illustrated in Chapter 2. Although plentiful voluntary initiatives have been promoted by various actors, including regional governments, industrial districts, research institutes and private companies, the level of public investments and strategic guidance by the national governance has so far been extremely limited.

6.1.2 Innovative partnerships for eco-innovation in Italy

Surprisingly, against an unfavourable domestic condition, Italy has been among the main beneficiaries of the Eco-Innovation Programme, with the second highest number of project leaders and amount of financing obtained, after Spain. The total number of private and public bodies that took part in the programme was among the highest too.

Thus, over the whole duration of the programme (2008–2013) implemented through four annual calls of proposals, Italian partners participated in 75 of the total of 185 projects co-financed by the programme, performing as lead partners for 45 of them. Overall, 105 Italian entities were involved, of which 77 private companies, 14 public entities including universities and 14 semi-public bodies, such as water boards, water and water consortia, etc.

As Figure 6.1 below shows, the majority of projects led by Italian partners concentrated on recycling and green business sectors with 14 and 13 projects respectively, followed by food and drink (7), water (6) and building and constructions (5). The overall number of projects in which Italian partners took part followed almost the same trend with 22 projects for green business, 21 for recycling, 12 for food and drink and 8 for the water sector. The only exception was the building and constructions sector in which the number of projects led by Italian partners was particularly low (Figure 6.1).

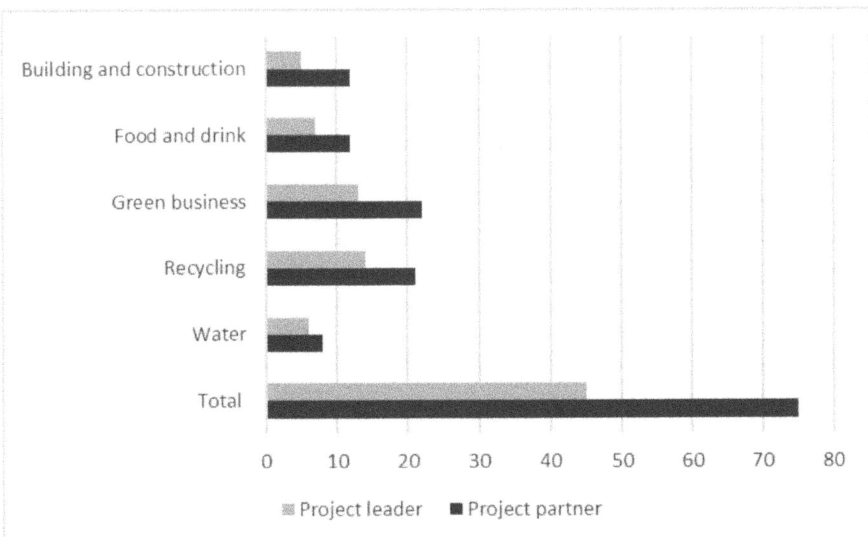

Figure 6.1 Italian coordinators and partners in eco-innovation projects by sector

Source: Author's elaboration on data from the eco-innovation database http://ec.europa.eu/environment/eco-innovation/index_en.htm

Table 6.1 Italian partners in eco-innovation projects by sector and typology

Sectors	*Private companies*	*Semi-public organisations*	*Public entities*	*Total*
Building and construction	10	4	0	**14**
Food and drink	18	1	3	**22**
Green business	26	5	5	**36**
Recycling	19	2	5	**26**
Water	5	1	1	**7**
	78	**13**	**14**	**105**

Source: Author's elaboration on data from the eco-innovation database http://ec.europa.eu/environment/eco-innovation/index_en.htm

As far as the composition of project partnerships promoted by Italian leaders is concerned, most of them were SME-research consortia (46%), followed by SMEs consortia (25%), large business (17%) and single SMEs 13%.

Overall, as Table 6.1. shows, the Italian partnership in eco-innovation projects have been quite mixed: private companies have constituted the majority but the participation of public and publicly owned entities (including universities) accounted for almost 30% of project participants coming from Italy. It is also worth pointing out that a relatively high number of projects included more than one Italian partner.

The potential of such partnerships for achieving the objective of enhanced learning, innovation and the market uptake of innovations appeared to be rather high, as beyond private companies they have also involved a wide range of entities normally performing research and innovation activities, such as research centres and universities, as well as other bodies that could contribute to a wider diffusion of innovative products and technologies, including chambers of commerce, consortia or specific sectoral agencies.

According to the data collected on a sample of 15 projects led by Italian partners, which developed process innovation, seven of them introduced substantial modification to existing technologies, five developed incremental improvements and 1 introduced a radical innovation (for two project the data was missing). Five of these projects were developed by SME-academia consortia, 3 by SME consortia, two by large businesses and two by individual SMEs. More in general, according to the data collected by the programme, in the vast majority of the projects, the organisation applying for the grants was either the initial and primary developer of the innovation (57%) or one of the several initial developers of the innovation (18%) (EACI, 2013), meaning that for around 75% of the projects, the applying organisation was actively involved in the development of innovations and had already developed a certain background experience in it.

Not only does this indicator reflect the high interest and commitment to eco-innovation objectives required from applicant companies and public entities, but it also confirms the availability of appropriate knowledge and capacity needed for developing ambitious projects at the transnational level. Thus, high ownership of EU objectives has been an inherent criterion for being eligible for the financial support provided by the programme. By the way, such commitment could hardly be symbolic, as the average budget of financed projects was between €800.000 and €1.6 million. Beneficiaries could obtain up to 50% of the total eligible costs from the programme, meaning that the remaining funding should be covered by themselves or other private or public sources, or come from income generated through the project. It should also be noted that a large number of innovations further elaborated on by the programme beneficiaries, had been initially developed with the funding of other EU funding initiatives (EACI, 2013).

Interestingly, rather an uneven territorial distribution of project partners has been observed across the country. As Table 6.2 below shows, the highest number of participating enterprises came from northern and central regions with respectively 58 and 29 project partners. Three regions were clearly leading, showing both the highest number of lead and ordinary partners: Lombardy (10/19), Emilia-Romagna (10/17) and Tuscany (4/16). Among the southern regions, Campania

Table 6.2 Breakdown of project partners by macro-areas and regions in Italy

	Regions	*Lead partners*	*Project partners*
North	Friuli Venezia Giulia	0	2
	Liguria	0	4
	Lombardy	10	19
	Piedmont	1	8
	Trentino Alto Adige	0	2
	Veneto	4	6
Centre	Abruzzi	4	2
	Emilia-Romagna	10	17
	Lazio	1	6
	Marche	2	4
	Molise	1	0
	Tuscany	4	16
	Umbria	1	1
South	Basilicata	0	2
	Calabria	0	1
	Campania	2	8
	Apulia	5	5
	Sicily	0	2
	Total	**45**	**105**

Source: Author's elaboration on data from the Eco-innovation database http://ec.europa.eu/environment/eco-innovation/index_en.htm

had the highest overall number of project participants, while Apulia showed the highest number of lead partners.

To a certain extent, such uneven territorial distribution can be explained by differences in the peculiar characteristics of economic and productive territorial sub-systems, as well as by the availability of specific policy initiatives promoted at the regional level.

Hence, Lombardy has the highest overall number of project partners and the same number of lead partners as Emilia-Romagna. Besides having among the highest GDP pro-capita at the national and EU levels, this Region is home to many multinational companies and has developed a multitude of instruments for promoting innovative research and investments. Recently, Lombardy has passed a Strategic Three-Year Programme for research, innovation and technological transfer (Regional Law 29/2016), whose objective is to increase public investments in R&D. However, neither has the Region introduced specific measure for environmental R&D, nor any dedicated legislative provisions have been approved in this field, except for an ambitious waste strategy package passed in June 2014, which included a number of ambitious eco-innovation targets: waste production-related tariffs for at least 20% of municipalities by 2020; 80% separated collection of waste by 2020; material recovery of at least 65% and energy recovery of 80% by 2020.

In contrast, Emilia-Romagna has the second highest number of lead partners, but is only in the 11th place among Italian Regions in terms of advancement of policies and investments for R&D (IRPET, 2013). However, as already illustrated in Chapter 4, the Region has developed rather advanced and multifaceted policy agenda for sustainable development, covering a wide range of structural measures potentially enhancing eco-innovation, such as the creation of clusters, direct financing and consultancy for innovative SMEs. Moreover, Emilia-Romagna has been among the first regions to develop a Circular Economy Package bill even before the EU legislative package was published in 2015, and dealing specifically with the eco-innovation in its Smart Specialisation Strategy.

Tuscany comes close to Emilia-Romagna with 16 project partners, although the number of lead partners coming from this region is rather low (4). Being on the sixth position of the regional index of research and innovation activities, Tuscany has also approved an advanced Circular Economy Package, aiming to reduce the overall amount of waste and achieve 70% waste separated collection, material recovery of at least 60%, increase energy recovery from 13% to 20%, and reduce landfills to 10% of urban waste from the current 42%.

Overall, the typical North-Centre vs. South divide emerges in the country, witnessing a rather advanced position of the Northern Regions, including, along with those already mentioned, Friuli Venezia Giulia, Piedmont and Veneto. These regions have traditionally invested higher than the national average percentage of their GDP to research and development, and have shown higher numbers of R&D employment and technological patents. The strategies of the Central regions, with the clear exception of Tuscany, were much less forward looking, as their overall resources for R&D measures were much more limited, and only intentions for developing measures for circular economy were announced by the Marche Region and Lazio. Among the Southern Regions, a more successful performance of Apulia and Campania also appears to be embedded in a wider context of research and innovation investments and the increasing attention to the reduction of waste and resource efficiency. Importantly, the Campania Region has registered the highest rate of investments in R&I among the Southern Italian Regions, which increased by 11% between 2010 and 2015, and amounts to 34% of the total investments in five Southern Regions.

The majority of enterprises that have been reached by the survey (18) and interviews (3) conducted for this research have shown high awareness about the role of technological innovation for green economy and market competiveness, and stated their long-term commitment to this objective.

Interestingly, the close linkage between the reduction of environmental impacts (water usage and pollution, etc.) and improvements in the process of production or products has been highlighted by some interviewees (Interview 17,18, 19). This linkage has been traced by the conditions of the call for proposals, but it was naturally embedded into many projects. For example, the Project B-Wool (Olimpias srl – IT) aimed at developing a totally innovative water and chemical-free industrially applied technology for anti-shrinkage wool, as the chemical currently used in industrial processes to get anti-shrinkage wool entails a substantial wastewater discharge strongly impacting on the environment. An even stronger positive environmental impact has been ensured by the WASATEX project (led by Europrogetti – IT) that used an innovative combination of well-tested technologies in water treatment in order to reuse up to 90% of water treated with Wasatex technology, in any part of the industrial processes. The production plant in Osjek-Croatia of group Benetton Tekstil was chosen for testing the technology that allows a significant savings in water itself, in costs associated to its discharge and to incoming water in the textile industry, and being re-adaptable to other water intensive productions such as paper, tannery or the agro-food sector.

Overall, a high degree of awareness and commitment to research and innovation activities promoted by the Programme have been observed among the enterprises that participated in the survey.

The strategic scenario of usage appears to prevail among the Italian beneficiaries, as they were able to clearly identify the additional opportunities (in terms of knowledge, technological development and financing) offered by the Programme. Most respondents (17/18) have declared to have had a medium to long experience of investment in research and innovation projects before joining the Eco-Innovation Programme. These activities included a wide range of environmental aspects concerning both product and process, concerning in particular the reduction of energy consumption and limiting CO_2 emissions (11/18), reusing or recycling of byproducts (12/18) and resource efficiency (10/18). 12 out of 18 companies have obtained international certifications pertaining to the quality of products and/or production processes, and some of them hold environmental certifications (such as 14001), which are an integral part of the EU Eco-Management and Audit Scheme (EMAS). At the same time, they have established a permanent

R&D unit or hired dedicated staff (12/18), although the percentage of their investments in research and innovation activities varied substantially (from 1% to 40%).

In addition, a learning dimension has also emerged from the analysis. Almost all companies have mentioned the possibility of consolidating the existing research and innovation activities by acquiring new knowledge on technologies, materials and products as the main motivation of participation in the Eco-Innovation Programme, although other benefits, such as new partnerships, networking and starting new research and development activities have also been considered important incentives to join. The outcomes of participation have also been very positively assessed by companies in terms of both learning opportunities though acquiring new knowledge, as well as strategic networking opportunities and collaborations for new research and development activities.

The process of learning involved not only technologically innovative activities but also strategic learning. Almost all companies have relied on external consultancies or research partners during the preparation and development of project activities, not only for the research and development part, but also with regard to project management. It has been highlighted that the internal staff in most companies was not prepared for dealing with very complex procedures attached to EU funding, whilst at the same time, the research and development part of project activities would not have been possible without the contribution of specialised research institutes and universities, as normally such a high degree of innovation capacity and expert knowledge is not available within companies. As one of the interviewed companies has stressed:

> the process of preparation and implementation of the project has implied different steps of learning. First we had to understand which characteristics (technical and strategic) our project had to have in order to obtain financing, then we had to implement project activities, monitor and report about its progress to the European Commission, and finally disseminate results. This was a gradual step-by-step process which has brought us from the call of proposals to concrete outcomes.
>
> (Interview 19)

This appears to be a very relevant aspect, as according to the survey, seven out of eighteen companies have learnt about the Eco-Innovation Programme from universities or research centres, six from consultancies and only three of them have found this opportunity autonomously. As far as project development and management activities are concerned, only six out of fourteen companies have mainly relied on their internal staff, while others have involved external experts at some stage.

Lastly, interviews have emphasised that the Eco-Innovation Programme has been crucial for obtaining additional funding for research and development activities that would not have been possible otherwise, since no similar national or regional funding schemes were available, while the high innovation costs could hardly be covered by enterprises alone. Bureaucratic obstacles have been mentioned among the main difficulties characterising the participation in the Programme, while surprisingly, a limit on duration (up to 36 months) restricted financial support of the EU and a lack of specific institutional support have been seen as less relevant obstacles. Overall, despite complexities and technical difficulties with the managing of projects of participation in the Programme, its implementation mechanism has been positively assessed compared to the function of national financial instruments, in particular in terms of celerity of procedures and disbursement of financing (Interviews 17, 18, 19). However, interviewees have also highlighted the need for major flexibility and attention to SMEs, as they possess huge potential but lack resources for developing eco-innovation activities. Therefore, small and medium-sized companies are particularly vulnerable in front of such challenges and had major difficulties in participating in the Programme compared to bigger ones, as the criteria for both project activities and company characteristics were very specific.

In sum, it seems feasible to suggest that besides the diffusion of specific policy ideas and knowledge related to environmental sustainability and green economy, the Eco-Innovation Programme has increased the awareness of companies about strategic cooperation opportunities existing within the European market space, which can be employed for increasing their competitive and innovation potential combined with higher environmental responsibility. In fact, some of the interviewed companies have stressed the relevance of the Programme for enhancing ownership of eco-innovation objectives, which should become the driving force for industrial transformations in the direction of major environmental sustainability.

Importantly, thanks to the participation in the Programme, all except one company have developed partnerships for new projects going beyond the framework of the Eco-Innovation Programme activities, and some of them applied for other EU funding schemes soon after the conclusion of their project, thanks to the acquired knowledge about how to build an international partnership and search for financing beyond national borders (11/18). Overall, companies believe that their participation in the Programme has contributed to increasing their visibility, in particular among consumers and, to a lesser extent, in the business and research environment.

6.2 The case of the UK

6.2.1 Domestic context: eco-innovation policies and performance

The UK context has offered completely different conditions for the implementation of the Eco-Innovation Programme. It has been one of the leaders at the EU level in the promotion of eco-innovation, the circular economy and new business models with environmental benefits (Eco-Innovation Observatory, 2017), potentially offering quite favourable conditions for enterprises to develop advanced environmental technologies and collaborative networks for innovation. Moreover, multiple organisations fostering systemic eco-innovation and a more circular economy have been established over the last decades, ensuring the delivery of financial support, advice and networking opportunities to innovative SMEs and public bodies at the regional and at the national level. Such organisations as Waste and Resources Action Programme (WRAP), Innovate UK, the Knowledge Transfer Network (KTN) and the Catapult Centres have been the most relevant of them.

More in general, the UK has shown an increasing long-term pattern of investment in research and development (R&D) since the early 1990s, currently amounting to around 1.7% of GDP, which mainly comes from the private sector (ONS, 2016). In the same way, employment in R&D has remained relatively high and stable in recent years despite some decrease due to the recent period of recession. The UK has performed very well in accessing EU direct funds. The most recent update from the consolidated FP7 Programme database shows that the UK has received the second largest share of funding, €5.205 million, and equivalent to 15.2% of the total (HMG, 2014). On the other hand, business investment in R&D has remained broadly static in relation to the size of the overall economy for a number of years, with the total expenditure by businesses representing approximately 1.1% of GDP in 2012.

Besides the two main strategic frameworks "The UK Sustainable Development Strategy (2005)" and "Securing the Future – delivering UK Sustainable Development Strategy (2006)" that have already been mentioned in the previous chapters, other relevant policy packages for resource efficiency, sustainable consumption and production have been approved, such as the "UK ETAP Roadmap", the "Building a low carbon economy: unlocking innovation and skills strategy" (2008), the Low-Carbon Industrial Strategy, and the Low-Carbon Transition Plan (2009). Overall, the policies addressing eco-innovation in the UK have been characterised by a double-fold approach aiming at promoting innovative solutions for pollution control and a greater resource and energy efficiency in industries on the one hand, and encouraging systemic transformations in production and consumption patterns on the other.

Such a consistent upgrade had taken place during the first decade of the 21st century, while in the 1990s the UK was the second main polluter in EU, responsible for around 771.7 million tonnes CO_2 equivalent, and significant energy intensive industry and an energy generation sector dominated by oil and coal. In 2008, the UK had already surpassed its Kyoto target, reaching a 19% emission reduction (Eco-Innovation Observatory, 2010b).

Between 2013 and 2014 alone, GHG emissions decreased by 7.7% in the UK, reaching a record low at 557.3 million tonnes of CO_2e. This was partly due to the reduction of coal burnt to generate electricity, with a 13.6% decrease in emissions generated by the energy supply sector. Coal imports reached their lowest value in 2014 – since 2010 – with 40 million tonnes, a 15% decrease compared to 2013 (DUKES, 2015). However, coal still represents 38.5% of the residual fuel mix. The UK has a mandatory target of a 15% share of renewables in its final energy consumption by 2020 under the EU Renewable Energy Directive. By the end of 2014, the UK was halfway towards meeting this target with renewable energy accounting for 7% of its capped gross final energy consumption. The growing number of public-private initiatives related to eco-innovation and the circular economy, enabled by a supportive policy landscape, represents a fertile ground for the UK to strengthen its performance in this area (Eco-Innovation Observatory, 2015).

More specifically, a range of financial programmes and governance instruments have been launched between 2008 and 2012 in order to foster systemic eco-innovation and transition to circular economy through the delivery of financial support, advice and networking opportunities to innovative SMEs and public bodies at the regional and at the national level. The following sub-sectors have been tackled in particular in this perspective:

i. Remanufacturing and new business models;
ii. Waste management and recycling;
iii. Sustainable use of natural resources and critical materials;
iv. Low-carbon transport, focusing in particular on ultra-low emission vehicles;
v. Clean and carbon abatement technologies.

Measures implemented across the aforementioned policy areas have contributed to improving the UK modest performance registered by the EU Eco-innovation Index between 2010 and 2012, and brought it on the leading positions in the EU28, swinging between the fourth (leading) and eighth (average – eco-performer) place in subsequent years. The index offers some further insights for contextualising the dynamics of participation of the UK companies in the Eco-Innovation Programme.

Hence, in terms of eco-innovation inputs, the UK has traditionally had one of the lowest scores of governmental spending on environmental and energy research and development in the EU, being higher only than the public spending on these sectors by Malta, Cyprus and Croatia. No substantial increase has had place afterwards: in 2015 it was 0.03% of GDP compared to Finland that topped the ranking with 0.10% of GDP. In contrast, the quantity of human resources and in particular R&D personnel and researchers has traditionally been above EU average, as well as the overall value of green early stage investments, which scored 232 in 2010 and 281 in 2013, although slightly decreasing in subsequent years (Eurostat, 2009).

The UK has been foremost among EU leaders in terms of eco-innovation activities that refer to the index of innovation with environmental benefits, which was introduced by enterprises, being obtained within the enterprise or by the end user. Instead, the diffusion of environmental certifications has been rather slow and international schemes were much more popular than those promoted by the EU. In fact, in 2011 the index obtained for ISO 14001 certification (the number of certified organisations per million inhabitants) considerably increased (110 against the EU average of 100) compared to 2010 when it scored 14, measured based on EMAS certification. In the same way, at the time of the implementation of the Eco-Innovation Programme, the UK performed rather poorly in some environmental outputs. In 2010 it scored 70, staying below EU average of 100 in the number of eco-innovation related patents and being at the bottom of the list (score 17) for the media coverage of eco-innovation issues. However, a higher than average index (129) was registered for eco-innovation related publications. In the same way, although remaining below EU average, the UK has progressively improved its position in terms of socio-economic outcomes of eco-innovation activities, increasing its comprehensive score from 81 in 2010 to 97 in 2015. The UK was among EU leaders with regard to resource efficiency outcomes, showing constantly the best comprehensive rates (above 175) of material, water and waste productivity and one of the lowest levels of emissions between 2011 and 2015 (Eco-Innovation Observatory, 2015). Domestic statistical data shows that waste recycling has increased across the country, with the highest rates for England (41.2%) and Scotland (43.6%) in 2011, and the country had reached one of the leading positions in material productivity between 2015 and 2016.

The construction industry in the UK has been one of the most critical sectors from the point of view of environmental impact. It accounts for 8% of the Gross Domestic Product (GDP) and provides employment for around 3 million workers, but at the same time it is the largest consumer of natural resources using over 400 million tonnes of material per year and is responsible for the production of over 100 million tonnes of construction, demolition and excavation waste every year – one third of all waste in the UK. According to some recent data, almost 13 million tonnes of this waste was landfilled without any form of recovery or reuse (WRAP, 2010). This industry has undergone significant transformations in recent years, being triggered by the governmental Strategy for sustainable construction published in 2008, worked by the WRAP and the Building Research Establishment Ltd (BRE), which have provided guidance and tools for the construction industry to embrace eco-innovation and make a significant contribution to sustainability of this sector in the UK.

Furthermore, a number of tools have been developed by enterprises at national level in order to encourage the reduction of waste production in the country, for example, the BREEAM (Building Research Establishment Environmental Assessment Method) assessment tool developed by the BRE, which has become the world's foremost environmental assessment method and rating system for buildings (Eco-Innovation Observatory, 2011). A number of voluntary schemes and tools for improving the environmental sustainability in the construction sector has spread in the country, including Designing Out Waste toolkit, the NetWaste Tool and the implementation of Site Waste Management Plans etc., providing information on sustainable design and products with recycled content, and driving a market need for high-quality construction products with recycled content. Moreover, a Materials Security Special Interest Group (SIG) has been established within the Technology Strategy Board (TSB – a governmental agency), with the objective of facilitating the adoption of innovative new business models and the rapid formation of new supply chains capable of delivering high impact and innovative solutions to material security challenges across multiple networks and sectors, including the WRAP, Innovate UK (Innovation Agency), the Knowledge Transfer Network (KTN) and the Catapult Centres to mention just a few.

Since 2008, these organisations have strongly supported eco-innovation research in universities, research centres, collaboration between academics and the industry, fostering international collaborations and supporting the training and career development of researchers (Eco-Innovation Observatory, 2015).

Lastly, a national strategic document "Enabling the transition to a green economy: government and business working together" (2011) has been jointly developed and published by DEFRA, Business, Innovation and Skills (BIS) and Energy and Climate Change (DECC), in response to requests from the private sector for greater clarity on the policies being put in place to achieve "green economy". This document aimed to shape opportunities for economic growth, stability and competitiveness, while generating wealth, reducing emissions and other environmental impacts, establishing the following priorities:

i. Use natural resources efficiently: effective demand management and efficiency measures for energy and other resources will be used in our homes, offices and businesses across the economy. Inputs of materials for production processes should be optimised and the level of waste to landfill should decrease. New processes and products will be required, creating new market opportunities.
ii. Be more resilient: The UK will have a reduced reliance on fossil fuels whilst maintaining secure supplies of energy and other natural resources. The economy will be more resilient and prepared for the implications of climate change and environmental risks such as floods and heat waves.
iii. Exploit Comparative Advantages: UK businesses will be well placed to take advantage of the expanding markets for greener goods and services.

Moreover, the UK has defined a clear business case for resource efficiency, demonstrating to industry that there is both a contribution to cost savings and reduced risk for businesses as well as diminishing impacts on the environment. The Pro-Environmental Behaviours Framework has helped to develop complementary policy to help consumers make more sustainable lifestyle choices, including the demand for more sustainable goods from manufacturers. The UK government has promoted a number of organisations in order to deliver eco-innovation and increase the knowledge transfer of technology into UK based businesses, including, in particular, KTNs funded by the TSB covering such areas as environmental sustainability, chemistry innovation, materials and modern built environment, which proved to be successful. As already mentioned in the previous paragraphs, green public procurement has been an important area of intervention, with the UK commitment to an EU target for 50% of relevant tendering procedures across the public sector to be "green" with the Government Buying Standards designed to make it easier for government buyers to buy sustainably.

According to the evaluation reports published by the Eco-observatory, some clear signs of improvement in the field of eco-innovation were observed between 2010 and 2012, in both production and consumption. It has been emphasised, however, that although the awareness about eco-innovation was growing (among policies, businesses and population), it was not yet on a sufficient level and there was still a lack of clarity in the understanding of eco-innovation challenges: "Many industries and organisations still saw resource efficiency and the greening of the economy as a cost rather than as an opportunity" (Eco-Innovation Observatory, 2011).

In sum, although a number of barriers to eco-innovation still exist in the country, it is outstandingly strongly engaged in the policy agenda for green and circular economy models, strongly underpinned by the principles of sustainability.

6.2.2 Innovative partnerships for eco-innovation in the UK

Within such a favourable context, the implementation of the Eco-Innovation Programme has been rather successful in the country, although it has generated much lower participation compared to Italy.

While a relatively low number of beneficiaries from the UK has participated in the first two calls for proposals (2008–2009), the UK has successfully caught up at a later stage, becoming the fourth largest beneficiary of the Programme and obtaining a consistent amount of projects and financing. Overall, only 21 projects were led by UK beneficiaries, while the total number of UK based project partners amounted to 60, with 11.1 million of euros of the total financing were obtained from the EU (Figure 6.2).

As Figure 6.2 shows, UK enterprises have been particularly active in the sector of building and construction, followed respectively by green business, recycling and food and drink. In this way, eco-innovation projects have been mainly promoted in the sectors within which the need for major eco-innovation investments was identified at the national level, and a number of domestic financial and

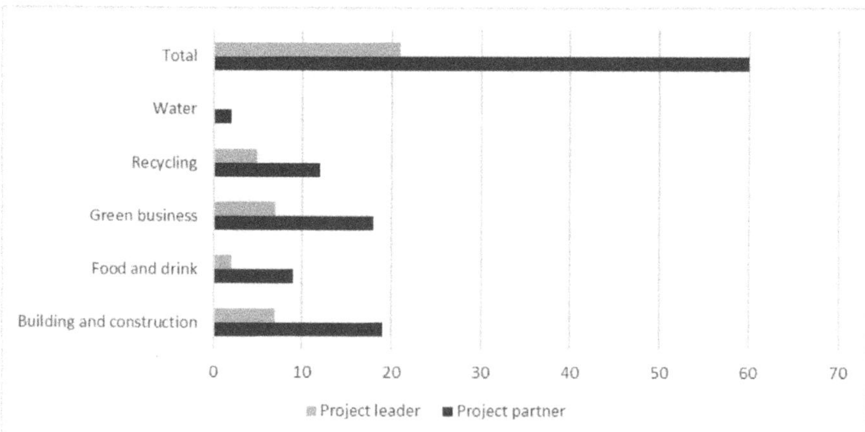

Figure 6.2 UK coordinators and partners in eco-innovation projects by sector

Source: Author's elaboration on data from the Eco-innovation database http://ec.europa.eu/environment/eco-innovation/index_en.htm

organisational initiatives were undertaken to support eco-innovation research and innovation activities, encourage the industrial uptake of technological innovations and enlarge international business opportunities.

The partnerships of projects with UK participants were mainly composed of SME consortia (60%), with less SME and academic consortia (30%) and a relatively high quota of large business (10%). In general, in contrast to Italy, private companies have largely prevailed in the composition of project partnerships (see Table 6.3).

The results of the survey show a mixed pattern of performance in and attitudes to certain aspects of the Programme, although the overall high ownership of the Programme's targets among all UK participants have been observed. All project partners reached by the survey have stated to have established a R&D unit or have hired dedicated staff (from two to five people), and invested a variable percentage of their profits (between 20% and 100%) into R&D activities. Most of them have developed research and innovation projects before participating in the Eco-Innovation Programme, investing in recyclability of products (4/10), resource efficiency and reducing utilisation of raw materials (4/10), reducing carbon emissions and energy consumption (2/10). Despite a medium to long experience (even more than ten years) in the field of eco-innovation projects by almost all respondents (9/10), none of the companies has ever obtained any kind of environmental certification. The figure of environmental manager was introduced only by three of them.

As for the motivation to participate in the Programme, the possibility to start up new activities for developing environmental technologies and knowledge has been recognised as its main trigger, along with obtaining additional resources for developing new technologies and knowledge, consolidating the innovation projects that have begun already and expanding international collaboration. Significantly, the respondents' expectations have been largely met, in particular with regard to the primarily important objective (obtaining additional resources for starting new innovation activities). In fact, the high relevance of innovative activities by UK led projects has been emphasised by the general Programme overview,

Table 6.3 UK partners in eco-innovation projects by sector and typology

Sectors	*Private companies*	*Semi-public organisations*	*Public entities*	*Total*
Buildings & constructions	9	0	1	10
Food and drink	9	0	0	9
Greening business	20	0	2	22
Recycling	13	0	1	14
Water	2	0	1	3
Total	**53**	**0**	**5**	**58**

Source: Author's elaboration on data from the Eco-innovation database http://ec.europa.eu/environment/eco-innovation/index_en.htm

according to which 3 out of 7 sampled projects were assessed as those that may generate radical innovation (product) (EACI, 2013). Most beneficiaries have stated to have acquired relevant knowledge on technologies and processes (8/10).

Although the opportunity to enhance international cooperation has not been considered the foremost priority, all respondents have declared that due to their participation in the Programme they developed wider international cooperation projects, mainly going beyond the scope of the Eco-Innovation Programme. Overall, developing partnerships has been mentioned as one of the main learning effects of the Programme. In contrast, the results of technical learning on new materials, technologies, processes and markets were mixed: half of the respondents stated that participation in the Programme led to acquiring new knowledge on the aforementioned aspects, while according to others it was only somewhat relevant. Furthermore, there is a perception that participation in the Programme has contributed to increase in the companies' visibility, mainly among industrial partners and research institutions, and to a lesser extent among policy makers and consumers.

As far as facilitating factors and obstacles for the participation in the Programme are concerned, proper financial resources and a good knowledge of EU policies have been mentioned among the preconditions, while the availability of specific technical expertise has been recognised as the most important one (4/10). The role of the internal R&D staff has been considered to be of limited importance. A mixed pattern emerges with regard to the staff policies related to project implementation too: in some cases, project relied on their internal staff (2/10), hired ad hoc staff (5/10) or used external expertise (3/10), and in all cases multilevel functional groups were created to implement project activities. Likewise, a variegated pattern of how beneficiaries have learnt about the Programme exists: three of them have found the opportunity to participate in the Programme autonomously, while others have learnt about it from partner universities or external consultants.

Complex administrative procedures have been considered one of the main difficulties related to participation in the Programme, while the factors of limited duration (up to 36 months) and restricted EU funding have not been considered relatively relevant. Finally, the majority of companies (except for two) state to have actively interacted and obtained the necessary support from the European Commission.

According to the evidence reported above, UK beneficiaries have clearly defined and pursued their objectives by strategically using the resources of the Programme. They have shown a strong sense of ownership of the Programme's objectives and targets, and have extensively invested in developing innovative environmental technologies within the framework of Programme activities. At the same time, the overall learning effect of the Programme appears to have been weaker compared to Italy, where project activities depended to a greater extent on external assistance and expertise. Importantly, most UK companies have autonomously learnt about the opportunities of the Programme, while most Italian partners that answered the survey have discovered about it from partner universities or external consultants.

Table 6.4 Breakdown of project partners by macro-areas and regions in the UK

Sub-state territorial units (Nations and LEPs in England)	*Lead partners*	*Project partners*
England		
South East	3	4
London	3	5
South West	2	6
East England	0	7
East Midlands	2	2
West Midlands	2	9
Yorkshire and the Humber	4	5
North East	1	5
North West	1	10
Scotland	1	1
Wales	1	3
Northern Ireland	1	1
Total number of lead partners	**21**	**58**

Source: Author's elaboration on data from the Eco-innovation database http://ec.europa.eu/environment/eco-innovation/index_en.htm

As Table 6.4 shows, the map of UK Programme beneficiaries is as patchy as the Italian one, with the highest number of applications from the North West and West Midlands, followed by the South West, London and Yorkshire and the Humber, and the North East.

Although, according to the respondents of the survey, the territorial variable has not been a relevant factor that might have encouraged or impeded the participation in the Programme, as in the case of Italy, there seems to be some linkage between the territorial concentration of the eco-innovation projects on the one hand, and the ambition of regional policies for environmental sustainability and specificities of economic and productive systems on the other.

Notably, the most significant investments by businesses in research and development (around 40%) has traditionally been registered in the South East and the East of England, where also about 41% of all full time equivalent research related jobs in the UK concentrates (UK PA, 39). However, if the total number of project partners was rather high (7) in the East of England, there were no lead partners among them. The South East has indeed shown a limited number of projects (4), although it was home to three lead partners. In contrast, the highest number of projects have been developed in the North West (10) and West Midlands (9), where the overall expenditure on R&D has been less consistent compared to the other two regions, but still relatively high: in 2012 it amounted to £1,874 million in the North West and £1,364 million in West Midlands. London registered a close rate of £1,477million with 5 projects, which is the same number of projects financed in the North East and Yorkshire and the Humber, where the concentration of lead partners was the highest. Such geographical traits seems to follow rather closely the map of the most important industrial regions in the UK, covering a piece of the North-East coast, Lancashire and the Birmingham Region, and Greater London (ONS, 2015).

The individual policies and approach to eco-innovation differed a lot across the country and all these activities are complicated to track. As far as England is concerned, Regional Development Agencies promoted and funded various activities for low-carbon economy before being dismantled in 2012. After their replacement by 24 new Local Enterprise Partnerships (LEPS), the regional landscape for eco-innovation has become much more fragmented and uncertain, as they are more business focused with limited financial resources (EPRC, 2016). As the LEPs continue to develop their business support programmes new opportunities may emerge; at least 12 of the LEPs are already pledging to support low-carbon or environmentally sustainable technologies, but progress has been slow (Eco-Innovation Observatory, 2011).

It is quite surprising that only one project, EcoADD (Sustainable Additives for Paints & Coatings & Concrete), came from Scotland. It was developed in the field of green business and its budget was among the highest in the whole programme (2.871.237 euro with 50% EU co-financing). EcoADD addressed the Greening Business Priority of the Eco-Innovation Programme in being the first application of a unique bio-based material – Curran. This material is a green sustainable multi-functional additive offering distinct advantages when substituted for products such as cellulose ethers in terms of environmental impact (through the use of up to 5 less chemicals during manufacture compared to cellulose ethers) and with improved performance characteristics (Eco-Innovation Programme, Project Gallery, 2013).

As already mentioned in Chapter 4, Scotland has not only shown an advanced sustainable developed strategy, but it has also quickly proceeded with the development of an ambitious Climate Change Act in 2009 and introduced advanced legislation to reduce emissions by at least 80% by 2050, aiming to drive eco-innovative solutions and build a sustainable low-carbon economy. More specifically, it has committed to climate change action in the Government Economic Strategy and National Performance Framework, setting out the following ambitious targets:

i. Generate 50% of Scotland's electricity from renewable sources by 2020 (~8 gigawatts) with an interim target of 31% by 2011(~5 gigawatts);
ii. 20% of Scotland's total energy use to come from renewables by 2020;
iii. Reduce the local and global environmental impact of Scotland's consumption and production.

Therefore, a system of supporting strategies was launched, including Low-Carbon Economic Strategy and Zero Waste Scotland. The Low-Carbon Economic

Strategy was published in 2010 and sets the policy direction for low-carbon economic opportunities with the ambition to better address producer responsibility to foster product designed for longer lifetimes, to foster the practice of reuse and repair, to accelerate the growth of the remanufacturing sector, to embed recycling and waste prevention into every business and household routine and to improve the use of biological resources. To this end, spreading good practices and behaviours, communication and the development of new skills have been considered of outmost importance. The Scotland's Zero Waste Plan was approved in 2011 with the purpose of developing a long-term strategy for a zero waste society. One of its flagship projects include the Scottish Institute for Remanufacture, jointly funded by the Scottish Funding Council, which has the objective "to accelerate the move to a circular economy in Scotland through product remanufacture, reconditioning, repair and reuse".

Finally, Scotland has widely invested in the improvement of water resources management, committing to deliver on its vision of Scotland as the world's first Hydro Nation. The Water Resources Scotland Act was passed in 2013, establishing a duty on the Scottish ministers and other public bodies take such reasonable steps as they consider appropriate for the purpose of ensuring the development of the value of Scotland's water resources. The Act has created an important overarching and broad policy framework aiming to manage the Scottish water environment to the best advantage, employ its knowledge and expertise effectively at home and internationally to increase the economic and on-economic value of Scotland's water resources. In fact, the Hydro Nation Forum was established, bringing together high-level experts from industry, academia and public sector to advise Scottish ministers on the overall direction and focus of the Hydro Nation agenda. Additionally, a new Hydro Nation Water Innovation Service was established in 2015 to assist the identification and exploitation of key opportunities for Scotland to bring forward new water technologies and processes to the reduction of costs for consumers and raising standards. The Hydro Nation International Programme was launched in order to enhance collaboration and respond to international business opportunities by sharing knowledge and expertise in the water sector internationally.

Furthermore, building on its "Scotland can do" initiative started in 2013 and setting up the region's ambition to become a "world-leading entrepreneurial and innovation-led nation", Scotland participates in the EU Vanguard Initiative – New Growth through Smart Specialisation launched in 2015. The objective of the project is to offer a new approach to growth and job creation in Europe by mobilising regional resources and ecosystems, aligned to smart specialisation strategies, enabling regions to address European priority areas in research, innovation and industrial policies'. It is worth mentioning that the Italian Regions of Lombardy and Emilia-Romagna are also part of this network.

More recently, Scotland has upgraded its commitment to the circular economy objectives by the publication of its first circular economy strategy "Making Things Last", along with a £70 million investment plan for a new strategy for manufacturing "A Manufacturing Future for Scotland" (Scottish Government, 2016). The circular economy strategy sets out ambitious priority actions in areas where the most significant environmental and economic benefits can be achieved, such as in remanufacturing, food and drink and the broader bio-economy, energy infrastructure and construction and the built environment. The core idea of the strategy has been to have all actors of society working together towards the creation of a more circular economy. The strategy's targets and ambitions build on previous Scottish strategies, the Zero Waste Plan and the Vanguard Initiatives.

Only three projects were co-financed by Eco-Innovation Programme in Wales, covering three different thematic strands: one in the water sector (REPHATER – Electrochemical waTER treatment pilot plant in the dairy industry with phosPHAte Recovery), one for Food and Drinks (SVAO – Sustainable vegetarian algae oil as alternative to krill oil health supplements) and one for the Green Business area (CLEANLEACH-Replication and deployment of a plan for treatment of leachates for plant nurseries in EU countries). Interestingly, all three projects were developed in partnership with Spanish enterprises. The aim of REPHATER was the development of a water treatment pilot plant based on the sequential combination of two innovative technologies. The novel prototypes developed by the consortium members will improve existing electrochemical solutions and will allow the take-up of such eco-effective techniques through the market, which are not currently used enough in most industrial sectors. The second project (SVAO) aimed at the production of Omega-3 EFA algae oil health supplement as an alternative to the use of krill derived oil and aiming on the reduction of carbon footprint of oil extraction. The CLEANLEACH project aimed to replicate and deploy a treatment system for recycling and treating leachates for plant nurseries, in order to avoid groundwater pollution and recycle nutrients and water.

The Welsh government produced "One Wales: One Planet" report in May 2009, which identified specific challenges and needs of Wales within the overall UK shared framework for sustainable development, and launched the Welsh strategy as already illustrated in Chapter 4. Wales was also an early adopter of Smart Specialisation and in 2013 it published Innovation Wales, the national innovation strategy, being, along with Scotland, partner of the Vanguard Initiative – New Growth Through Smart Specialisation.

The only project presented for the Eco-Innovation Programme in Ireland was developed in the building and construction sector. It comes as no surprise, as the Northern Ireland's (NI) Sustainable Development Strategy was formulated rather late compared to others nations. Its main document "Everyone's Involved" was published in 2010 with the objective to put in place the structures and policies needed for upgrading interventions for sustainable development (Northern Ireland Executive, 2010). The Strategy has been heavily influenced by the necessity to relaunch Northern Ireland's economy in respect of the environment and referred to the following principles:

i. Living within environmental limits;
ii. Ensuring a strong, healthy, just and equal society;
iii. Achieving a sustainable economy;

iv. Promoting good governance;
v. Using sound science responsibly;
vi. Promoting opportunity and innovation.

Accordingly, the implementation plan "Focus on the Future" was produced in response to this strategy, clarifying the division of competences and functions between central government departments and local governments. Although such objectives as resource efficiency, technological innovation for environment and the reduction of carbon footprint from productive activities have been included in both documents, no specific priorities for eco-innovation have been formulated.

In summary, the usage of the Eco-Innovation Programme has been characterised by significant differences not only between but also within the countries, with stronger concentration of programme participants in those areas where historical manufacturing districts exist. More general contextual factors, such as the amount of R&D investments at the regional level, as well as the ambition and the degree of consolidation of the regional political agenda for eco-innovation, circular economy, etc. appear to be relevant factors too, although they often do not explain the variation at the local scale. It seems feasible to suggest, therefore, that policy variables related to the established kind of entrepreneurial culture, resources and previous experience in the field of eco-innovation have been principal triggers of participation in this EU programme. As already mentioned, elements of strategic usage have characterised the participation of project participants from both countries, while in the case of Italian enterprises the ideational dimension has been involved too.

References

Ambrosetti Club (2017). *L'ecosistema per l'innovazione: quali strade per la crescita delle imprese e del Paese*. Technology Forum. Available at: www.ambrosetti.eu/ricerche-e-presentazioni/technology-forum-rapporto-finale.

Digest of United Kingdom Energy Statistics (DUKES, 2015), Supply and consumption of coal (DUKES 2.4). Department of Energy & Climate Change. Available at: https://www.gov.uk/government/statistics/solid-fuels-and-derived-gases-chapter-2-digestof-united-kingdom-energy-statistics-dukes.

Eco-Innovation Observatory (2010a). EIO country brief 2010: Italy. Available at: https://ec.europa.eu/environment/ecoap/italy_en.

Eco-Innovation Observatory (2010b). EIO Country Report: United Kingdom 2010. Available at: https://ec.europa.eu/environment/ecoap/sites/ecoap_stayconnected/files/field/field-country-files/eio_country_brief_2010_uk.pdf.

Eco-Innovation Observatory (2011). EIO Country profile 2011: United Kingdom. Available at: https://ec.europa.eu/environment/ecoap/sites/ecoap_stayconnected/files/field/field-country-files/eio_country_brief_2011_uk.pdf.

Eco-Innovation Observatory (2014). EIO country brief 2014: Italy. Available at: https://ec.europa.eu/environment/ecoap/italy_en.

Eco-Innovation Observatory (2015). EIO Country Report 2015 United Kingdom. Available at: https://ec.europa.eu/environment/ecoap/sites/ecoap_stayconnected/files/field/field-country-files/uk_eco-innovation_2015.pdf.

Eco-Innovation Observatory (2017). Eco-innovation in United Kingdom. EIO Country Profile 2016-2017. Available at: https://ec.europa.eu/environment/ecoap/sites/ecoap_stayconnected/files/field/field-country-files/uk_eio_country_profile_2016-2017.pdf

Eco-Innovation Programme (2013), Project Gallery. Available at:http://ec.europa.eu/environment/eco-innovation/projects

European Commission (2015). EU Resource Efficiency Scoreboard 2015. Available at: http://ec.europa.eu/environment/resource_efficiency/targets_indicators/scoreboard/pdf/EU%20Resource%20Efficiency%20Scoreboard%202015.pdf [Accessed 19 June 2018].

European Commission (2016). Analysing the success drivers of EMAS in selected member states case study on Italy. Available at: http://ec.europa.eu/environment/emas/pdf/other/IT_EMAS-CaseStudy.pdf.

European Policies Research Centre (EPRC) (2016). *Negotiating development? Contracts, agreements and deals in the governance of regional policy in Europe*. EoRPA Policy Briefing, University of Strathclyde.

Executive Agency for Competitiveness & Innovation (EACI) (2013). Analysing and reporting on the results achieved by CIP Eco-Innovation market replication projects, Final Report. Available at: http://ec.europa.eu/environment/eco-innovation/files/docs/publi/report-eco-innovation-results.pdf.

Eurostat (2009). Community innovation survey. Available at: https://ec.europa.eu/eurostat/web/microdata/community-innovation-survey.

Fondazione per lo Sviluppo Sostenibile (2017). Green Economy Report. Available at: https://www.fondazionesvilupposostenibile.org/pubblicazioni.

HMG (2011). Enabling the transition to a green economy: Government and business working together. Available at: www.gov.uk/government/publications/enabling-the-transition-to-a-green-economy.

HMG (2014). United Kingdom Partnership Agreement Part 1 (Sections 1 and 2). Available at: www.gov.uk/government/uploads/system/uploads/attachment_data/file/368808/bis-14-1179-united-kingdom-partnership-agreement-part-one.pdf.

Istituto Regionale Programmazione Economica Toscana (IRPET) (2013). Le politiche per le imprese e l'innovazione in Italia: le scelte delle regioni. Available at: www.regione.toscana.it/-/ricerca-e-innovazione-toscana-tech-il-27-e-28-febbraio-al-palacongressi-di-firenze.

KTN's website: www.ktn-uk.co.uk/about/.

Ministero dell'ambiente e della tutela del territorio e del mare (MATTM) (2013). The Italian Environmental Footprint Programme. Available at: www.minambiente.it/pagina/italian-environmental-footprint-program.

Northern Ireland Executive (2010). Everyone's involved. Sustainable development strategy. Available at: https://www.nienvironmentlink.org/cmsfiles/policy-hub/files/documentation/Waste/Sustainable-Development-Strategy.pdf

Office for National Statistics (ONS) (2015). The spatial distribution of industries in Great Britain. Available at: www.ons.gov.uk.

Office for National Statistics (ONS) (2016). Statistical bulletin: Gross domestic expenditure on research and development, UK. Available at: www.ons.gov.uk/economy/governmentpublicsectorandtaxes/researchanddevelopmentexpenditure/bulletins/.

Scottish Government (2016). A Manufacturing future for Scotland. Available at: https://beta.gov.scot/policies/manufacturing/

WRAP (2010). Reducing your construction waste. Guidance for small and medium size constructors. Available at: www.wrap.org.uk/content/about-us.

Conclusions

The EU is currently passing through perhaps the worst political turmoil in its history, as the scenario of "Europe 'à la carte" dominated by national political interests and preferences is emerging, accompanied by decreasing popular support and growing Eurosceptic movements across member states. Besides the long-term problems related to a limited legitimacy and low trust of citizens in European institutions, the EU has not managed to effectively address a number of highly demanding political challenges including, in particular, the economic recession after the economic crisis of 2008–2009 and the increased migration flows as consequence of intensified instability and military conflicts in the Middle East and North Africa. It is rather obvious that an enormous political effort is required to relaunch the integration project in Europe and that the EU institutions have underestimated the relevance of a number of political dimensions of how "Europe matters" not only for national states, that have largely used European integration for solving domestic problems, but most importantly, for all other actors including regional and local governments, private companies and local communities.

In this perspective, not only does the agenda for sustainable development represents an insightful case for reflecting on strengths and weaknesses of the EU in its capacity to deal with complex policy programmes, but it crucially embraces all those policy areas in which European societies currently face dramatic challenges individually and as a big whole. These include economic development and well-being, depletion of natural resources and climate change, welfare and migration. Since the end of the 1970s, the international community has committed itself to finding a new equilibrium among these pillars, being aware about the limits of old policy paradigms.

The analysis presented in this book has brought to light a number of relevant insights about the direction and relevance of EU action in mainstreaming sustainable development objectives across various policy sectors with the purpose of encouraging national, regional and local governments, and private companies to commit to common objectives and transform their strategies in order to achieve shared targets.

Overall, the ambition of the EU policy strategy seems to have shrunk, and an evident misbalance has emerged as the legal foundations of the principle of environmental policy integration has been strengthened, along with the decreasing political commitment to this principle and a paramount priority to the dimension of economic growth, which has translated into the diffusion of numerous overlapping policy narratives, such as green economy, circular economy, smart growth, etc. The normative foundations of the EU SD policy agenda appear not to be solid enough, and its substantive and operational principles are still characterised by a substantial degree of ambiguity. Indeed, a paradigmatic shift (Hall, 1993) appears to have taken place, as the objectives and instruments of the EU internal policies for sustainable development have been replaced at once, being more and more confined to the Lisbon priorities. The vision underpinning the Europe 2020 Agenda seems to have definitely consolidated this trend by strongly enhancing the dimension of economic growth and establishing the related policy and governance mechanisms that, among others, include a system of progressive monitoring and evaluation. Surprisingly, no systematic review of the progress of the strategy for sustainable development has been carried out since 2006. Although plenty of data has been collected by Eurostat for a wide range of sustainable development indicators illustrating member states' performance, no clear linkage exists between this data and a set of EU policies and programmers that announced the objective to promote sustainable development objectives across various sectors. In this perspective, it is certainly alarming that concerns have been expressed about the effectiveness of the better regulation instrument that has been the only de-facto tool allowing for the ex-ante integration of SD into EU policies. Finally, no reference to the concept of SD has been made in the While Paper on the Future of Europe – confirming that Europe has no strategy in place for the end of this decade, and no real instruments to pursue an ambitious agenda in economic, social and environmental terms (Renda, 2017).

Regardless of the aforementioned inconsistences, evidence has been provided that EU policy programmes have largely shaped policy actors' strategies, encouraging policy and governance transformation and ultimately contributing to increasing policy convergence across different territorial scales. A set of policy variables has been helpful for tracing and explaining the different scenario of usage of EU resources by target actors, illustrating how and why the selected EU policy programmes have brought about different scenario of change between and within the countries.

Contrary to what could be logically expected, the existence of facilitating factors within domestic contexts does not seem to determine a more pro-active policy response of target actors to EU policy initiatives. Very different scenarios of policy change have been observed at the regional and local levels with regard to the EU sustainable development agenda, where sub-state actors have developed more advanced strategies in view of EU policy objectives than those that would normally be expected taking into account the availability of additional domestic incentives.

In fact, a clearly symbolic commitment to the EU strategy has characterised the position of Italy for over a decade. As the empirical analysis has shown, except for the early and quite formal rather than substantive steps to launch the NSDS in the beginning of the 2000s, the Italian national efforts to develop appropriate policy instruments and measures have been rather sporadic and poor, being characterised by an extremely low sense of ownership of and political interest to the suitability agenda. A few initiatives have been promoted in the country by individual institutional actors, including governmental agencies, research bodies and private foundations in the absence of a consistent nation-wide political guidance in this field. In contrast, the UK has actively committed to a sustainable development agenda since the end of the 1990s, joining first the group of leaders and then becoming one of EU pioneers – thereby legitimising its previous political choices. As a consequence, a clear political strategy together with a multitude of policies and programmes have been developed in the country in order to enhance policy and governance transformations at different territorial levels (regional and local), and ensure the diffusion of pro-sustainability behavioural change among individuals and social and economic actors.

It appears surprising against this background that the Italian regions, cities and enterprises have comprehensively shown the same or even more pro-active attitude towards the EU policy programmes as their UK counterparts. However, a number of differences have been observed in the strategies of individual policy actors across domestic contexts.

More specifically, as far as the objective of SUD is concerned, against a mixed symbolic-cognitive trend in the programming of EU structural funds in Italy and its legitimising usage in the UK, the scenario has differed significantly between all four regions. They all have strategically deployed the resources offered by EU structural funds by formulating a set of their own policy goals in the perspective of EU priorities and explaining how the attainment of these goals will contribute to the economic and social development of the respective territories. Accordingly, they have settled and managed regional bids in order to invest the assigned amount of funding into concrete projects and entirely spent the financial allocations for the 2007–2013 programming period; most likely all funding will be spent in the current programming period as well. However, significant differences have arisen between the four regions in the way they have deployed the EU policy guidance for selecting their priorities and designing operational measures. From this viewpoint, Emilia-Romagna in Italy and Scotland in the UK have shown a major EU ideational impact in terms of policy objectives, while following the legitimising path as far as governance settings were concerned. Both regions have identified Urban Authorities for implementing SUD actions, without adopting EU territorial governance instruments (CLLD and ITI). In contrast, England was the only region to adopt the new integrated territorial governance instruments (CLLD and ITI) for its ERDF programme, while its programming priorities tended to legitimise the existing polices rather than adopt new policy ideas borrowed from the EU. The Veneto Region has presented a few policy innovations, although a clear evidence has been provided that the objective of sustainable development and in particular SUD were introduced in the regional programming following EU policy input. Remarkably, Emilia-Romagna has managed to bring about much more autonomous choices in the selection of policy objectives and targets by using the EU guidance than the Veneto Region that has rather closely followed the national policy guidance. In general, previous research on the UK explains that the governments of Scotland, Wales and Northern Ireland have put in strong efforts in designing their own sustainable development strategies in order to considerably distinguish themselves from Whitehall (Hogwood, 2013).

Likewise, the implementation path of the Covenant of Mayors has diverged a lot between and across the countries. Although the overall interest in the initiative has been much higher in Italy, the UK cities that joined it have shown high commitment to the initiative and have strategically deployed it in order to either improve their local sustainable energy policies that have mainly been developed within the framework of domestic initiatives or to expand their international visibility and collaborative networks. However, substantial difference between the municipal strategies have been observed (Glasgow and Poole), mainly depending on such factors as the existence of previous local strategy in this field, political leadership, resources and capacities mobilised for the implementation of the initiative at the local level. Hence, in the case of Glasgow, the legitimating kind of usage has been mainly in place, although the city has substantially upgraded its local suitable energy and climate strategy by strategically deploying the CoM network and methodology for obtaining financing from the EU Horizon Programme developed in partnership with other three European cities. Instead, Poole has developed its SEAP from scratch soon after it joined the initiative, by building an extremely pro-active strategy at the local level and mobilising the community networks around the SEAP actions. Although both cities recognise a limited usefulness of the initiative in terms of shaping priorities, developing SEAP measures and methodologies, they have greatly explored the relational and networking potential of the programme, recognising its relevance for empowering the local level and increasing its visibility at the EU level. The Italian cities of Padua and Bologna have used the CoM strategically in order to consolidate and revise their local sustainable energy plans that had to be prepared in accordance with national law dating back to 1991, but for which neither general political guidance nor specific technical instruments were provided at the national level. Therefore, the municipalities have intensely used the CoM resources to shape their local sustainable energy strategies in the long run, identify clear targets and build knowledge-based measures for achieving the established objectives. Moreover, the city of Padua has obtained a number of EU grants not only for developing its preliminary strategy that has laid down the basis for the local SEAP, but also for promoting a range of activities related to SEAP implementation. Political and administrative leadership and capacity have been clearly the most important factors for the smooth launch and progressive consolidation of Padua participation in the initiative. In contrast, Bologna's path to participate in the CoM has been much more cumbersome. Due to changes in the political majority in the local council, the preparation of Bologna SEAP was stuck for some years shortly after its application for membership was submitted to the CoM. subsequently, its participation in the CoM was relaunched, thanks to new political leadership and strong administrative commitment. Unlike the municipality of Padova, the city of Bologna has taken part in a few EU projects but has developed a very dense network of cooperation at the regional level by closely involving the local partnership in the implementation of the SEAP. Thus, both municipalities have shown high ownership of the Programme objectives and have gone through the process of learning in order to comply with its priorities and targets. Importantly, both Regions (Emilia-Romagna and Veneto) have introduced specific support measures for municipalities that have developed their SEAPs within the framework of their regional operational programmes co-financed by the ERDF. All municipalities state to have interacted with the CoM office and increased their knowledge and awareness about the role of city networks in Europe.

Finally, the Eco-Innovation Programme has exhibited somewhat similar trends, with a high number of participants coming from Italy and less numerous partnerships from the UK. Such high activism of Italian beneficiaries is again surprising, as eco-innovation policies have been rather underdeveloped in the country and few public incentives exist for companies to invest in this sphere, or in R&D in general. Interestingly, there has been rather an evident concentration of implemented projects in some local areas in both countries, mainly coinciding with historical industrial districts, which also normally show comparatively higher levels of investment in research and development as well as higher employment rates in this sector at the national level. Overall, the programme appears to have met the expectations of beneficiaries by offering strategic opportunities for developing innovative environmental technologies, increasing specific expert knowledge on processes, materials and markets, enlarging and consolidating collaborative networks within and across countries and between private and public entities. However, some interesting differences in the scenario of usage of this programme has emerged between the countries, in particular with regard to the composition of project partnerships, the degree of its internationalisation, motivations for participation and learning outcomes. In this way, in projects led by Italian partners, there was a large quota of SME and academic research partnerships (46%) and a relevant number of large businesses (17%). Obtaining resources for consolidating the existing R&D activities, acquiring new knowledge and enlarging collaborative partnerships were among their main motivations to participate. Interestingly, the share of foreign partners in projects involving Italian beneficiaries was rather small (49 of the total of 165), meaning that more than one Italian partner were involved in the same project. In contrast, projects with UK participants were more international, having a balanced representation of foreign (47) and domestic (46) partners in the total of 93. The UK led project partnerships were mainly composed of SME consortia (60%), with a smaller quota (30%) of SME-academia partnerships. For UK beneficiaries, the possibility of obtaining additional resources for starting up new innovation activities was the main motivation behind joining the Programme. Importantly, although most beneficiaries from both countries were active in the field of eco-innovation long before joining the Programme, they all recognise a relevant learning effect of their participation in the Programme for acquiring new expertise on materials, technologies and their market uptake. In the case of UK partners, a relevant impact in terms of the development of new research in the field of environmental technologies has been observed too, thus making ownership of the Programme targets higher than among Italian participants. Almost all companies reached by our survey have developed other new projects and networks by strategically using their Eco-Innovation Programme partnerships and the networking skills acquired due to their project activities.

To sum up, a number of interesting conclusions can be drawn from the above analysis. First, despite a significant gap in the Italian domestic policy and legislation on sustainable development, which has been only partly recovered by the country over the last years, the target actors analysed by this research have actively deployed various instruments provided by EU programmes and increasingly aligned their strategies to the priorities and targets established by the EU. Indeed, the empirical analysis has shown that the actors under examination have used a variety of EU instruments (funding, guidance, cooperative networks, etc.) to compensate the lack of domestic policies in terms of ideas, knowledge, specific methodologies, expertise or strategic opportunities of networking at the EU level. In fact, in Italy, a mixed scenario of usage combining strategic and ideational elements has mainly prevailed, contributing to policy learning and enhancing ownership of EU objectives.

In contrast, the policy response of UK target actors has been mainly shaped by a mix of strategic and legitimating features, as in all three cases they have developed previous experience or strategies in the context of similar policy initiatives implemented at the national level. However, against an overall low interest in the EU programmes under examination, the group of UK policy addressees who joined the initiatives have shown high commitment to and ownership of EU objectives. They developed those additional elements (e.g. EU scale partnerships, new technologies, funding, etc.) that were not covered by domestic policy strategies or used the EU programmes to consolidate or upgrade their existing strategies or plans in the respective fields.

Interestingly, the empirical findings collected by this research show that the map of local participation (CoM and Eco-Innovation Programme) has largely coincided with the areas that were more favourable to remain in the EU at the Brexit referendum, including London area, Manchester, Bristol, Leeds, Newcastle, Glasgow, etc. Remarkably, only three eco-innovation projects and one SEAP was developed by target actors in Wales, which, by the way, has received substantial funding from EU structural funds over the last decades.

Theoretically speaking, these findings bring to limelight the important evidence of how agency matters in the process of policy implementation and how policy variable can be helpfully used for tracing the condition of policy success and failures across different contexts. The empirical analysis has shown that although domestic policy legacies in the two countries have more generally influenced the degree of policy actors' activation within the framework of EU programmes, other relevant variables related to policy actors' motivations, interests, resources, capacities and knowledge have determined the specific patterns of usage of EU related regulatory, relational, learning and financial resources. Such conclusions confirm the relevance of a bottom-up perspective of policy analysis, providing especially useful insights for understanding the success and failure of EU policy experiments and their actual relevance for both the quality of policy implementation in the EU and the legitimation of policy solutions promoted at the EU level. The main analytical challenge of this research path is evidently related to the lack of reliable and comprehensive quantitative and qualitative data allowing for the comparison of a representative number of EU countries.

Furthermore, this comparison brings about several insights in more practical and pragmatic terms. It clearly shows, as the example of the NSDS and the EU structural funds programming have illustrated, the trend to maintain a strong gatekeeping position and the propensity to legitimise rather than to modify positions on the part of national governments. In contrast, sub-state authorities are more prone to adjust their policies and indeed often use EU initiatives to empower themselves not only by developing more advanced programmes and plans that are strongly oriented on EU targets but also by encouraging their local stakeholders to build linkages with the EU arena. According to the evidence collected by this research, the main perceived weakness of the EU policy initiatives under analysis have been their complexity and a diffused lack of capacity among policy addressees to correctly put into practice the desired policy and governance innovations, which has not been adequately compensated by the EU Commission support and guidance.

The issue of additionality of EU action also clearly comes out from the research results, as the value and the impact of EU interventions seems to be directly related to the EU capacity to fill in the policy gaps existing in domestic policy regimes by providing target actors with complementary and not overlapping policy instruments. The possibility of supporting the development or implementation of local SEAPs with specific funding schemes available through direct thematic programmes such as Life or the Framework Research programmes (currently Horizon 2020) and the ERDF appear to be a well-functioning example.

The overall effort for mainstreaming sustainable development objectives across regional and local strategies appear to have been rather successful, as specific actions were introduced (or consolidated) in target actors' strategies along with at least the three main pillars: greening of economy (R&D, in particular eco-innovation), sustainable energy (reduction of emissions, energy efficiency and renewable energy), resource efficiency and recycling. Multiple connections and complementarities emerge between and across the actions promoted through the three programmes, although they are not self-evident for their addressees.

Last but not least, EU programmes have proved to provide an important socialisation tool that contributed to enhancing convergence to common policy objectives, mutual knowledge and trust among those involved, for example, by encouraging to share local SEAPs and their monitoring in the website of the CoM or by building eco-innovation projects based on international partnerships. Obviously, this kind of impact is still limited, as it is relevant only for those involved in the programmes, which is far from reaching the total EU population of local authorities in the case of the CoM or enterprises for the Eco-Innovation Programme.

To sum up, based on the above analysis of the overall strategy and the experience implementation of specific policy programmes several general conclusions can be drawn regarding EU governing capacity in the field of sustainable development. First, the EU agenda for sustainable development has progressively expanded over the last decades and a number of fundamental principles have consolidated therein, shaping also EU policy programmes and individual policy instruments. However, a strong political commitment and leadership of the strategy has been missing at the level of EU institutions since the mid-2000. The strategy has so far been struggling to delineate clear roles and responsibilities, where its objectives and goals have oftentimes overlapped, producing excessively complex and somewhat ambiguous policy agendas. Second, the empirical analysis has shown that the essence of policies for sustainable development cannot be taken for granted, but it should be questioned and checked in terms of specific content, actions and impacts in order to be able to claim for strong EU leadership in this field. Third, further quantitative and qualitative research is needed to appraise the real potential of coordination and learning tools that the EU has extensively promoted with the purpose of enhancing policy and governance change for sustainable development across member states. Consistently with conclusions drawn from previous research on this issue (Radaelli, 2008), our empirical findings confirm that there has been a limited and slow process of policy convergence at the national level. More dynamic transformations have been observed, however, among regional and local authorities and private companies, in terms of diffusion of shared policy goals, operational principles and expert knowledge related to various dimensions of sustainability. Such evidence is an encouragement in carrying on the analytical endeavours for understanding the conditions under which soft coordination and bottom-up learning may lead to policy and governance convergence. Needless to say, the credibility of EU action in this field clearly depends on its capacity to solve this puzzle, identifying a strong European added value in its policy agenda, which speaks to the needs and expectations of its citizens.

References

Hall, R. (1993). Policy paradigms, social learning, and the state. *Comparative Politics*, 25 (3), pp. 975–296.

Hogwood, P. (2013). The UK's devolved authorities and the European sustainability discourse: Between identity and actor hierarchy. In: Barnes, P.M. and Hoerber, T.C. eds., *Sustainable Development and Governance in Europe: The Evolution of the Discourse on Sustainability*. London and New York: Routledge.

Radaelli, C. (2008). Europeanization, policy learning, and new modes of governance. *Journal of Comparative Policy Analysis*, 10 (3), pp. 239–254.

Renda, A. (2017). How can sustainable development goals be 'mainstreamed' in the EU's better regulation agenda? *CEPS, Policy Insights*. Available at: www.ceps.eu/publications/

Index

For Product Safety Concerns and Information please contact our EU
representative GPSR@taylorandfrancis.com
Taylor & Francis Verlag GmbH, Kaufingerstraße 24, 80331 München, Germany

www.ingramcontent.com/pod-product-compliance
Ingram Content Group UK Ltd.
Pitfield, Milton Keynes, MK11 3LW, UK
UKHW011012180926
475701UK00004B/706
* 9 7 8 0 3 6 7 6 6 4 6 9 5 *